From Roosevelt
to Roosevelt

THE LITERATURE OF HISTORY

Richard L. Rapson
General Editor

*Revolution, Confederation, and
Constitution*

STUART GERRY BROWN

*From Roosevelt to Roosevelt:
American Politics and Diplomacy,
1901–1941*

OTIS L. GRAHAM, JR.

*The Civil War and
Reconstruction, 1850–1877*

I. A. NEWBY

*Major Interpretations of the
American Past*

RICHARD L. RAPSON

Goldentree Books

From Roosevelt to Roosevelt

American Politics and Diplomacy, 1901-1941

edited by

OTIS L. GRAHAM, JR.
University of California, Santa Barbara

NEW YORK

APPLETON-CENTURY-CROFTS
EDUCATIONAL DIVISION
MEREDITH CORPORATION

General Editor's Foreword

History abounds with a literature of excitement, great power, and controversy; and increasing numbers of students are being given access to it. That compendious dispenser of data, the textbook, served long and usefully as a substitute for reading original interpretive works by influential historians. It dispensed history as a mass of proven and uncontroversial fact, predigested and given to readers at second hand. But history, despite its attempts at thoroughness and accuracy, is not strictly classifiable as another branch of science. Because it asks unanswerable questions about the meaning of man's existence by looking at and pondering what man has done, a catalog of memorizable dates, names, and facts represents an unsatisfactory and unstimulating rendering of history. The few textbooks that have endured over time are those in which the voice of a questioning historian may be heard through the walls of facts. And these voices speak out even more distinctly in books written to get at certain truths, as that historian sees them, rather than in books which must cover the material comprehensively. Before the paperback revolution, the instructor found it nearly impossible to assign the "great" books of his field of study to his classes: even if a sufficient number of copies could be found in print, the cost was prohibitive. These are now available and within the means of most students.

The LITERATURE OF HISTORY is a series of books-about-books. It is designed to bring into sharper focus the many outstanding paperbacks read increasingly in undergraduate and graduate courses. By force of habit, students often approach these seminal books as if they were texts, with little awareness of their importance to the study of history, of what theses are being propounded and challenged, of the scholarly milieu at the time of their writing, of the controversy they frequently aroused. Scholarly introductions occasionally furnish some of this information; but most of the original works read for history courses are read in an intellectual vacuum.

For each volume in the series, the editor has chosen what he believes are the most important and widely read books on a given subject. Such a choice is of necessity an interpretation, perhaps an idiosyncratic one. For each of these important books the editor has gathered together the best book reviews, review articles, and critical commentaries about that book.

Reviews are a neglected form of historical writing—and for the most part deservedly so. They are too often pallid summaries of a book's argument, combined with a list of a few factual errors found by the reviewer, and concluding with some polite consoling generalizations. Nevertheless, one occasionally encounters thoughtful commentaries of genuine intellectual merit. These are expressed in a peculiarly personal form of historical dialogue since serious scholars are analyzing the thinking and writing of their fellow scholars.

The intent of THE LITERATURE OF HISTORY is to enhance independent reading; in no instances do the critiques serve as a substitute for reading the original work. Plot summaries and such have been excised; the portions retained are those that make a unique intellectual contribution, those that engage a student's critical faculties, those that raise questions as to *why* and *how* certain books are important. After eliminating the vapid reviews and the book summaries, we find stimulating, succinct, valuable arguments and counter-arguments, opinions and new suggestions about the ideas contained in our best books of history. Many reviews are little unmined gems of historical expression.

The editors in this series are practicing scholars in the subject of their particular volumes. For this reason they have been encouraged to enter the controversy—in the full historiographical essay at the outset and in the briefer introductions to each book discussed—to make judgments and offer new interpretations. The reader should read these contributions with the same critical spirit we would have him bring to the many outstanding books which have inspired this series. Historians have been described as cannibals in their scholarly relations with one another; it is only fitting that students should now have an opportunity to join in the feast.

RICHARD L. RAPSON

Contents

From Roosevelt
to Roosevelt

Who cares to open a book that is without defect or amiable weakness?

Carl Becker

Introduction

Books of this sort, usually called "readers," are supposed to write themselves. I expected to select approximately ten important, controversial, and widely read books and let those who have reviewed or discussed them in print do the rest. Such pleasant speculations ended when I began work on the project, and discovered the occasion piled high with difficulty. For a time I considered writing a critical introductory essay on the state of reviewing in the historical profession, but I have little taste for treason, and furthermore find that my own hands are not clean. Still, I was shocked to find so many important books so skimpily discussed in print. Fortunately there are many important books, and I had no difficulty in compiling a book of this size. My chief pain was in parting company with many books which had much to recommend them, but which for one reason or another had little or no career in the journals and other literature of our trade. Perhaps I may be allowed a brooding word about some of them before going on.

Some important books, such as William E. Leuchtenburg's *Perils of Prosperity 1914–1932*, or John D. Hicks' *Republican Ascendancy 1921–1933*, generated bland reviews.[1] Their arguments were apparently so unimpeachable that no extended criticism was possible; also, because these were broad syntheses with no single thesis, the reviewers did not know where to concentrate. At any rate, I gave them up for the purposes of this project. Other books started wonderful arguments—Charles Beard's *President Roosevelt and the Coming of War, 1941*, for example, which in addition to heated reviews drew a book-length rebuttal from Basil Rauch in his *Roosevelt: From Munich to Pearl Harbor*.[2] But Beard's book is no longer read. Indeed, there are

[1] Leuchtenburg (Chicago, University of Chicago Press, 1958); Hicks (New York, Harper & Row, 1960).
[2] Beard (New Haven, Yale University Press, 1948); Rauch (New York, Creative Age Press, 1950).

1

important books which have never been read by students and presumably never will be, such as the massive two-volumed work by William S. Langer and S. Everett Gleason, *The Challenge to Isolation, 1937–1940*, and *The Undeclared War, 1940–1941*.[3]

Other books had the wrong shape. A book like Gabriel Kolko's *Wealth and Power in America*[4] contains material on the period 1900–1941 but most of its argument applies to post-World War II America, a period assigned to another author in this series. The same is true of *The Autobiography of Malcolm X*, or William Appleman Williams' *The Tragedy of American Diplomacy*.[5] And some of the best writing came in a form which meant it would not be reviewed—for example, Arthur S. Link's influential article, "What Happened To The Progressive Movement in the 1920s?"[6]

There are a number of older books of lasting value which, thanks to paperback publishing, are still read and reread by students of history. I think of Fred Howe's *The Confessions of a Reformer*, of Lincoln Steffens' *The Autobiography of Lincoln Steffens*, or of Frederick Lewis Allen's little masterpiece, *Only Yesterday*.[7] Largely because of the date of their appearance and their anecdotal, personal character, these books were accorded almost no serious, extended critical commentary among historians. They were in fact not intended for historians, and while this is part of their virtue, they stimulated little comment worth reprinting.[8] Different considerations ruled out a number of other books I have read and assigned. One of the monumental scholarly efforts of recent years is Arthur S. Link's multivolume biography of Woodrow Wilson (now at five volumes), a work which has inspired controversy as well as praise, but unfortunately it is a difficult work to grasp in the whole. Another landmark book, A. A. Berle and Gardiner Means, *The Modern Corporation and*

---

[3] (New York, Harper, 1952); (New York, Harper, 1953).

[4] (New York, Praeger, 1962).

[5] Malcolm X (New York, Grove Press, 1964); Williams (Cleveland, World Publishing, 1959).

[6] *American Historical Review*, 64 (July 1959), 833–51.

[7] Howe (New York, Scribner's, 1925); Steffens (New York, Harcourt, Brace, 1931); Allen (New York, Harper, 1931).

[8] The existence of a very uneven but now classic group of comments on Howe's book almost made me select the book to reprint the comments; see the symposium, "Where Are the Pre-War Radicals?" *The Survey*, 55 (February 1926), 536–66. But the comments, by some old reformers and exreformers, do not illuminate Howe's book so much as they do the state of progressivism in 1926.

Private Property, seemed to me too technical, and the controversy it produced more technical still.[9]

To go on enumerating titles reluctantly put by would only remind me of my original difficulties. Persons offended by the exclusion of a favorite book will now perhaps be hobbled by a small sympathy. Despite problems of selection, the idea of this series is one of great merit. Students of history who read an assigned book are usually intimidated by its scholarly argument. They either take it or leave it— an unenviable poverty of alternatives. This series will make available to them the critical reception of the book so that their use of it may be more discriminating. I have discovered that the scholarly community does not always produce a substantial critical evaluation of even its most valued books, but there are many such books (even after subtracting those students hardly ever read) and for many of them an intelligent critical reputation has built up in published form. I have selected eleven of these.

To another type of criticism I am entirely vulnerable. The books chosen lean strongly in the direction of "political" history and American foreign relations. Among areas slighted would be the lives of the laboring classes (where I might have used Irving Bernstein's admirable book, *The Lean Years*[10]); the history of radical movements (where I might have chosen James Weinstein's provocative new book, *The Decline of Socialism in America: 1912–1925,* or Irving Howe and Lewis Coser, *The American Communist Party*[11]); business or entrepreneurial history (where I might have used Allan Nevins and Frank E. Hill, *Ford: The Times, the Man, the Company,* or Forrest McDonald's *Insull*[12]); state and local histories (where one might well have turned to George Mowry's exemplary book, *The California Progressives*[13]); religion, the arts, popular culture, technology, science, education, and so on. To such criticism I can only plead that this book is designed to supplement history courses in American colleges and universities, and its tastes are the predominant tastes in surveys of American history and in the twentieth-century period courses. The political and diplomatic focus of such courses may not be entirely defensible, but

[9] (New York, Macmillan, 1932).
[10] (Boston, Houghton Mifflin, 1960).
[11] Weinstein (New York, Monthly Review Press, 1967); Howe and Coser (New York, Praeger, 1962).
[12] Nevins and Hill (New York, Scribner, 1954): McDonald (Chicago, University of Chicago Press, 1962).
[13] (Berkeley, University of California Press, 1951).

it greatly narrowed the range of my own torment. I stood in no need of titles from cultural and social history when, for example, I could not even find room to include an unfortunately little-known book, *Conservation and the Gospel of Efficiency*, by one of the most influential "political" historians of twentieth-century America, Samuel P. Hays.[14] I have taken consolation in the merit and broad influence of the eleven books selected, and the opportunity in this introduction to describe the burdens under which the editor of such a book must labor.

Despite the ideal of detached scholarship, written history is powerfully shaped by the social milieu in which it is conceived. A few historians write as if they have been unaffected by the events and social currents of their own era, but most show clearly the era's intellectual marks. Historians have not agreed whether this is good or bad, or whether anything can be done about it in any event, but they generally agree that it is true. A consequence is that one should never read history without adding to one's critical apparatus the date of publication. These eleven books were published between 1950 and 1967. If we reflect on the collective experience of American intellectuals in those years we are certain to read these books more intelligently.

In the half century before 1950 the average historian was stirred by the political and intellectual currents of the progressive and New Deal reform eras, with which he was usually sympathetic. This was especially true after the First World War, when young men from the Midwest and the urban East began to outnumber the conservative sons of Brahmin New England among publishing historians. The "liberal" tradition got the upper hand intellectually (in all disciplines, not just history), a tradition which encouraged men to see in American political and economic development a conflict between two relatively unified groups—the elites of large-scale business against the mass of small farmers, urban laborers, and exploited consumers. Leading historians developed rather clear social sympathies. They hoped the champions of The People would press their conflict with antisocial business elites until the social order was thoroughly reformed. These were their political views, as citizens. Having such views, they had a natural tendency to see in the past the sort of social struggles they witnessed at first hand, and they had little doubt as to the heroes of

[14] (Cambridge, Harvard University Press, 1959).

American democracy's long struggle toward fulfillment. The commanding figures in this historiography were men like Charles Beard, Vernon L. Parrington, and Matthew Josephson, and the best examples of the transference of progressive outlook into progressive history would be Parrington's *Main Currents of American Thought,* Claude Bowers' *Jefferson and Hamilton,* or Arthur M. Schlesinger, Jr.'s *The Age of Jackson.*[15]

Within a few years after the end of World War II America found herself in the Cold War, a state of seige in which her institutions and national beliefs seemed to face mortal challenges. At home, McCarthyism and a revived Republican Party appeared to threaten the welfare state and liberal internationalism. Everything seemed in jeopardy. It was a time for caution and social unity, a time when many intellectuals developed a strong appreciation of the common ground upon which Americans might stand in a hostile world. Emotionally as well as politically on the defensive, intellectuals were appalled that public leadership seemed to have fallen into the hands of men of absolutist, reckless mentality, such as John Foster Dulles or Senators Joseph McCarthy, John Bricker, and William Knowland. A mood of pessimism was general, along with a feeling that agitation and social criticism probably came from the totalitarian Left or Right—and in either case was unwelcome.

History, along with every other intellectual activity, was strongly affected by these developments.[16] The contemporary suspicion of mass movements and simplified, ideological thinking, natural for people who lived in a world populated by Stalin, McCarthy, and General Curtis LeMay, seems to have produced among historians a tendency to be critical of the Great Simplifiers—Bryan, Wilson, La Follette—and to be much more sensitive to the reactionary possibilities inherent in mass movements. The progressive viewpoint now appeared too uncritical of mass movements and too prone to emphasize (always favorably) the frequency of social and class conflict in America. Class conflict was muted in the 1950s, and any serious internal divisions would not have been generally welcome, considering the apparent threat from world

[15] Parrington (New York, Harcourt, Brace, 1927–1930, 2 vols.); Bowers (Boston, Little, Brown, 1933); Schlesinger, Jr. (Boston, Little, Brown, 1945).

[16] A good review of the shift away from progressive historiography is John Higham, "American History," Part III of John Higham, Leonard Krieger, and Felix Gilbert, *History* (Englewood Cliffs, N.J., Prentice-Hall, 1965).

communism. Thus it is not surprising that written history in the 1950s, with some notable exceptions,[17] minimized social and intellectual conflict in America, and showed a distaste for all absolutist modes of thought and a tendency to find more to criticize than to praise in mass politics. This reaction might take the mild form of a critical biography of some popular political leader whose appeals, while reformist, had also been emotional and simplistic; at an extreme, it took the form of outright chauvinism, as when Samuel Eliot Morison in 1950 urged his fellow historians to write the kind of history "that would make a man want to fight for his country." [18] John Higham described this mood in an important article in 1959 as the "cult of the American consensus," citing as leading examples the work of three of America's most highly regarded historians, Richard Hofstadter, Louis Hartz, and Daniel Boorstin.[19] These and other scholars in the late 1940s and the 1950s, according to Higham, conducted "a massive grading operation to smooth over America's social convulsions." They found in the American past less social conflict than the progressive historians, more flaws in mass movements, and more to regret in the growing influence during the modern period of mass opinion on the making of foreign policy.

In this intellectual setting John Higham wrote his study of nativism, Schlesinger his admiring study of a President who steered America clear of radical demagogues of Left and Right, George Kennan his brooding indictment of democratic diplomacy, Richard Hofstadter his brilliant but unflattering portrait of American liberal reformers.

The 1960s, as few need to be reminded, were different. The decade was full of the discovery of American shortcomings, of ideological and political conflict of Americans against Americans. Critics

[17] An example would be Eric Goldman's popular *Rendezvous with Destiny* (New York, Alfred A. Knopf, 1952) which despite the date of publication was squarely in the progressive tradition.
[18] See Morison, "The Faith of an Historian," *American Historical Review,* 56 (January 1951), 270.
[19] Higham, "The Cult of 'The American Consensus,'" *Commentary,* 27 (February 1959), 93–100. A book which not only described but welcomed the recent absence of ideological conflict in America was Daniel Bell's *The End of Ideology* (New York, Free Press, 1960). A splendid discussion of the intellectual development of American historians since World War II may be found in Richard Hofstadter, *The Progressive Historians* (New York, Alfred A. Knopf, 1968), Chapter 12, "Conflict and Consensus in American History," and in the bibliographical essay. This should not be missed.

protested the country's racism, her complacent acceptance of poverty, the conservative purposes of her universities, her profligate environmental pollution, her aggressive foreign policy in Vietnam and the Caribbean. The protests seemed to change nothing, improve nothing, and the result was a high level of tension and dissatisfaction. Such a milieu might have led historians to write conservative history—placing emphasis upon authority and stability, now that these seemed so widely threatened. Perhaps this will be true in the 1970s, if the student protests which began in the late 1960s continue to alarm a formerly sympathetic faculty (which contains nearly all the nation's historians). But judging by the published work of the 1960s, historians shared the critical mood of the period rather than reacting against it. They increased their attention to the history of American blacks, probed American foreign policy for its economic and moralistic sources, and began a critical reassessment of the relationship between business and government under the "welfare state."

Inevitably there were some historians, principally the older ones, whose interests did not much reflect the public life of the 1960s. They published books, as they always had, in which America's social conflicts appeared to have been modest in scale and successfully managed, in which her foreign policy seemed fashioned in the best national traditions of humanitarianism and a realistic appraisal of the needs of national security. The ideal of scholarly detachment may account for this lack of change less than the familiar tendency of a person's social outlook to resist modification when the world around him changes. But then one expects intellectual disciplines to show a certain independence and resistance to short-run cultural pressures. What was surprising was the extent of the impact of a decade in which America appeared as a huge, bureaucratic, militarized society with great extremes of poverty and wealth and also of ideology.

The most publicized effect among historians was the rise of a New Left history, described in some detail by Irwin Unger in an article in the *American Historical Review* in 1967, and anthologized, among other places, in Barton J. Bernstein (ed.), *Towards a New Past: Dissenting Essays in American History.*[20] Less publicized but more important—since New Left historians were very few in number and included only a small minority of the most gifted historians of

---

[20] Irwin Unger, "The New Left and American History: Some Recent Trends in United States Historiography," *American Historical Review*, 72 (July 1967), 1237–63; Bernstein, *Towards a New Past* (New York, Pantheon, 1968).

the country—was the range of new perspectives and interests among scholars of all ages and political leanings. C. Vann Woodward did not exaggerate when he described the beginnings of an "Age of Reinterpretation" at the start of the 1960s, an age that would leave many a textbook and set of lecture notes out of date.[21]

The largest changes were in the treatment of slavery and racial history generally, the abolitionist record, and recent American foreign policy. But portions of the 1901–1941 period were also convincingly reinterpreted. The older view held that a democratic movement called progressivism had brought a measure of social justice, an improved and democraticized political system, and a balance among economic interest groups which was more conducive to the public interest than the unreformed system of the 1890s and before. The 1920s were seen as a strikingly different and generally deplorable (conservative, also frivolous) interlude. The New Deal had continued the defense of the public interest and the protection of the disadvantaged by completing the building of the "welfare state" begun some thirty years before. As for foreign policy, the traditional view was that in the first half of the century enlightened political leaders had led the American people by gradual stages to assume their proper twentieth-century role as international guardians of democracy and the principle of peaceful resolution of disputes. But this synthesis, which I have slightly caricatured—but not much, especially if one reads the textbooks published in the period—could hardly be expected to satisfy a generation of historians who had in the 1960s been surprised and even reluctant to learn how the "welfare state" had left America a country of a few royal fortunes but millions in poverty, and who had watched in apparent helplessness as the liberal governments from 1960 through 1968 indulged in colossal military spending and were quick to use their armed might to halt social change in small, underdeveloped countries.

One would have expected also much criticism of the liberal historians' interpretation of the 1930s, the crucible of the "welfare state," but essay-length studies by Paul Conkin and Barton J. Bernstein, and a few unconvincing sallies by young radical historians were all that the 1960s produced.[22] Revisionist writing was concentrated in the progressive era and it was impressive both in scope and quality.

[21] Woodward, "The Age of Reinterpretation," *American Historical Review,* 66 (October 1960), 1–19.
[22] See Paul Conkin, *The New Deal* (New York, Crowell, 1967); Barton J. Bernstein, "The New Deal: The Conservative Achievements of Liberal Reform," in Bernstein (ed.), *Towards a New Past* (New York, Pantheon,

Progressivism seen from the 1960s was no longer a virtual social revolution by morally aroused preachers, journalists, and social workers, but a reasonably successful effort by large businessmen and university and professional "experts" who, while they might occasionally differ, shared a desire to bring stability and efficiency to modern industrial society. Revisionist historians did not deny the presence of muckrakers, social-gospel preachers, settlement workers, and others who talked of democracy and justice; it was just that their new perspective made such types seem peripheral. Seen from the 1960s, the *results* of prewar and wartime changes—larger and fewer corporations, the co-optation of radical demands and subsequent atrophy of radical movements, the remarkable persistence of the old patterns of wealth and income distribution—led the new historians to emphasize those reformers who brought efficiency to city government, scientific management to industry, and at the national level created governmental institutions to bring coordination and friendly regulation to large industry. The new sense of what had been accomplished during the progressive era, and by whom, came in two rather distinct theoretical formulations—one best expressed by Gabriel Kolko, the other by Robert Wiebe. The work of these authors is discussed below.

While no other aspect or portion of the 1900–1941 period was quite as altered by the work of the 1960s as was the progressive era, other areas and problems were importantly affected. More books were published on urban themes, on conservation, and most especially on various aspects of the history of the American Negro in the twentieth century. The 1960s produced a large crop of biographies of radical political leaders—for example Emma Goldman, Norman Thomas, W. E. B. Du Bois, Henry A. Wallace (in his Progressive Party phase), Eugene Debs, and Vito Marcantonio (but also good biographies of Calvin Coolidge and Alfred M. Landon!). In American diplomatic history one could discern changes which seemed to correlate in a rough way with changes in the international and domestic situation of the United States after Eisenhower left the presidency, but the pattern was uneven. There was an increase in scholarly interest in relations between the United States and both Latin America and the Orient (two sensitive areas for the State Department in the 1960s), and

---

1968); Jerold S. Auerbach, "New Deal, Old Deal, or Raw Deal: Some Thoughts on New Left Historiography," *Journal of Southern History*, 35 (February 1969), 18–30.

there was also a tendency for historians to be increasingly aware of the influence of economic pressures on the formulation of American policy.[23] At least three books on U.S. relations with Mexico during the Mexican revolution, and several more on U.S.–Soviet relations, testified to a growing preoccupation with the response of American governments to revolutionary social change abroad, a natural interest for men who lived in a decade when American handling of revolutionary nations seemed awkward and ineffective at best. In a general way one detects in writing on American foreign relations less defensiveness, less anticommunism, a greater sympathy with popular revolutionary movements even if they are Marxist-Leninist, and a greater willingness to find fault with heroes of liberal internationalism like Woodrow Wilson and Franklin D. Roosevelt.

Yet these are only tendencies and trends; they are far from general, and may not become so. American diplomatic historians still come in all varieties. The 1960s have not raised up any single, simple interpretation (William Appleman Williams' economic interpretation was advanced in the 1950s, and still seems to be regarded with respectful skepticism, or just plain skepticism). Despite the widespread uneasiness with what most intellectuals see as an overextended American policy in the 1960s, the isolationists of the 1930s have not been rehabilitated.[24] Despite the spreading revulsion against war as an instrument of policy, scholars who treat Wilson's war decision in 1917 still tend to approve it. Ernest May's *The World War and American Isolation, 1914–1917,* the best recent review of American intervention, showed a strong tragic sense but generally approved of Wilson's

[23] See for example Lloyd Gardner's *The Economic Aspects of New Deal Diplomacy* (Madison, University of Wisconsin Press, 1963). Arno J. Mayer has written two brilliant books on Wilson's diplomacy in which he not only utilizes a multinational perspective but describes Wilsonian policy-making against a background of domestic political and economic problems and a contest of international ideologies; see *The Political Origins of the New Diplomacy* (New Haven, Yale University Press, 1959) and *The Politics and Diplomacy of Peacemaking* (Princeton, Princeton University Press, 1967). A focus on Wilson's fears of Bolshevism as the key to his postwar diplomacy distinguishes N. Gordon Levin's *Woodrow Wilson and World Politics* (New York, Oxford University Press, 1968), a prize-winning book which I perversely continue to find both stylistically and intellectually a trifle boring.
[24] A young historian recently restudied the isolationists, and in spite of a genuine sympathy he left their reputations about where they were twenty years before, which is not very high: see Manfred Jonas, *Isolationism in America* (Ithaca, N.Y., Cornell University Press, 1966).

diplomacy, and the book was shaped more by a new methodological approach to the problem than by any presentist perspective.[25]

Perhaps the best example of the sort of changes one observed as the post–World War II perspectives began to give way to those of the 1960s would be the difference between Herbert Feis' *The Road to Pearl Harbor* and Paul Schroeder's *The Axis Alliance and Japanese–American Relations, 1941.* Feis, after exhaustive research, was unable to discern a better line of diplomacy for the United States, given the circumstances. Schroeder, writing in the late 1950s, worked his way to a moderate criticism of Roosevelt and Hull for a form of moralism which he could easily have detected in Washington in the years after Feis brought out his own account.

An informed awareness of the general intellectual climate in which a book was produced is a vital part of the critical equipment necessary to take its full measure. But full evaluation of any piece of written history, and appreciation of its contribution and its deficiencies, requires more than understanding the milieu in which it was conceived. As we have noted, many books (meaning their authors) seem relatively impervious to influences of this sort. In any case, an intelligent appraisal requires that the reader know something of the subject and the historical controversy surrounding it. He should also be critically attuned to the methodological and conceptual techniques involved: the nature and use of evidence, the presence and extent of bias, the appropriateness of scale and focus, the underlying theoretical assumptions. I have tried to provide some discussion of historiographical background and methodological and conceptual foundations in the headnotes introducing each set of reviews, as no common discussion of these factors could be managed for eleven different books. The heart of this volume, of course, is the selected critical commentaries in which professional historians offer their own appraisal. With these resources one may read these books as they ought to be read—not (as all of us have at times been forced to do) as an embarrassed naïf who can only choose between uncritical awe or a boredom that masks his inadequacy and preserves his self-respect—but as a person in a position to think intelligently and independently about the past.

O. L. G., Jr.

[25] (Cambridge, Harvard University Press, 1959.)

RICHARD HOFSTADTER

~~~~~~~~~~~~~~~~~~~~~~~~~~~~~~~~~~~

The Age of Reform
[1955]

Chapters I-III [Populism]
Chapters IV-VII [Progressivism]

F OR FIFTEEN YEARS," a senior colleague from an upper-midwest university once said to me, "my graduate students seem to have read, and reread, only one book—*The Age of Reform*." His tone combined admiration and censure. Among recent American historians few have exerted an influence to match that of Richard Hofstadter, and while each of his seven books has been widely read and discussed, *The Age of Reform* has had the greatest impact. It constitutes a series of essays on modern reform movements—Populism, progressivism, and New Deal liberalism—and from the moment of its publication all the older interpretations were eclipsed. As its influence spread the book was paraphrased hundreds of times in print, yet it is almost impossible to summarize with reasonable fidelity. The book itself, while it conveyed a powerful and distinctive argument about American reform, was a complex, tentative, and well-balanced piece of writing. But its success put it into the hands of many translators with more enthusiastic and less subtle minds than Hofstadter's, the thousands of teachers and writers with an interest in recent American history. Their *The Age of Reform* was simpler, more devastating to old reputations, and, incidentally, highly irritating to some. Many historians, such as my Midwestern colleague, found the reputation of the book immensely stifling, and yearned for different answers, even different questions.

They did not have long to wait. After a few years of deceptive calm in which it seemed that virtually everyone endorsed *The Age of Reform* as the final word on modern liberal reform, a flood of articles and books showed that the book had stimulated an extensive scholarly reexamination of Populism and progressivism, bringing into these slightly stale historical periods a new speculative fertility and a greater degree of methodological rigor.

From today's perspective it is clear that the best work

Richard Hofstadter, *The Age of Reform: From Bryan to F. D. R.* (New York, Alfred A. Knopf, 1955. Paper: Vintage Books).

as well as the most work in populism and progressivism has been done since 1955, and while some of this increased attention was a result of natural factors such as growth in the number of professional historians, *The Age of Reform* deserves a major share of the credit. As readers of the following tiny sample of the *Age of Reform* debate will see, if there is a problem now, it is not the problem of any stifling orthodoxy, but of an embarrassment of new data and of theories as to what the data mean.

Hofstadter's discussion of Populism assumed a reading of the earlier historical literature, in particular John D. Hicks' *The Populist Revolt*.[1] In view of the existence of what he explicitly acknowledged as a solid and valuable body of narrative political studies of Populism, Hofstadter was attempting not another history of the farmers' revolt but rather an essay which would supplement and in important respects alter the existing interpretation. Others had written of the Populists' insights and their lasting beneficial influence. Hofstadter, granting these things,[2] wrote primarily of the sources of their ideology, and of some of their intellectual and temperamental deficiencies. In addition to this critical dimension, his treatment had both the power and the vulnerability of the essay form—it was literate and compact, and employed documentation sparingly, to illustrate the argument, rather than copiously, to compel agreement by sheer weight of evidence. He was in the main reporting new thinking, not new reading.

Hofstadter's was a revisionist argument in a persuasive form, and it made countless converts. But it also produced many critics with lengthy objections. No book should undertake such fundamental and seminal generalization, some historians felt, while relying upon sources which were largely secondary, too few in number, and probably unrepresentative. Others thought Hofstadter's preoccupation with the reactionary or "seamy side" of what had always been seen as a liberal popular movement derived less from the nature of his evidence than from the circumstances in which he conceived the book. McCarthyism, they said, had frightened urban

---

[1] (Minneapolis, University of Minnesota Press, 1931).

[2] Hofstadter gave credit to the Populists handsomely, explicitly, and, apparently, forgettably, on pp. 12–22, 60–61, and 94–96 of *The Age of Reform.*

intellectuals and caused them to project their current suspicion of popular movements back upon the Populists, another movement of protest arising in rural, Midwestern America. This latter criticism of Hofstadter as an Eastern urban elitist with antidemocratic sentiments has produced some bitter, insensitive, and generally useless language which those who pursue these debates may or may not find entertaining.[3] Unfortunately, it is a part of the record. But most of the critical record is what it should be—thoughtful questions about the representativeness of Hofstadter's evidence; whether he exaggerated certain reactionary tendencies among the Populists in view not only of their admitted humanitarian and liberal concerns but also in view of the fairly high level of nativism in the entire society in the 1890s; whether the irrational element in Populist thinking limited their effectiveness in an important way, and whether Hofstadter in discussing it at all did not inadvertently convey the impression that the farmers' *primary* problems were psychic and emotional rather than economic. These critics have produced some challenging new studies of Populism themselves, making the past fifteen years a rich harvest for those interested in agrarian political movements at the turn of the century. Norman Pollack, probably Hofstadter's angriest critic, published his *The Populist Response to Industrial America* in 1962;[4] Walter T. K. Nugent brought out a fine study of Kansas Populism, *The Tolerant Populists* (1963);[5] C. Vann Woodward, author of a brilliant biography of an important Southern Populist, Tom Watson (1938), brought his enormous erudition to bear on the argument in an essay, "The Populist Heritage and the Intellectual," in Woodward (ed.),

[3] Much of the criticism is, in fact, directed at a group of social scientists who adopted something resembling Hofstadter's viewpoint and used it to help argue for a broad distrust of rural uprisings—or even any popular uprisings. See for example, V. C. Ferkiss, "Populist Influences on American Fascism," *Western Political Quarterly,* 10 (1957); the essays by Peter Viereck and Seymour M. Lipset in Daniel Bell (ed.), *The New American Right* (New York, Criterion Books, 1955); more careful criticisms of the Populists appeared in Edward A. Shils, *The Torment of Secrecy* (Glencoe, Free Press, 1956) and Oscar Handlin, *Race and Nationality in American Life* (Boston, Little, Brown, 1957).

[4] (Cambridge, Harvard University Press, 1962).

[5] (Chicago, University of Chicago Press, 1963).

The Burden of Southern History (1960);[6] and Michael Rogin brought out in 1968 a full-length study of the relation of Populism and progressivism to McCarthyism, *The Intellectuals and McCarthy: The Radical Spectre* (1968).[7]

The seasoned student of history will not be surprised to find the argument unresolved. Hofstadter's critics have made some of their indictments stick, but his general argument has strong scholarly defenders. One important result of the controversy has been the completion of a number of empirical studies of exactly who the Populists were at the rank-and-file level, including data such as level of formal education, mortgage indebtedness (by volume and by type), recency of immigration, political affiliation and experience, and so on.[8] These studies thus far present a complex picture, but they seem for the moment to leave intact Hofstadter's notion that what bothered the Populists was not only economic deprivation but also the fact that they were the rearguard members of a social class in involuntary and largely uncomprehending transit from a simple society to a complicated, morally relativistic one. Economic data, it appears, do not entirely explain Populism, and concepts such as social alienation may ultimately have to be used even by historians most sympathetic to the ordeal of farmers in the early industrial age.[9] It has been a lively fifteen years for the reputation of Populism, but, despite the acrimony and the growth of data without an emerging pattern, we are much, much closer to an understanding of the Populists than in the years before 1955, when Populism had been pretty much "solved."

[6] (New York, Macmillan, 1938). Woodward's essay first appeared in *The American Scholar,* 29 (Winter 1959–60), 55–72. *The Burden of Southern History* was published in 1960 by Louisiana State University Press.

[7] (Cambridge, Massachusetts Institute of Technology Press, 1968).

[8] A good example is Stanley Parsons, "Who Were the Nebraska Populists?" *Nebraska History,* 44 (July 1963), 83–99.

[9] See the review by J. Rogers Hollingsworth, in the *Agricultural History* symposium, op. cit., 81–85. A useful anthology is Raymond J. Cunningham (ed.), *The Populists in Historical Perspective* (Boston, D. C. Heath, 1968). Some of the critical commentary reprinted below is from an important symposium on Populism published in *Agricultural History,* 29 (April 1965), 59–85.

Chapters I-III (Populism)

CRITICAL COMMENTARIES

WALTER T. K. NUGENT

The Tolerant Populists
[1963]

Only one writer of the fifties dealt with Populism directly rather than as contributory to some other study, and he has been its most influential critic—the historian, Richard Hofstadter. In a Pulitzer Prize book, *The Age of Reform: From Bryan to F.D.R.* (1955), Hofstadter did many things. He fitted Populism into a general interpretation of American liberal reform since the late nineteenth century. He arrived at many of the same conclusions as the social scientist critics but in a much more coherent and striking manner. He added fresh insights and new indictments to the case. He placed such social psychological concepts as scapegoat-seeking and status resentment at the core of his

From *The Tolerant Populists* (Chicago, University of Chicago Press, 1963), 16–27, 231. Reprinted by permission of the author and the University of Chicago Press. (Footnotes have been omitted, and reprinted sections slightly abridged.)

Walter T. K. Nugent teaches history at Indiana University, and is Associate Dean, College of Arts and Sciences.

argument. And all this he achieved so convincingly that the reader could set the book down with the impression that the scapegoat-seekers had become themselves scapegoats for many of the most censurable elements in American life today.

Very possibly this impression was not intended, because Hofstadter often pointed out that Populism had a rational, productive, valuable side and that he was simply interested in showing that it had "an ambiguous character." He praised the "reform tradition" for discovering "real and serious deficiencies in our economic system," and Populism, as "the first such movement to attack seriously the problems created by industrialism," for trying to remedy these deficiencies. . . .

Hofstadter's book went some distance toward a balanced view of Populism not only by presenting warnings such as these to less cautious critics but also by some insights that call for solid endorsement. As his book pointed out, the Populists were heirs and perpetuators of the American "agrarian myth," a view of life to which a once-rural country could naturally assent, a view that glamorized farming, country life, the self-sufficient yeoman, an economy of freeholders, as things peculiarly and supremely conducive to virtue, both moral and civic. Hofstadter did not remind his readers, however, that since in the Populists' day most Americans still lived in rural areas, their devotion to rural values was not so surprising; but he did render a service by recalling the deep roots of this outlook, from Jefferson, Crèvecoeur, Paine, and Freneau through the nineteenth century.

Another useful insight of Hofstadter's was that this agrarian myth existed alongside a very practical devotion to money-making through the cultivation and marketing of crops. If the farmer was a yeoman in theory, said Hofstadter, he was an entrepreneur in practice, and such a "double personality" led him to use the rhetoric of the agrarian myth to protect his commercial existence.

Hofstadter made two other points in his book that were all to the good in revising the previous writing on Populism. In the first place, *The Age of Reform* freed Populism from the toils of the Turner frontier thesis, through both direct criticism and the suggestion of a plausible alternative. Secondly, it declared that "liberal intellectuals . . . readily succumb to a tendency to sentimentalize the folk . . . [and] remake the image of popular rebellion closer to their heart's desire." Previous writers on Populism may well have taken too romantic a view, and a stronger dose of realism would not be out of place.

These helpful insights and careful qualifications did much to make *The Age of Reform* the valuable book that it is. But along with them went some severe criticisms. The Populists were conspiracy-minded, nativists, chauvinists and jingoes, anti-Semites, part of a long-time "undercurrent of provincial resentments," founders of a legacy of virulence, part of a credulous age but more credulous and vicious than their contemporaries, rebellious, suspicious, irrational. To arrive at these criticisms Hofstadter seems to have relied heavily and consistently on three things: several behavioral science concepts, especially status mobility; a somewhat elitist frame of reference in dealing with social structures; and what has been called the consensus approach to American history.

Populist conspiracy-mindedness, the suspicion that a gang of knife-in-teeth plutocrats threatened their every act, was an irrational outgrowth of the agrarian myth: The agrarian myth encouraged farmers to believe that they were not themselves an organic part of the whole order of business enterprise and speculation that flourished in the city, partaking of its character and sharing in its risks, but rather the innocent pastoral victims of a conspiracy hatched in the distance.

The Populists, Hofstadter maintained, particularly "loved the secret plot and the conspiratorial meeting," believed that "all American history since the Civil War could be understood as a sustained conspiracy of the international money power," felt the need of a melodramatic villain or scapegoat, and blamed this villany not simply on the domestic enemy, Wall Street, but on a foreign conspirator, Lombard Street, as well. No one could deny that there have been conspiracies in history, but the Populists went overboard by "saying that history *is,* in effect, a conspiracy"; therefore they were not just "singling out those conspiratorial acts that do on occasion occur" but were "weaving a vast fabric of social explanation out of nothing but skeins of evil plots." For these conclusions, *The Age of Reform* gave as primary sources eight references from four books by Populist or radical writers, especially S. E. V. Emery.

Populist nativism also sprang from the agrarian myth, said Hofstadter, who was the only critic of Populism discussed [in *The Tolerant Populists*] to make a firm allegation of nativism, although others had hinted at it, and in his view it was perhaps their chief fault. If the Populists were dedicated to agrarian life and "personal entrepreneurship and individual opportunity," they also wanted to "maintain a homogeneous Yankee civilization." Populism, coming as it did in an age of mass immigration, was "in considerable part colored by the reaction to this immigrant stream among the native elements of the population" and rose out of "the indigenous Yankee-Protestant political traditions." It in turn left a legacy of "hatred of Europe and Europeans, racial, religious, and nativist phobias" that has seemingly reappeared in "the cranky pseudo-conservatism of our time." Populism's connections with "nativism and nationalism" have been overlooked up until now, Hofstadter declared: The conspiratorial theory and the associated Anglophobic and Judophobic feelings were part of a larger complex of fear and suspicion of the stranger that haunted, and still tragically haunts, the nativist American mind. This feeling, though hardly confined to Populists and Bryanites, was none the less exhibited by them in a particularly virulent form.

To document these charges, *The Age of Reform* listed several pages in a book by Mary E. Lease (which were written at a time when she was only very tenuously connected with the People's party and which were cited elsewhere in support of conspiracy-mindedness) and one page each from a book by Tom Watson and a book by "Coin" Harvey. . . .

Aside from four books by three authors (Mary E. Lease, "Coin" Harvey, and Gordon Clark) brought in elsewhere in *The Age of Reform* to establish the case for conspiracy-mindedness and nativism, Hofstadter cited two sources for the charge of anti-Semitism: a statement by a New Jersey granger at the Second National Silver Convention in Washington in 1892 and the same novel that Handlin had flayed, Ignatius Donnelly's *Caesar's Column.*

Finally, the fact that Populism so effortlessly jettisoned the great bulk of its reform program to embrace fusion with the Democrats in 1896 on the previously secondary issue of "free silver" indicated their fundamental lack of principle—that their vaunted program was just a cover for a drive to regain agrarian power and prestige.

In *The Age of Reform,* three interlocking points form a base from which the qualifications, the valuable insights, and the severe criticisms rise in a cohesive structure. These three points are an adherence to the consensus approach, a querulous view of popular movements, which seem to threaten the leadership of an urbanized, often academic, intelligentsia or elite, and the use of concepts that originated in the behavioral sciences. Given proper analysis and careful application, each of the three may become a very useful tool for understanding the past; in particular, the use of behavioral concepts is quickly becoming a *sine qua non* in many areas of historical writing. Yet some exceptions seem to be in order regarding the use of these points in *The Age of Reform.*

The book exhibits the consensus approach mainly in three ways.

In the first place, American farmers (including the Populists) are for the first time described as strongly entrepreneurial and devoted to commercial enterprise. Although their agrarian myth came to deviate from it, their practical economic orientation was much the same as everybody else's: the Populists, in practice if not in theory, were part of the American consensus on economic beliefs. Secondly, although liberal historiography seemed to fix the Populists irrevocably in a stance of protest against an established order, as a group obviously out of the mainstream, the whole period they lived in was "an age of reform." Therefore, the Populists were not protestants against the evils of their time but exemplars of its chief trend. True enough, the Populists battled certain other groups very vigorously, but both of the contending elements agreed on important fundamentals (profit-taking, especially) and really should be interpreted as parts of a consensus rather than as opposites in a dialectic. When consensus history replaced New Dealish dualistic history in this way, the ideologies of the Populists and their opponents became not the uniforms of warring armies, but different patches on the same quilt of history, beneath which the two elements jostled each other for the bigger half of the same good old American bed.

The third use of consensus placed the Populists at some disadvantage. To the extent that they actually believed the agrarian myth and became oversold by their own propaganda, they engendered in themselves the neurotic aberrations of nativism, anti-Semitism, chauvinism, and conspiracy-mindedness; they deluded themselves with dualisms, golden ages, and conspiracies, and thus placed themselves outside the serene, cautious, capitalistic consensus. Such a deviation, and much of the resulting protest, became in Hofstadter's view irrational—to such an extent, in fact, that the rational roots of the whole Populist movement were obscured. Since his book omitted any discussion of the Populist reform program and its basis in actual historical conditions, since his discussion was pitched entirely at the subliminal level of the group and its place in an assumed age of reform, it thereby located the Populists outside the consensus as a lunatic fringe mainly deserving reproof.

Perhaps it is worth adding a comment. It is one thing to say that a consensus on some vague, broad fundamentals existed among the political parties and movements of the eighties and nineties (although there certainly were plenty of differences in the programs and origins of many of them); it is another to assert some consensus between one or all of these movements, on the one hand, and present-day American thinking, on the other. This is an error that leads easily to the mistaken belief that minority protests were a matter of rabble-rousing, not reform. Furthermore, he who commits it lays himself open to the charges of being anti-intellectual (since fresh ideas in economic or political affairs would become worse than useless) and unhistorical (since it effectually denies both specific causation and intrinsic differentiation between phenomena). . . .

Perhaps it is ironic that while consensus may have been good enough for interpreting the past in the contemporary crisis of the early fifties it was a dualism that mattered—a dualism with hyper-democracy, provinciality, and social and political irresponsibility, on one side, conspiring against rationality, well-being, public safety, and an educated intellectual elite, on the other. The valid place of education, responsible elites, and the rule of law in a democratic society is beyond doubt, but to seek to describe that place, as a philosophic problem alone and without reference to history, requires much more discussion than any single author, or obviously a line or two here, can possibly give. In fact, to strike a balance among the legitimate claims of classes and masses, of individual citizens, minority groups of whatever type, and the total community, has been a constant issue in the United States beginning at least as early as the First Continental Congress. And it ought to be an issue in any society that is not to be static. One may hope rather than fear that it will never be settled conclusively in favor of either side of the argument. The point is that the values of elites and majorities to each other and to an organic society are not absolute but a function of shifting historical contexts; and surely the context shifted greatly from the time of Populism to that of McCarthyism. . . .

The old writers on Populism, most of them inheritors of Wilsonian idealism, practitioners of Turnerian historiography, and participants in the reform urge of the thirties, erred by investing the Populists with an aureole of democratic dedication and by pointing out their grimy overalls and shiny frock coats. But Hofstadter and the other new critics also erred. They sketched too starkly what they took to be Populism's tendency toward a dull gray *petit bourgeois* authoritarianism running roughshod over the rights of individuals and minorities. With the demagogue McCarthy enjoying the support of one out of every two Americans in the year preceding the publication of *The Age of Reform,* it is easy to understand how the strength of popular

movements might suddenly become frightening and how the democratic impulse itself, together with such an outstanding example of it
as Populism, might become suspect.

The third basic point that underlies *The Age of Reform* is a
series of concepts that originated in the behavioral sciences. Four of
these are particularly important. First is status resentment: social
groups have at any time a certain place, or status, in a social hier-
archy, are very conscious of this status, and if their status becomes
lower (i.e., if they are "downwardly mobile") they tend to resent it.
As Hofstadter saw it, farmers were downwardly mobile, and Populism
was an expression of their status resentment. The second concept is
scapegoat-seeking: the status-losing group attempts to fix the blame
for its downward mobility on some definite minority group, or scapegoat, which may or may not have anything to do with the real causes
of their status loss. The Populists, according to Hofstadter, found a
scapegoat in the "money power," foreign elements, and so on. Third,
scapegoat-seeking and status resentment are pervasive: they are not
restricted to isolated attitudes or actions but underlie a general state of
mind tending toward neurosis of a paranoid type. Populist conspiracy-
mindedness, Anglophobia, and anti-Semitism were "part of a larger
complex of fear and suspicion of the stranger that haunted . . . the
nativist American mind." The fourth concept is irrationality of motivation: the conscious actions of an individual or a group may or may
not be well founded in reality, but in any case they spring from the
irrational, subconscious, libidinous, or psychopathological drives inherent in everybody, which increase in significance as the person or
group shuns reality and moves toward neurosis. *The Age of Reform*
gave very little notice to the concrete economic and political reality
involved in Populism and therefore left it to be viewed fundamentally
in terms of the psychopathological and irrational.

A study by certain prominent behavioral scientists of prejudice,
nativism, and anti-Semitism [among Populists in Kansas] contradicts
Hofstadter's views, but perhaps it is worth reiterating here that *The
Age of Reform* was not in any sense a diatribe or a one-man mudsling-
ing contest. It is a significant reassessment of a critical problem in
American historiography. It warned the reader against extreme or
overly simple views. It was a reinterpretation that contained many
new and valuable insights and in some ways was a fresh contribution
to historical methodology. Like any historical interpretation, however,
it must end with a question mark. Hofstadter cannot be blamed if,

after the book left his hands, the question mark was answered with so resounding a "yes" that the qualifications were drowned out, that a new, demoniacal stereotype rushed to replace the overly angelic one of earlier liberal historians. So while *The Age of Reform* improved our knowledge of Populism in several ways, it still left us in need of a corrective. This corrective should be more than simply the striking of a mean between Hicks and Hofstadter. It should try to answer both of their sets of questions and some new ones. In particular, it must emanate from a more direct and thorough contact with the primary sources. This book is not that corrective, but I hope it is at least a step in the right direction.

Although a sizable body of literature appeared during the 1950s that asserted that the Populists were deeply hostile to things non-American, the Kansas story does not support those assertions. In fact, it supports something more like the opposite of each of the outstanding points of criticism.

The Populists have been accused of nativism, both of a personal kind and of an ideological kind; instead, they were friendlier and more receptive to foreign persons and foreign institutions than the average of their contemporary political opponents. They have been accused of "conspiracy-mindedness"; for them, however, tangible fact quite eclipsed neurotic fiction. They have been accused of anti-Semitism, both personal and ideological; instead they consistently got along well with their Jewish neighbors and consistently refrained from extending their dislike of certain financiers, who happened to be Jews, to Jews in general. They have been accused of chauvinism and jingoism, especially with reference to the Spanish-American War; instead, such lukewarm support as they gave collectively to Cuban intervention was based on quite different grounds, and as a group they strongly opposed the imperialism that the war engendered. Finally, they have been accused of selling out their vaunted reform principles by seeking political fusion with the Democratic party, especially in 1896, and thus of revealing a neurotic instability; but instead, fusion was for them a legitimate means to the accomplishment of real, if limited, reform. In the case of Kansas, the largest of the wheatbelt Populist states, the five principal criticisms of Populism voiced by recent writers not only do not square with the facts, but should be replaced with a viewpoint so much in contrast as to be practically the opposite.

NORMAN POLLACK

Symposium on Populism
[1965]

Populists sought the establishment of a just social order founded on a democratized industrial system and a transformation of social values, each reinforcing the other in the direction of greater concern for the welfare of all. They rejected unbridled individualism and the competitive mentality, maintaining instead that neither a few nor a class should enjoy the benefits of civilization. The quality of life of the masses was the index by which to measure social improvement. . . .

Populism was not a retrogressive social force. It did not seek to restore a lost world of yeomen farmers and village artisans. The reverse was true. Of course Populists borrowed from the past, but they borrowed selectively . . . their gaze was directed to what lay ahead rather than to what lay behind.

In seeking to democratize rather than abolish industrialism, Populism was a progressive social force. Yet its orientation was progressive not only because it based its remedies on an accommodation to social change, but also because in pursuing these policies it adopted a highly affirmative stance. . . . Woven into the texture of their thought was the insistence that men *could* consciously make their future. Populists contended that there is nothing inevitable about misery and squalor, nothing irreversible about the tendencies toward the concentration of wealth and the legitimation of corporate power.

From *Agricultural History,* 39 (April 1965), 59–85. Reprinted by permission of the author and the Agricultural History Society. This selection, and the two which follow, are taken from a Symposium on Populism in *Agricultural History,* April 1965. All footnotes have been omitted, with the exception of one footnote in the Unger essay which is essential to an intelligent reading of the text.

Norman Pollack teaches history at Michigan State University, and is the author of *The Populist Response to Industrial America* (Cambridge, Harvard University Press, 1962). His essay has been slightly abridged.

Not the impersonal tendency but men themselves are responsible for the contemporary society, and for this reason men can—according to Populists, must—alter the course of that society in a humanistic direction. What stands out, then, about the Populist mind is an affirmation of man, a faith in man's capability to shape his own history. . . .

From this brief overview of Populist thought, with the emphasis on its rational, humane and affirmative qualities, it is clear the speaker dissents from the recent interpretation of Populism as the source of American anti-Semitism and proto-fascistic behavior. He does not find the movement xenophobic, irrational, opportunistic and in search of a scapegoat, and he does not transform its social protest into status striving, its discontent into the addiction to conspiratorial delusions, its attempts at farmer-labor alliances into retrogressive utopianism. In sum, he does not conceive Populism as an authoritarian social force. It is not necessary to review the critical literature here. Who the writers are and what they have said is by now common knowledge, as perhaps are my views on Professor Hofstadter's work, on the incidence of anti-Semitism in the movement, and my positive statement on the nature of Midwestern Populism. . . .

I did not come here today to rehash the controversies of the past, but to look to the future. I submit that the time for bickering is over, and that the following should be conceded by all, so that we can go on to more pressing problems as historians: one, the past decade and a half has witnessed the unwarranted denigration of Populism, and because Populism has served as the type-form for radicalism, we have also seen the unwarranted denigration of the reform tradition in America as well; two, the critics not only have not worked in the primary materials, but have ignored an impressive array of books, monographs and articles which flatly contradict their case; three, that whatever their motives, and I should like to think these centered upon a commendable endeavor, to ascertain the roots of authoritarianism in American life, they have not only failed to explain the rise of proto-fascism—and have so obscured the picture that we know less today than we did at the start of the 1950s—but historians have turned against the very currents of democracy and humanism resisting its rise. Opposed to scapegoating, these historians have nonetheless, and with no evidence, found their own scapegoat, the Populist movement.

I take these three considerations as no longer open to doubt, and will not stop to offer point-by-point refutations of the critical literature, or summarize the writings of Professors Hicks, Woodward, Destler, Arnett, and a host of others to show the humane character of Populism, or the fact that times were hard, and hence that Populists did not respond to non-existent grievances. Therefore the question must now be asked, why—despite overwhelming evidence to the contrary—did historians embark on the denigration of Populism, and why did the recent interpretation gain such widespread acceptance? Given the facts that critics neither refuted earlier scholarly works nor presented new evidence, given the facts that these earlier works saw not irrationality but the concern for human dignity, and not one pointed to anti-Semitism, given the facts that Populism expressed compassion for the under-privileged, both Negro and white, and that historians had agreed in viewing the movement as the summation of a whole century of American radical thought, where Man, written large, was at the center of the political universe, given this and more, much more, I think it can be said that the justification for the reinterpretation lies not in history but in the mind of the historian, and more specifically, the historian who feels compelled to rewrite the past with a vengeance.

When Professor Woodward suggests in "The Populist Heritage and the Intellectual" that critical currents in historical writing were a response to McCarthyism in the early 1950s, I think his explanation for what has happened is too charitable. I submit that there is a world of difference between standing up against McCarthyism and seeking to understand its roots unencumbered by predispositions as to where to look, on one hand; and not only capitulating but then turning on one's own philosophic heritage by identifying with the hated object, Mc-Carthyism, on the other. Yet, the latter is precisely what happened. Since there was no objective basis for singling out Populism, one can only conclude that the ultimate destructive force of McCarthyism was not to keep men silent, but to make them purge the very tradition of humanitarianism and radicalism for which the Populist movement stood as a notable example in the American experience. It is no coincidence that Professor Hofstadter's archetypal radical turns out to be not the man who protests against social injustice or economic inequality, but one who wants only a larger share of the pie, who wants to scramble up the ladder, who is governed in short by the capitalist-on-the-make mentality. The judgment is revealing. I see here not only a preoccupation with present-day values, and the attempt to read them back into the past, but also the rock-bottom of cynicism and disillusionment over man.

Now, I do not deny that the historian is influenced by the present when writing about the past. Whether Professor Carr in *What Is History?* specified the interaction between present and past to everyone's satisfaction is less important than his insight on how the historian must be aware of the dominant trends of his age when exploring the past. Still, by no stretch of the imagination does this reciprocal relation permit one cavalierly to disregard the past and write solely from the present, which I feel the critics of Populism have done. . . .

I have left the original question hanging, of why the denigration of Populism. . . . The standard literature on the middle classes provides ample testimony that the strains of modern society are not confined to the agrarian sector. The writings of Max Weber, Hans Speier, Franz Neumann, Robert K. Merton and C. Wright Mills, just to name a few, are too substantial and too familiar to have been overlooked by students of authoritarianism. Likewise, it seems highly unlikely that a post–World War II scholar could be unaware of the historical and sociological trends contributing to the breakdown of Weimar Germany and the rise of Nazism. The point is that in both cases—the corpus of writings on the nature of industrial society; and the principal example where proto-fascism erupted into its fully matured form—the signs lead directly to the middle and lower middle classes as the most volatile and unstable stratum in modern times.

The next step, it appears to me, one naturally evolving out of the discussion of the topic, would be to follow through on these insights. Yet, despite such obvious signs of non-agrarian authoritarianism, historians resolutely refused to investigate these other social forces. . . . [This] is due in part to the sociological backgrounds of historians themselves. . . . [but] is by no means the key to the problem, [although] it is important. If in fact there are distinctly urban and middle class sources of proto-fascism in the United States, as *is* the case in Western European societies, then historians whose roots are urban and middle class would find it difficult, indeed distasteful, to contemplate such a possibility. . . .

Historians currently engaged in rewriting the past, I suggest, are torn within themselves on viewing the post-war world as both distasteful and pleasant, and in this, they mirror a larger ambivalence in the American mind itself. Our society too is torn. As I see it, the essence of the Enlightenment heritage, the affirmation of the rationality of man and the confidence in his ability to make the world over, is being dessicated under the glaring sun of Cold War stresses. Torn between fear on one hand, and self-glorification on the other, the chief casualty in this ambivalent process has been our faith in human potentiality.

Herein lies the meaning of the denigration of Populism. Why

have historians been so quick to strike down the Populist movement, and why have the allegations, although without foundation, enjoyed such widespread acceptance? The question can no longer be evaded. Specifically, I submit that Populism represents all that we are not; it stands for the very affirmation we no longer feel; and because we do not find within ourselves the internal sources of strength to face the modern world, we have turned swiftly and relentlessly on the movement for possessing the courage and other qualities which we today lack. Critics of Populism write from a clearer present-day perspective than they realize. For what we project onto Populism is no more than our own times. . . .

In taking stock, I think we can dismiss the critics as being of little importance. Just as there would have been McCarthyism (under whatever label) had the junior senator from Wisconsin not been on the scene, there would also have been an attempt to purge the American past of dissident elements had several scholars not made their respective contributions. The ground swell was too overwhelming to be the work of any one man or group of men. To blame a handful provides too simplistic a solution, for the problem touches on the nature of society and not on the activities of a few historians.

The reasons underlying the denigration of Populism are complex, and cannot be more than tentatively blocked out in this paper. My remark a moment ago that historians are purging the past of dissident elements—a point I made four years ago in connection with *The Age of Reform*—can serve as a point of departure. We have witnessed over the last dozen years a trend in historical writing which superimposes a straitjacket of consensus on the American past. By that I meant in 1960, and still mean, that all traces of social protest are being eradicated in favor of a model which characterizes the historical development of the United States as no more than a euphonious assertion of capitalist-on-the-make values. There was no conflict, only harmony; and certainly not the existence of hard times which might give rise to genuine grievances. In sum, our society exhibits a pattern of splendid equilibrium.

Four years ago, I could not see beyond this point. Today, I should like to ask, what are the larger implications of the consensus framework? Is it a temporary response to Cold War conditions? If so, how does one account for our excessive fear over admitting that social protest existed in the past, or our zeal in superimposing a pattern of equilibrium on that past, or finally our alacrity in accepting the charges against Populism? In a word, does not the quest for consensus reflect a deeper anxiety than that stemming from a concern over McCarthyism at home and tensions on the international scene?

Perhaps the clue to the disease lies in its symptoms. Consensus tells us a great deal about the society receptive to its message. First, it is an unmistakable sign of stereotypic thinking. There is not only the tendency rigidly to categorize data, as a substitute for the analysis of specific evidence in a unique historical situation, but also the endeavor to categorize the entire span of our history in the same mold. We now know that stereotypy is a dangerous trait, and not just the mark of intellectual carelessness. Stereotypy signifies that the capacity for individuated experience is absent; facts are not treated in their own right, but only in terms of pre-arranged categories. In a nutshell, the significance of this pattern of thinking is that it represents the desire to eliminate uncertainty from one's existence. Rigid ego-defenses are erected as a barrier against seeing what one does not want to see. Conflict cannot be tolerated. Contrary ideas cannot be admitted, for fear that they will threaten one's very identity.

Second, consensus militates against adopting an intraceptive outlook. We are afraid to look inward, afraid to confront our past in all of its intricacies—in all of its blemishes as well as strong points. Anti-intraception betrays an attitude which places a premium on process and form, rather than on what is human in history. Fearing what we might find in ourselves, we regard the problems of man as an unsafe subject of discussion. The same barrenness of ego comes through as in the case of stereotype thinking. All men, the noble and the base alike, are reduced to a common formula, and made over into the image of ourselves. Populists and Jacksonians are capitalists-on-the-make because we are capitalists-on-the-make. For them to be different, to have dreams and aspirations which differ from our own, might serve as a reproach to our own values. Whether this represents self-glorification of present-day America, or self-loathing, or both, is less important than the larger picture which anti-intraception suggests. American society lacks the confidence in itself to take a close hard look at its past, both the best as well as the worst in that past.

Finally, consensus reveals an even more disturbing trait. By characterizing the American past in terms of a homogeneity in values, experiences and goals, we have promoted the myth of national purity. This is different from the chosen-people strain in our history, for the emphasis has shifted. We are no longer John Winthrop's city upon the hill for all to see and take heart in, nor even the turn of the century expansionists who want to civilize the little brown brother to the South and across the Pacific, although no doubt each of these sentiments persists down into our own times. Rather, the stress is upon uniformity for its own sake. The impulse is entirely negative. For it serves to bring cohesion out of chaos, a sense of belonging where that sense is not felt, in sum, a belief in homogeneity which provides the feeling of self-identification with the ingroup as opposed to the other, the stranger, all those who lie outside the national experience.

Hence, consensus contributes directly to ethnocentric patterns of thought. Through the assertion of purity comes the erection of mental walls, with a rigid ingroup-outgroup dichotomy defining who shall be on either side of the barriers. In such a situation, with stereotypic thinking and anti-intraception as derivative responses, further impetus is given to maintaining homogeneity, past as well as present, at all costs. This uniformity of outlook becomes a crutch; our past stands for fundamental agreement, marking the progressive realization of the expectant capitalist. We now have a sense of continuity between present and past, and the added reassurance that present-day institutions and values are the product of universal approval on this side of the wall, that is, among the ingroup. From here it is but a short step to maintaining that social protest upsets the equilibrium, threatens the consensus, denies the homogeneity of the nation, and thus is a form of treasonable conduct.

It is difficult to escape the conclusion that the critics of Populism and the society which finds the charges so congenial to its temperament exhibit the very traits of authoritarianism they impute to others. Not willing to admit the existence of authoritarian currents in ourselves and in our society, we project them onto others—the outgroup, the Populists, indeed reform tradition in America.

Thus, Populism becomes for the historian and the larger society what the Jew is for the anti-Semite. Both historian and anti-Semite require a scapegoat, and the character of that scapegoat is incidental. For each hates not Populists or Jews but himself. Each cannot affirm man, each has little faith in human potentiality or confidence in man's ability to shape the future and rationally control society, each cannot confront the possibilities of self-fulfillment in humanity—and frightened by these thoughts, each turns blindly to dependence on the homogeneous folk or the static past. In the final analysis, the denigration of Populism signifies the fear of man.

When I suggest that the consensus framework and McCarthyism are, far from being at opposite poles, actually one and the same underlying trend, I am of course not directing these remarks so much to the critics of Populism as to the society they faithfully mirror. Populism stands as the conscience of modern America. It means frank and full discussion over essentials, and not blind submission to the status quo; it means the people, indeed the much maligned common man, can take the future in hand and make a better world, and not elitist despair over human nature and contempt for popular movements as being degenerate mobs; it means taking the earlier democratic values of American society at face value and trying to implement them, and not the cynical, amoral pragmatism of today which finds the very notion of ideological commitment to be a sign of the crackpot. Populism is our conscience, and we cannot face it.

When I point to similarities of response in the critic and the anti-Semite, I do not mean the former (and society at large) is necessarily anti-Semitic. One need not be an overt anti-Semite to reflect the authoritarian thought patterns outlined here. To call the critic an anti-Semite misses the point, for both share in common a deeper negation of man. We have only begun, since World War II, to appreciate fully that anti-Semitism itself is more basically dehumanizing than an attack solely on Jews. Simply put, we know from psychoanalytic studies that ethnocentrism, stereotypy and anti-intraception, found in critic and anti-Semite alike, constitute the core of the authoritarian personality.

In the comparison I am drawing between the critic (and the society he reflects) and the anti-Semite, I know of no more penetrating analysis of this underlying authoritarianism than that presented by Jean-Paul Sartre in "The Portrait of the Anti-Semite." It is this statement of the problem which best explains what is happening in American society, why so much stress is placed on consensus, and why at bottom we have witnessed the denigration of Populism. When Sartre speaks of the anti-Semite, we could just as readily insert the critic of Populism, or better yet, the form such criticism takes.

For both critic and anti-Semite share in the search for uniformity. And both deny the efficacy and wisdom of social protest, not only out of cynicism of man's desire for human betterment and his ability to achieve improvement (utopian is a term of reproach for both), but also out of the fear that protest leads to change and change means the end to stability and certainty in one's life. Thus both cling to present-day values because they cannot plan for the future. They enshrine the status quo as a means of escaping from the responsibilities of living. Sartre describes this defeatist outlook as the product of men "who are attracted by the durability of stone."

What is consensus but this state of mind? The static equilibrium, the ahistorical consensus, these alone provide reassurance. We see an orientation here, to quote Sartre, "in which one never seeks but that which one has already found, in which one never becomes other than what one already was." And to insure this equilibrium, I might add, both must have a scapegoat. Balance is attained by eradicating the evil one. Then all is well again. . . .

Indeed if Populism is the conscience of modern America, I submit we should look to the heritage and take pride in what we see. The Cassandras of despair have had their day. The time has come to call a halt to the erosion of human values, and to the denigration not only of Populism but of man himself. Why fear today and tomorrow when we as a nation have had our share of splendid yesterdays? America has in Populism a rich tradition for moving in the direction of the affirmation of man.

OSCAR HANDLIN

Symposium on Populism
[1965]

The treatment of American populism in the last three decades reveals the extent to which history is still far from being a cumulative science which steadily refines the understanding of the past through successive scholarly discoveries. If any figure of speech is appropriate, it is that of the treadmill, with regressions and standstills as frequent as advances. A good deal has been written on the subject; progress, alas, has been slight.

Most of the difficulty arises from a pervasive Manicheanism

From *Agricultural History,* 39 (April 1965), 59–85. Reprinted by permission of the author and the Agricultural History Society.
Oscar Handlin teaches history at Harvard University, and has written many books on American immigration.

which interprets history as the battlefield between the forces of light and those of darkness—the good guys against the bad guys. In this drama, which can be pushed indefinitely back into the past, the honest, the altruistic and the patriotic constantly battle the greedy and the corrupt in defense of national virtue. This formulation has the virtue of simplicity and of clear identification of heroes and villains; its drawback lies in its slight correspondence with actuality.

The heated emotions the Populist movement aroused among contemporaries have extended into the historical literature. Although the political issues of the 1890s have faded, the heat they engendered persists. . . .

The need to cast the Populists as either heroes or villains turned the discussion about the false question of whether they were proto-Nazis or tolerant. Richard Hofstadter, using essentially the same evidence as I, added the pejorative designation "anti-Semitism," although he qualified his characterization more carefully than his critics think. The choice of that term was unfortunate for it stirred up a hornet's nest. Vann Woodward, Norman Pollack, John Higham and Walter T. K. Nugent in their zeal to defend the populists have thoroughly befogged the issue.

The tortuous apologetics of the defenders are wider of the mark than Hofstadter's blanket indictment. . . .

The same defensive attitude has confused his critics with reference to a much more important element in Hofstadter's account—the incisive analysis of the irrational element in Populist thought. The idea that politicians were subject to other than rationally calculated drives is not after all in itself startling; Populists, like Democrats and Republicans, were human beings. Yet the suggestion that their agrarianism or their belief in an Anglo-Wall Street conspiracy did not rest on pure reason alone has evoked an instinctive response which justifies them as farsighted men whose analysis of the problems of their time was essentially correct. Professor Pollack, for instance, feels compelled to demonstrate that they were progressive (or radical or socialist) in order to prove that they were not a "source for later proto-fascist groups, McCarthyism, anti-Semitism, xenophobia, and anti-intellectualism."

The techniques of defense are significant. The standards of judgment applied to the Populists differ from those used for their opponents. There is an assumption that the reforms proposed were self-evidently valid. And indefensible ideas were written off as irrelevant eccentricities. . . .

Too often . . . the defenders have uncritically assumed that the Populists were correct in their assessment of the problems they faced and the reforms they advocated. Certainly in the periods of falling prices and depression of the 1880s and 1890s, American farmers, like American laborers, had genuine grievances; but it does not follow that they understood their own situation or that their "folk-wisdom" provided them with simple solutions to complex philosophical questions.

"What really irked them," writes Professor Nugent, "was not commerce, but the abuse of commerce, not loans and interest but usury, not banking but special privilege, not enterprise but speculation"—as if those differentiations were clear and precise. It is easy enough to paraphrase the Populist literature in denunciations of "monopoly" and in demands for the "equitable distribution of wealth"; it is not so easy to determine just what those concepts meant.

When it comes to specifics, the failure of analysis is glaring. "More and more wealth of all kinds was concentrating in fewer and fewer hands." "Who does not know that no man can be nominated for president by either party who is not approved by the money power of New York and Boston? Who does not know that the railroad barons, democrats and republicans though they be, are ONE in the halls of Congress?" The Senate was a corrupt rich men's club; political machines perverted democracy; not overproduction but plutocratic monopoly, deflation and excessive distribution costs caused the farmers' difficulties. These judgments are accepted as statements of fact with scarcely any effort to go beyond the data presented by their advocates. Nor is there any more careful scrutiny of the remedies proposed. The direct election of senators and the primary would reform politics; monetary inflation, cooperatives and government ownership would raise farm incomes and lower consumer prices.

Can we assume that the advocates of those changes were wiser, more enlightened, more concerned with the public welfare than the opponents? In the perspective of the experience of the past half-century, these propositions are by no means self-evident. Direct election has not altered the character of the Senate and the primary has not weakened the political machine. Agricultural surpluses have not disappeared, cooperatives have had a negligible effect on distribution costs, and government ownership, to the extent that it was adopted, caused no cures. The discrepancy between results and expectations is not decisive—conditions have changed since the 1890s—but it is a warning against the passive assumption that the Populists understood what ailed them or knew what was good for them. It certainly leaves open the possibility that the Populists may have clung to their nostrums for reasons that were as non-rational as those which attached the goldbug or Bourbon to his own.

IRWIN UNGER

Symposium on Populism
[1965]

Norman Pollack is the victim of a serious self-deception. He wants desperately to uncover a viable American tradition of the left, and since he cannot, for various reasons, find it in the Marxism of De Leon, Debs, and Hillquit, Populism will have to do.

Populism, he says in effect, attempted to deal with industrialism as today's new left—readers of *Dissent,* say, or *Studies on the Left*— might have done. His very language betrays him. "Dignity," "dehumanization," "loss of autonomy"; these terms were not used in 1892. They are the verbal small change of twentieth century academic radicalism, and they reveal Mr. Pollack's inadmissible present-mindedness. Pollack is trying to do for the Populists what Arthur M. Schlesinger, Jr., attempted for the Jacksonians, with, I think, as little success. Won't we ever give up trying to impose the present on the past?

In justice to Pollack it must be said that several of his opponents have fallen into the same trap—though one differently baited—when they accuse the Populists of proto-Fascist sympathies. Fascism, I would suggest, like neo-radicalism, is the product of special twentieth

From *Agricultural History,* 39 (April 1965), 59–85. Reprinted by permission of the author and the Agricultural History Society.

Irwin Unger, who teaches history at New York University, won a Pulitzer Prize for *The Greenback Era: A Social and Political History of American Finance 1865–1879* (Princeton, Princeton University Press, 1965).

century circumstances. It has no direct precursors, certainly not in America, though no doubt—like all political movements—it drew on the past for certain useful ideas and even more obviously for its rhetoric.

But by directing the main force of his attack against a small group of social and political scientists who see proto-Hitlers and Mussolinis behind James Weaver, Jerry Simpson, and Mrs. Mary Lease, Pollack is not being fair to his opponents. The most influential re-interpretation of the Populists, Richard Hofstadter's *Age of Reform,* does not fall into this error. Hofstadter has never called the Populists Fascists; nor is he unwilling to acknowledge that they were indeed deeply concerned with the industrial problems of their day. What Hofstadter says, I believe, is that they were agrarian men with a limited understanding of the complexities of their era. They proposed solutions to current problems which often reflected their ignorance, their isolation from the best thought of the day, and their profound sense of frustration at the intractability of their social and economic environment. Clearly, he implies, we today, in a still more complex world, cannot expect inspiration from such a parochial and limited social vision. . . .

In a word, much of the recent criticism of late nineteenth century agrarianism is valid, although often overstated. This being the case—to adopt one of Mr. Pollack's rhetorical styles—we have already explained, without elaborate psychoanalyzing, the origins of the new view of Populism. There is no mystery about it. Populism had a dark side as well as a light one, and the recent critics of Populism have merely detected and described it. And yet Pollack is surely engaged in a legitimate enterprise in seeking to uncover the origins of the new views. The quest may tell us little about Populism substantively but it does, I believe, reveal much about the nature of the historical profession in America in 1964.

Unfortunately, as an historiographic undertaking Pollack's effort suffers from two fatal flaws: it is too limited in scope; and it is wrong. To begin with, what Pollack doesn't see is that his knife cuts two ways. We must not only ask why recent historians have been so critical of Populism; we must also ask why earlier historians were so uncritical of it. The answer, I believe, is very largely that the social origins of American historians have changed. With the exception of Mr. Pollack, who comes to the issue, as I have suggested, with special concerns, the disagreement over Populism among historians today measures the difference between Buffalo and Brooklyn on the one hand and Vanndale, Arkansas, and Pickering, Missouri, on the other.[1]

The new history of Populism is urban history, and to a large extent, if the urban men can detect the dark side of Populism, it is because they—like urban men in 1892 and 1896—cannot identify with rural, naive, simplistic agrarianism. Pollack, of course, has noted this urban factor, but he says it produced anti-Populism because intellectuals cannot bear to blame themselves for twentieth century Fascism. But since when haven't urban intellectuals been able to indulge in self-hate? Indeed, the advent of McCarthyism permitted them for the first time in years the refreshing alternative of hating someone else! No. I think it is the inadequacy of Populism for the complex urban world the urban historian sees around him, rather than his own failings, that makes him unreceptive to the style and ideology of Populism.

But beyond this urban rejection of rural values there does loom the very real, though perhaps exaggerated, response of intellectuals to the radical right. Who can forget the fact that those very areas that were like tinder before the Populist configuration have also burned for Barry? Who can ignore the attacks of the extreme right on the eastern, university educated "establishment," the universities themselves and the literate big city press? And when we extend our memories to the thirties, the overlap between Populism and right wing demagoguery becomes still clearer. Who will deny that both Father Coughlin and Huey Long owed an immense debt to Populism for both their rhetoric and their program? The fit between the Irish priest and Ignatius Donnelly is uncanny.

But I am not falling here into the trap of present-mindedness. I do not believe Huey Long, or Father Coughlin, or Barry Goldwater are either Populists or Fascists. But that they share some of the style, stance, support, and suppositions of Populism is clear, and this resemblance (and this is my point) explains in part why twentieth century intellectuals find Populism so badly flawed. Targets for the last decade of a constant barrage from Oklahoma fundamentalists, Midwestern rural Congressmen, and small town newspapers, for their supposed left wing sympathies, their Godlessness, their immorality, is it surprising that the Professors should regard with something less

[1] I am, of course, referring to Richard Hofstadter, Oscar Handlin, C. Vann Woodward, and John Hicks, respectively.

than total enthusiasm those groups in our past whose relationship to cosmopolitanism and urbanity was similar?

It is entirely possible that the urban intellectuals are mistaken in all this analogizing. The parallels between Huey Long and Jerry Simpson may not be valid. But if so, the error is an honest one. . . . Let us give Mr. Pollack the benefit of the doubt and say that he does not wish to be unfair to his opponents; he merely fails to understand them. Pollack calls those men who have detected a basic consensus in America apologists for the conservative *status quo*. He may be right about some of them being right. But many of them are really left, and if some critics of Populism have detected a basic consensus in American life, it is often with a sense of regret. Their mood is one of disappointment with the Populists for not offering a true alternative to *laissez-faire capitalism,* or so alloying it with intolerance, ignorance, fanaticism, and bad temper, as to make it impossible to use.

But do those who attack Populism insist on consensus? They don't deny that Populists were angry and disturbed. They do question whether they were angry and disturbed in a completely rational way, or at the right things. Was it rational to make the gold standard or the bankers villains? Was the city or the East the real enemy of the farmer? As I understand it, all that has been claimed by those who have asserted the consensual nature of American politics is that the range of American political life as compared with contemporary Europe was limited. We had no royalists; we had few serious socialists. We all accepted private property and private profit; we all favored universal male suffrage. There were no deMaistre's or Marx's in America. Who will deny these facts except those, who like the Populists themselves, must see the world in Manichean terms, as an eternal struggle between God and the Devil?

THE EARLIER HISTORIANS of the progressive era had never been much interested in why men became reformers. They generally took the progressives at their word on the matter, assuming that the flagrant social maladjustments of the day simply shocked the younger generation of decent, literate Americans into protest and reform. Such historians occupied themselves in describing what the progressives attempted and accomplished. Hofstadter, noticing that the enormous social problems of the 1880s and 1890s had produced nothing comparable to the progressive uprising of the Theodore Roosevelt–Wilson years, thought the timing of the reform impulse suggested the presence of motivating forces quite apart from the heartlessness of industrialism and the crimes of urban bosses. His account of reform motivation combined many familiar factors in an unusually comprehensive argument—the growth of trusts, urban poverty, class polarization of American society, a steady rise in prices after the Spanish War, the Protestant conscience, a revolution in journalism. But the most striking part of his analysis—indeed, people often forgot the rest—was his suggestion, based on a concept familiar to social psychologists, that the reform impulse was in part a function of declining social status among certain groups in middle-class society. With this sense of what had brought the progressives to their revolt, Hofstadter quite naturally was led to emphasize in their corrective activities those reforms which defended the economic interests, reinforced the moral beliefs, and reassured the anxieties of the Protestant middle class.

The general impression created by *The Age of Reform* was of a movement with some intellectual shortcomings we had not quite appreciated earlier—despite the critical remarks of Walter Weyl, Walter Lippmann, John Chamberlain, and, in his study of California progressives, George Mowry. None of these writers, all of whom had been to some degree critical of progressivism, had matched Hofstadter's erudition, intellectual intensity, and stylistic brilliance. None had sketched the progressives—their class origins, their characteristic modes of thought, their intellectual and tactical ambivalence —so fully.

Most reviewers paid generous tribute to Hofstadter's unmatched talents, and were persuaded by his argument. It is hard to overestimate the influence of the portions of the book dealing with progressivism. But reviews must be written before certain questions raised by a book may be looked into adequately; over the years, a substantial body of criticism has built up. Some early critics could not forgive Hofstadter for assuming that the "social evils" of early twentieth-century America might not be an entirely sufficient explanation of the reform impulse. They wished to keep the eyes of their students and the reading public fixed upon these evils (undoubtedly, and understandably, so that capitalism might be further reformed), and they saw Hofstadter's motivational inquiries as depreciating the extent of social injustice in recent American history, which of course in strict logic they did not. Some critics denied that historians should be allowed to make use of psychological or sociopsychological evidence or theories, an argument which seemed deplorably reactionary and which made few converts. Another early critic who attacked along unpromising lines was Andrew Scott, who argued that progressives were far more interested in "social justice" than in the defense of middle-class interests.[1] Scott reminded his readers in rather warm tones of the Progressive Platform of 1912, and concluded with a sweeping reassertion of the radicalism of the progressives, but his argument was stronger on passion than on evidence, and has not been tried again. The most effective criticism of *The Age of Reform* was not to come from scholars who accused Hofstadter of implying that the social order of prewar America had no serious flaws (especially as a close reading of the book revealed that this was a position he explicitly disavowed). Nor would it come from those who thought he had grossly underestimated the radicalism (or altruism) of the progressives, for such critics, to put it charitably, have not been supported by the work of the leading scholars of the period—Robert Wiebe, Samuel P. Hays, Roy Lubove, George Mowry, Richard Abrams, Gabriel

[1] "The Progressive Era in Perspective," *Journal of Politics,* 21 (November 1959) 685–701.

Kolko, James Weinstein.[2] Instead, the most effective criticism came from those who argued that Hofstadter had made certain methodological errors.

The status revolution theory, actually a small part of the book, occasioned a flood of studies designed to test its validity. These studies, of which Richard B. Sherman's was the first, have in the main revealed that had Hofstadter checked the profile of a control group of the "conservatives" (or antireformers) in the progressive era he would have found it to be substantially the same as that of the reformers. Some have felt that this discovery disposes of the status revolution thesis. I cannot agree—although the thesis does seem unusable in its present form. The idea that status decline may have sharp effects upon political attitudes has found support in some recent studies in social psychology. The fact that many members of groups who are or who feel themselves to be threatened by shifts in patterns of deference and power nonetheless remain politically apathetic does not "contradict" any theory relating status decline to political attitudes. The theory does not require every such person to run a higher political temperature than might be judged normal. If one finds a tendency *for this group as a whole* to be more politically active than one might expect (judging this by the political behavior of comparable groups, or of the same group at a time prior to the onset of status anxieties), then one has a suggestive correlation and perhaps a causal explanation. If it is true that much more must be done than Hofstadter did in order to make a strong case for the status revolution theory, it is also true that his critics who have checked the conservative side of the political equation, granting the value

[2] Robert Wiebe, *The Search for Order* (New York, Hill and Wang, 1967); Samuel P. Hays, various articles, including the one partially reprinted below, and his book, *Conservation and the Gospel of Efficiency* (Cambridge, Harvard University Press, 1959); Roy Lubove, *The Progressives and the Slums* (Pittsburgh, University of Pittsburgh Press, 1962) and *The Struggle for Social Security* (Cambridge, Harvard University Press, 1968); George Mowry, *The California Progressives* (Berkeley, University of California Press, 1951): Richard Abrams, "The Failure of Progressivism," paper read at the American Historical Association meeting, December 1967; Gabriel Kolko, *The Triumph of Conservatism* (New York, Free Press, 1963); James Weinstein, *The Corporate Ideal in the Liberal State* (Boston, Beacon Press, 1968).

of their work, are far from having demonstrated that no case may be made for the theory at all. If study showed that a sudden shift in group status did in fact seem to precede, and have a causal relation to, a heightened susceptibility to new social and political ideas and habits for the group as a whole, one would then need to know what other factor or factors distinguished the individual in this group who became a reformer from the one who remained basically satisfied with the society despite his own difficulties. Any number of factors might turn out to be operative—birth order, relationship to parents and/or siblings, a timely exposure to broader cultural horizons, and so on. The status revolution theory stands disproven only if one insists that all those experiencing it respond in the same way, and that it alone controls political attitude, a view which is not only unreasonably restrictive but one which I do not find in *The Age of Reform*. Another view of the possible usefulness of the theory is advanced below by Bernstein and Matusow.

Thus the status revolution controversy is at something of a standoff. But that theory has perhaps preoccupied us overmuch. Hofstadter had more important things to say about progressivism, and the most fundamental challenge to the book has been made by scholars who understood this, and ignoring the status revolution problem, argued that Hofstadter had concentrated upon an unrepresentative type of reformer. This error, they argue, led him to see reform as in large part aimed at psychological relief when in fact the real goals of reformers, while no less self-regarding, had primarily to do with the more rational pursuit of the political, economic, and occupational dominance of rising professional and business classes. At issue was the identity of the reformers, a vital issue which *The Age of Reform* pushed to the forefront of scholarly activity.

Hofstadter's interpretation was of course largely controlled by the men and women he had identified as reformers—which is to say, by his sampling procedures. These procedures, as with most historical work, were largely unsystematic and intuitive, and netted him a familiar group of intellectuals and political figures. But he had also used the results of two pioneering collective biographies compiled by George Mowry (in 1949) and Alfred D. Chandler (in 1954).

Combining these studies with his own research in primary and secondary sources, Hofstadter created a vivid composite portrait of the reformer—young, well educated, Anglo-Saxon, old-stock, by heritage and by personal occupation a member of the old New England elite of lawyers, doctors, clergymen, teachers, and independent businessmen. This reformer's most effective critics would be those historians who, because of different selection procedures (which might be either a matter of conscious methodology or of simply having pursued their researches into some different sector of the movement, and via different sources), thought Hofstadter's progressives far from typical of the movement. This critical approach to *The Age of Reform* rarely appeared in reviews since the work on which such criticism would be based had not been completed. Portions of Samuel P. Hays' article express such criticism.

Scholars like Hays and Robert Wiebe find the typical progressive to be a member of the "new" rather than the "old" middle classes—upwardly mobile professionals with legal or scientific skills in great demand in an urban, technocratic society; businessmen with expanding commercial horizons; in short, an energetic elite on the offensive rather than the defensive, eager to expand the role of government so that men of their type might impose organization and rationality upon a wasteful and disorderly society.[3] There have also been some brief attempts, like that of J. Joseph Huthmacher, to argue that both elitist views, old and new, are wrong and that progressivism was a movement with strong lower-class support.[4] This argument has been revived periodically, but without much success, since there are few sectors of the reform experience where even the most devoted friend of the lower classes could find them the primary source of progressive activism. Huthmacher made a thinly documented but plausible case that the lower classes in New York and Boston participated in the progressive movement in those cities, and recent studies suggest that the same may have been true for

[3] Wiebe's work is considered in detail in "Robert Wiebe: The Search for Order," pp. 112–23.

[4] J. Joseph Huthmacher, "Urban Liberalism and the Age of Reform," *Mississippi Valley Historical Review,* 69 (September 1962), 231–41.

brief periods (usually toward the end of the progressive era) in other cities.[5] But there is more and more evidence that the lower classes were usually the victims, sometimes the resisting victims, of progressive efforts (to close the saloons or abolish the ward system of city governments, for example). At any rate, Hofstadter's views are not necessarily incompatible with the interpretations of Hays, Wiebe, or even Huthmacher. Reformers came from all classes, and the movement was immensely varied. The difficulty lies in formulating an acceptable generalization about the class origins, motivations, and accomplishments of progressives, a generalization neither too sweeping to be compatible with known evidence to the contrary, nor too restrictive to satisfy our desire—which we may one day have to give up—for a coherent general theory of American progressive reform.

The final portion of *The Age of Reform* discusses the New Deal, and is best known for the argument that progressivism and the New Deal were substantially different, both intellectually and emotionally. This thesis, too, has been widely influential and vigorously controverted. Students whose interest in this question is only whetted by the critical commentary reprinted here may compare the review essay by Richard Kirkendall, "The Great Depression: Another Watershed in American History?," where Hofstadter's interpretation is challenged, with my own book, *An Encore for Reform*, which reviews the literature and presents evidence which tends to support Hofstadter's sense of discontinuity between the two reform movements.[6]

[5] The most determined spokesman for the view that urban, non-WASP and presumably middle and lower class groups were an important source of progressivism is now John D. Buenker; see for example his "The New Stock Politicians of 1912," *Journal of The Illinois Historical Society,* 62 (Spring, 1969). See also Melvin G. Holli, *Reform in Detroit: Hazen S. Pingree and Urban Politics* (New York: Oxford University Press, 1969), and Michael Rogin, "Progressivism and the California Electorate," *Journal of American History,* 55 (September, 1968).

[6] Kirkendall's essay appears in John Braeman, Robert Bremner and Everett Walters (eds.), *Change and Continuity in 20th Century America* (Columbus, Ohio State University Press, 1964); Otis L. Graham, Jr., *An Encore for Reform: The Old Progressives and the New Deal* (New York, Oxford University Press, 1967).

The Age of Reform is a remarkably durable book. It has been subjected to a degree of concentrated criticism rivaling that which was directed against Beard's book on the Constitution, yet one rereads it with amazement at the sophistication of its arguments and the variety of its insights. Few scholars are likely to enter more fully into the mental world of a certain type of progressive, or to combine detachment, sympathy, and resolute criticism with such felicity and balance. Along with George Mowry, Hofstadter persuaded readers of the 1950s of the essential conservatism of the progressive movement, and subsequent scholarship has reinforced this perspective. Whatever the fate of its various interpretive positions, *The Age of Reform* has been for a generation of historians their most demanding and stimulating mentor, demonstrating what no critic will ever contest—the value of literary craftsmanship, of thinking deeply and originally about what is known and presumably understood, of uniting for the purposes of historical study the techniques and interests not only of both the political and the intellectual historian, but of the more scientific disciplines engaged in the study of man.

Chapters IV-VII (Progressivism)

CRITICAL COMMENTARIES

GEORGE E. MOWRY
[*1956*]

This highly original and important volume departs from the usual survey of recent reform groups in several distinct ways. In the introduction the author states that his theme "is the conception the participants had of their own work and the place it would occupy in the larger stream of our history." Thus, the book, the author says, is "primarily a study of political thinking and political moods." He is far too modest. This study contains not only the public and private record of what the reform leaders thought, but also innumerable suggestions of what they felt but would not vocalize, and even what they would not admit to feeling. What Mr. Hofstadter has done is to write the history of recent reform groups in terms of both their perceptions and feelings as they moved up and down relative to other competitive units in the power and prestige complex of American life. In short, the volume

From *The Mississippi Valley Historical Review,* 42 (March 1956), 768–69. Reprinted by permission of the Organization of American Historians.
George Mowry, author of a number of respected books in the history of the progressive era, teaches history at the University of North Carolina.

is a brilliant foray into the psychology of reform groups and as such leans heavily upon the techniques and sometimes the vocabulary of social anthropology and social psychology. But whether one agrees with most of the author's arching generalizations or not—and the reviewer does—there is always a nagging question of certitude in applying scholarly techniques designed for use in the present to a past where the possibility of check and verification is small indeed.

The volume is distinctive in a second way. Up until the very recent present most writers of American history have approached their subject with a decided agrarian bias reflecting, in the author's words, a deep-seated belief in the "agrarian myth" that "rural life and farming was something sacred." This has been particularly true of historians of reform movements, since most such movements, at least in the nineteenth century, either welled up or found a good share of their support in agricultural sections. To the contrary, this is an urban-centered book, and as a consequence it is sharply critical of Populism and the agrarian side of progressivism as few other books on recent reform movements have been.

As such it is a valuable corrective and also a substantial additive to works that have preceded it, in the sense that Mr. Hofstadter analyzes agricultural aspirations and frustrations from viewpoints that have never before been so precisely and so persuasively put. But one has the feeling at times that the author occasionally fails to understand the agrarian mind and that he is making some of his judgments about Populism and agrarian progressivism not in terms of the conflicts of the past, but rather more fully in terms of the author's urban present.

Many historians will want to modify, or at least question, some of the author's generalizations, for example, such statements as that the Populists and the Roosevelt progressives were ready for war in 1898 because they hoped "it would unseat the money power," or that the Populist leaders sold out to the silver movement because of needed finances, or that the World War was the fundamental reason for the death of progressivism. In discussing the causation of the progressive movement the author has perhaps overstressed the "sense of guilt" factor, and has overlooked the place of American women in the movement, and the function of the rapid secularization of a religious fundamentalism. But such criticisms of this volume really do it an injustice, because it is full of sparkling new viewpoints, insightful remarks, lively quotations, and sharply etched characterizations. This book simply demands consideration for the Pulitzer Prize.

ANDREW M. SCOTT

The Progressive Era in Perspective
[1959]

Hofstadter's interpretation of the New Deal is closely associated with his treatment of the progressive era. Since he views the earlier period as conservative and sees little in it that was new, he is more or less forced to attribute all significant innovation to the New Deal. In this way he is drawn into a second major error. Along with underestimating the contributions and the radicalism of the Progressive Era, he exaggerates the radicalism and the contributions of the New Deal. . . . There were differences between the two, to be sure, but they were not always as he conceives them.

Hofstadter is right in noting that none of the previous reform movements had had to grapple with a depression like that facing the New Deal. Nevertheless, a number of the ways in which the New Deal sought to cope with the depression were foreshadowed during the progressive period. Passage of the Income Tax Amendment in 1913 helped prepare the way for the large budgets of the later period. Planned deficit spending was a New Deal innovation but the principle that the resources of a country should be used to promote the general welfare was not. The handling of relief and other programs on a national scale is an obvious extension of the principle that problems that have expanded beyond the reach of individual states should be handled at the national level. The 1912 Socialist Party Platform demanded a program of "useful public works" as a means of dealing with unemployment, the lending of funds to the states and municipalities by the federal government for public works, and the establishment of governmental employment bureaus.

From *The Journal of Politics,* 21 (November 1959) 685–701. Reprinted by permission of *The Journal of Politics.* (Footnotes have been deleted.)
Andrew M. Scott teaches political science at the University of North Carolina.

In trying to stress the difference between the progressive era and the New Deal Hofstadter declares that the latter period sidestepped "those two *betes noires* of the progressive mind, the machines and the trusts." On the matter of the trusts, however, it is hard not to be struck by the similarity of treatment during the two periods. Both were ambivalent, torn between regulation on the one hand and trust-busting on the other. Elsewhere in his volume Hofstadter concedes the similarity.

The New Deal never developed a clear or consistent line on business consolidation, and New Dealers fought over the subject in terms that were at times reminiscent of the old battles between the trust-busters and the trust regulators.

The parallel is understandable since New Deal thinking on the trust question had advanced very little beyond the point to which it was carried during the progressive era.

The SEC [Securities Exchange Commission], an important part of the New Deal program for dealing with corporations, had been called for in unmistakeable terms two decades earlier by the Report of the Pujo Committee and by the platform of the Progressive Party. . . .

Hofstadter notes that the New Deal did not concern itself with bossism, but this calls attention to a difference between the two periods only at the cost of emphasizing that progressivism was radical on a broader front than was the New Deal. The same could be said of Hofstadter's observation that the New Deal was "almost completely free" of any crusading for direct democracy. The New Deal has nothing to weigh in the scales with women's suffrage, direct election of senators, or the agitation about the initiative, referendum and recall.

Hofstadter finds another feature that he believes distinguishes the New Deal from earlier reform movements. "The demands of a large and powerful labor movement, coupled with the interests of the unemployed, gave the later New Deal a social-democratic tinge that had never before been present in American reform movements." This social-democratic flavor is supposed to have changed the nature of American reformism.

Hitherto concerned very largely with reforms of an essentially entrepreneurial sort and only marginally with social legislation, American political reformism was fated henceforth to take responsibility on a large scale for social security, unemployment insurance, wages and hours, and housing.

These are puzzling passages. The progressive era was not concerned "marginally" with social legislation but centrally. This is a point about which there need be no confusion. It can be documented almost indefinitely but perhaps the easiest way to clear the matter up is to draw attention to the section on SOCIAL AND INDUSTRIAL JUSTICE in the Progressive Platform. Social security, unemployment insurance, and wages and hours, which Hofstadter speaks of, are specifically referred to along with an array of other demands that had been agitated successfully enough to warrant inclusion. . . .

Hofstadter . . . says the New Deal was almost bereft of new social and political thought. . . . The New Deal could proceed without a Wilson, a Croly, or a Brandeis, because such men had already done their work. The task of criticizing the old ideas and shaping the new had largely been completed *during the progressive era.* It was because the basic thinking had already been done that the general approach to the crisis, as distinct from particular programs, could be agreed upon so quickly and with so little need for agonizing reappraisal. Franklin Roosevelt could restate the ideas of Theodore Roosevelt or Woodrow Wilson and seem moderately bold while he was, in fact, returning to ideas that had gone a long way toward gaining respectability several decades earlier. Scores of passages in Wilson's speeches can be laid alongside parallel selections from Franklin Roosevelt's and not suffer by comparison, as Roosevelt well knew. . . . Progressivism had become a part of the American political tradition, and the New Deal profited enormously from this fact.

The progressive era was more original than the New Deal and more daring as well.

RICHARD B. SHERMAN

The Status Revolution and
Massachusetts Progressive Leadership
[1963]

In *The Age of Reform,* Richard Hofstadter has advanced a provocative thesis about the "status revolution" and the motivation of
progressive leaders. His analysis draws heavily upon two significant
surveys of progressive leadership, one by Alfred D. Chandler, Jr. for
260 Progressive Party leaders throughout the United States and another by George E. Mowry for California. Although there are some
regional variations, the conclusions of both surveys are similar. Progressive leaders did not represent the population at large; rather they
had some distinct and special characteristics. Thus progressive leaders
were likely to be from urban, upper middle class backgrounds. They
were generally rather young native-born Protestants of old Anglo-
American stock. Many of them were college graduates. Most of them
were either professional men, particularly lawyers or businessmen
who represented neither the very largest nor the very smallest busi-
nesses. In New England especially they were likely to be managers of
older established firms, not aggressive entrepreneurs. Hofstadter, for
one, has used such summaries in presenting his notion of status
anxiety as a major force in motivating men towards progressivism,
and his thesis certainly has been influential in recent revaluations of
the progressive era. In the following analysis of Massachusetts a few
reservations are suggested about the usefulness of the concept of the
status revolution.

From *Political Science Quarterly,* 78 (March 1963), 59–65. Reprinted with
permission from the *Political Science Quarterly,* 77 (March 1963), 59–65.
(Footnotes have been deleted.)
    Richard B. Sherman teaches history at the College of William and
Mary.

In general the Massachusetts Progressive Party leader resembles the "progressive profile" drawn by Mowry and Chandler. However, neither of these scholars has presented comparable surveys of other political leaders at that time, so there is no basis for knowing how special the characteristics of progressive leaders were other than the fact that they clearly were not representative of the population at large. In my study of Massachusetts, Progressive Party leadership has been compared with that of the regular Republican and Democratic parties. The result suggests that the Progressive leader, particularly in comparison with his Republican counterpart, has essentially similar class characteristics. . . .

The typical Massachusetts Progressive Party leader was fairly young. As of the end of 1912 the average age was 45.2 years, and a sizeable number of important men were in their early thirties. While Progressives came from all parts of the state, a leader was most likely to live in an eastern city. Only five of the fifty were foreign-born (including one born in Paris of American citizens). Of the native-born Americans, twenty-five were from Massachusetts, and nearly all the rest came from New England or the Northeast. British surnames abound, and many Progressive leaders traced their ancestry back to colonial America. Of thirty-five whose religious preference is known, twenty-nine were Protestant and six Catholic. The educational background is known for forty-seven of the group. Of these, thirty (63.8 per cent) attended college or some special training institution beyond secondary school, and sixteen studied at Harvard. Slightly over half of them were professionals, including sixteen lawyers and a few ministers, professors, and physicians. Businessmen of various kinds made up nearly all of the rest. Of these none was connected with the very large national corporations; most worked for or owned firms of medium size in which they played a prominent role. Some led family companies, but at least six were "self-made" men, rising from poor backgrounds. But no laborers, skilled or otherwise, and no routine white-collar workers were among the group. The Massachusetts Progressive Party leaders were relatively inexperienced in organized politics. Twenty-six of the fifty had no record of previous political activity at the time they joined the Roosevelt movement in 1912, and very few of the others had more than very limited experience in local or state politics.

Such a summary fits in reasonably well with the picture of the progressive presented by Chandler and Mowry, but it also bears very strong resemblance to the description of the regular Republican leader in Massachusetts. Republican leaders were slightly older than the Progressives, averaging 50.5 years at the end of 1912. All of the thirty-six Republicans studied were born in the United States, and twenty-five came from Massachusetts, a much higher proportion than among the Progressives. Most of them worked in the general vicinity of their birthplace, and more than a third came from the Boston area. Even more Republican leaders than Progressives had British surnames, and of those whose ancestry is known, seventeen traced their families back to the colonial era. Every one of the twenty-five for whom a religious preference is known was Protestant, with Episcopalian and Unitarian the most frequently listed denominations. Twenty-eight of the thirty-six (77.8 per cent, a higher figure than that for the Progressives) attended college or some post-secondary school. Of these, fourteen went to Harvard, four to Amherst and three to other Ivy League colleges, while eleven undertook graduate study of some kind. The professional pattern was also similar to that of the Progressives. Although none of the Republicans was drawn from teaching or medicine, the regular Republican leadership claimed twenty lawyers, seven manufacturers, four bankers, five journalists and a scattering of other occupations, including a few duplications where two professions were listed. The most obvious difference between the Progressive and Republican leaders was the degree of political experience. As a slightly older group in actual control of the dominant party in the state, the Republicans had considerably more experience in politics. All of them had been active before 1912, and two-thirds had engaged in state or local politics before 1901. But as for their class origins, the regular Republican leaders of Massachusetts, even more than the Progressives, came from Yankee, Protestant, well-placed backgrounds.

The leadership of the Democratic Party in Massachusetts was drawn from much more diverse backgrounds than that of either the Progressives or the Republicans, and it clearly reflected the nineteenth-century immigrant impact. But even it was remarkably well-placed in many ways. . . .

This brief survey of the leaders of the Progressive, Republican and Democratic parties in Massachusetts indicates a considerable similarity between the first two, and a high level of educational and occupational attainment in the case of the third. For Massachusetts at least the leaders of *all three* parties were far from being anything like a reflection of the population at large as far as nativity, education, and occupation were concerned. Now this picture of Massachusetts leaders raises some questions about the explanation of progressives' motivation in terms of a status revolution. . . . In the case of Massachusetts at least, it appears that political leadership in general, especially of the regular Republican, was well placed in society. At any rate the Progressive leaders by comparison no longer appear to have such distinct and special characteristics. . . .

As most of the leaders of the regular Republicans came from backgrounds very similar to those of the Progressives, why did some men become Progressives, while others did not? If there was a status revolution, how do we explain the difference in reaction to it? Possibly the Massachusetts situation was a special case. Indeed one could well argue that the regular Republican leadership had shown a considerable amount of progressive conservatism in the past in terms of its legislative record. Still, given the conditions of 1912, one would hardly label as progressive such men as Winthrup Murray Crane, Eben S. Draper, John W. Weeks, Samuel W. McCall, and many others holding similar views. This survey of the political leadership in Massachusetts does not, of course, prove that Progressive leaders were not concerned about apparent threats to their class status. I believe that some, at least, certainly were. But clearly we must be cautious in drawing conclusions from a class analysis of progressives alone, for in Massachusetts their status was not an independent variable. Much more needs to be learned about the individuals involved and the many factors that motivated such men before a more adequate explanation of progressive leadership can be made.

STAUGHTON LYND

Jane Addams and
the Radical Impulse
[1961]

The impulse to radicalism has been getting a bad press. Students are being told that John Brown had "reasoning paranoia," that abolitionists and progressives were middle-class men who felt their status threatened by centralized industrialism, that Populism was anti-Semitic and paranoid, that Woodrow Wilson's insistence on Article 10 was Presbyterian rigidity, and that when Jane Addams was a little girl she would get up in the night to tell her father she had told a lie. Indeed the scholars who are seeking to psychologize out of existence that radicalism which will not rest until, in Blake's words, "we build Jerusalem in England's green and pleasant land," the motive-changers who have occupied the temple of divine discontent, have made Jane Addams a principal exhibit in their collection of curious cases.

For Jane Addams had the temerity to proclaim, in an article written in 1893, that the settlement movement was as much a "subjective necessity" for its participants as it was an objective necessity for society as a whole. The physical segregation of rich and poor in our great cities, she wrote, impoverishes the children of the rich as well as the children of the poor. "It is inevitable," she said,

that those who feel most keenly this insincerity and partial living should be our young people, our so-called educated young people who accomplish little toward the solution of this social problem, and

From *Commentary,* 32 (July 1961), 54–55. Reprinted from *Commentary,* by permission; Copyright © 1961 by the American Jewish Committee.

Staughton Lynd has written on the American Revolution, the Cold War, and the history of American radicalism. He has taught at Spelman College and at Yale University. He is at present a resident of Chicago, Illinois.

who bear the brunt of being cultivated into unnourished, over-sensitive lives. They have been shut off from the common labor by which they live. . . . They feel a fatal want of harmony between their theory and their lives. . . . They hear constantly of the great social maladjustment, but no way is provided for them to change it, and their uselessness hangs about them heavily.

In this essay, as throughout her writings, Miss Addams pointed to the great unused motive of the desire to do good.

I think it is hard for us to realize how seriously many of them are taking to the notion of human brotherhood, how eagerly they long to give tangible expression to the democratic ideal. . . . There is a heritage of noble obligation which young people accept and long to perpetuate. The desire for action, the wish to right wrong and alleviate suffering, haunts them daily. Society smiles at it indulgently instead of making it of value to itself.

It is easy to see how such a frank confession of personal need to do good by a do-gooder provides an opening for those who have been questioning the validity of radical action by exploring its psychic origins.

Thus Richard Hofstadter, in his brilliant and influential book, *The Age of Reform,* calls this essay by Jane Addams "fine," but puts it in the context of the progressives' sense of guilt. The context, it seems to me, erodes the adjective. Does he mean to say that it was wrong or abnormal for a member of the urban middle class in 1900 (or for that matter, today) to feel guilt about living in comfort when millions of immigrant families battled tuberculosis and the sweatshop in filthy and overcrowded tenements? In some of the Mulberry Bend tenements, finally destroyed after a decade of agitation led by Jacob Riis, the infant death rate was one in five. What exactly is one meant to conclude about the reform activity of a John Brown, a Henry Demarest Lloyd, or a Jane Addams, when told that they suffered from a sense of guilt? It hardly "explains" the uniqueness of a Jane Addams. Social-psychological generalizations which may in some rough fashion explain the behavior of masses of men in conventional circumstances fall down just at that point where the radical impulse comes into play: in unusual persons, and in circumstances which compel ordinary persons to improvise action to meet elemental needs.

Another way to view Jane Addams's essay on "The Subjective Necessity for Social Settlements" is to see in it the kind of mood which swept Russian youth in the last decades of the 19th century, the youth of Israel between the two World Wars, and the young people of Japan and of so many underdeveloped countries today. A mood, that is, which condemns the material exploitation and spiritual poverty of bourgeois society, and which strikes out desperately for an opposition way of life. In these youth movements one finds characteristically a mystique of the people and the land, a desire to go among common people, and by sharing their life to learn from them a simple intuitive wisdom. Characteristic above all of this mood and these movements is a relentless desire that the radical impulse shall find its outlet in action, that every detail of daily life be purged in its purifying fire: so girls cut their hair short, a brutal honesty is practiced in all the commonplace exchanges of the day, brilliant lawyers and doctors throw up their careers and take up manual labor. Whether of this century or the last, of the West or the East, Communists or Christians, these young people ask, in reality, one question: Is there then no longer a place for the totally committed life?

RAY GINGER

Essays on Sources
[1965]

Richard Hofstadter, *The Age of Reform: From Bryan to F.D.R.* (1955) is not as bad as might be inferred from Norman Pollack, "Hofstadter on Populism: A Critique of 'The Age of Reform,'" *Journal of Southern History,* vol. 26 (1960), 478–500, but neither is it as good as has been widely claimed. On three major points

From *The Age of Excess* (New York, Macmillan, 1965), 343–46. Reprinted with permission of The Macmillan Company from *The Age of Excess* by Ray Ginger. © 1965 by Ray Ginger.
    Ray Ginger, author of *The Age of Excess* and a number of other books, among them a biography of Eugene Debs, teaches history at Wayne State University.

it seems to me basically right: (1) Jingoism and imperialism were so rampant in Populist regions in the years leading to the Spanish-American War that the notion of an "isolationist" Midwest at that time is highly suspect. (2) Make-believe was a major element in the progressive era; on crucial problems what the movement sought was "a purely ceremonial solution" (Hofstadter, p. 243); and Roosevelt's success in satisfying that mood was central to his popularity. (3) Very probably most progressive leaders were white middle-class Protestants in the cities.

Minor matters aside, *The Age of Reform* has major defects. Its analysis depends on minimizing the economic problems of both the Populist and progressive periods. (a) Hofstadter: The Populists failed to realize that their plight was a result of world wide overproduction of certain staples. True, but it was also a result of Federal policy. For Populism as "farm interest politics," see C. Vann Woodward, "The Populist Heritage and the Intellectual," *American Scholar,* vol. 29 (1959–1960), especially p. 63. (b) Having barely noted the devastating squeeze on farmers in a period of "rubber money and iron debts," Hofstadter presents them as a parochial bunch (they were) beset by status anxieties (a doubtful point) that were manifested in anti-Semitism and other types of xenophobia. He writes: "It is not too much to say the Greenback-Populist tradition activated most of what we have of modern popular anti-Semitism in the United States." (p. 80). In contrast David M. Potter has written: ". . . the evidence of a high correlation between Populism and anti-Semitism is flimsy." I agree; see Norman Pollack, "The Myth of Populist Anti-Semitism," *American Historical Review,* vol. 68 (1962–1963), 76–80, and Walter T. K. Nugent, *The Tolerant Populists: Kansas Populism and Nativism* (1963).

(c) Hofstadter: Progressivism was provoked chiefly by a status revolution that lowered the position in society of white Protestant Anglo-Saxons among the urban middle classes. He writes: "Curiously, the progressive revolt—even when we have made allowance for the brief panic of 1907 and the downward turn in business in 1913—took place almost entirely during a period of sustained and general prosperity." (pp. 134–135) Compare Cochran, *The American Business System;* pp. 22–23: "The progressive movement, for example, reached its height during the years 1908 to 1914 when for nonagricultural sectors of the economy recession or depression was more the rule than prosperity." Both statements are exaggerated. The best statistics we have show that real Gross National Product on a per capita basis was growing from 1907 to 1911, but at less than half as rapid a rate as from 1902 to 1906. In the progressive era millions of Americans lived in extreme poverty. Many middle-class persons suffered losses in income as well as in status from the combination movement: for small businessmen the point is obvious, and in *Altgeld's America* I tried to show how ordinary lawyers—important in the leadership of any political movement—lost sizable portions of their law practices because of changes in the business world. (d) Neither Chandler nor Mowry, the students on whom Hofstadter relies in describing the traits of progressive leaders, used a control group in his study; that is, neither proved that the same traits would not characterize the leadership of, say, the Old Guard Republicans. Surely a demonstration of this point would be useful in showing that a status revolution was correlated with progressivism. (e) Hofstadter implies that the same social group that produced progressive leadership also provided its mass support among voters. No compelling evidence on this point has been produced, and I think we should heed the warning in another connection about "the confusion that has come often from interpolating from its leadership the nature of the Federalist party as a party." (Shaw Livermore, Jr., *The Twilight of Federalism,* 1962, p. 6). (f) Hofstadter: "In politics, then, the immigrant was usually at odds with the reform aspirations of the American progressive." (pp. 180–181) Here again *The Age of Reform* seems to be coarse-grained, aimed more at working out the implications of certain psychological and sociological assumptions than at working into the historical record; see J. Joseph Huthmacher, "Urban Liberalism and the Age of Reform," *Mississippi Valley Historical Review,* vol. 49 (1962–1963), 231–241. The insistent demand now current in some historical circles for "revisionism" is not a valid reason to brush aside older scholarship in order to embrace ideas that are startlingly original but mistaken, and evidence contrary to much of Hofstadter's argument is available in many careful studies.

BARTON J. BERNSTEIN
AND ALLEN J. MATUSOW

Twentieth Century America:
Recent Interpretations
[1969]

Among the studies other than Hays' that criticize the "status revolution" (the theory that status anxiety greatly contributed to, or produced, progressivism) are Richard B. Sherman's "The Status Revolution and Massachusetts Progressive Leadership," *Political Science Quarterly,* 78 (March 1963), 59–65; E. Daniel Potts' "The Progressive Profile in Iowa," *Mid-America,* 47 (Oct. 1965), 257–68 and Jack Tager's "Progressives, Conservatives and the Theory of the Status Revolution." *Mid-America,* 48 (July 1966), 162–75. These writers generally conclude that state progressive political leaders did not differ significantly in social profile from Republican leaders. The theory of the status revolution, however, might be partly redeemed if status is defined by the individual reformer's *own* perception; but then there is still a need to explain why such perceptions were so different from those of others in the *same objective* positions. What is needed to test the interpretation that a status revolution contributed to the making of progressives is a collective biography of progressive and nonprogressive leaders that will delve beyond objective criteria of social position (such as education, religion, occupation) to examine through diaries, reports, and other sources, the views that these men held of their own position, and whether they thought they were rising or falling on the social scale.

From *Twentieth Century America: Recent Interpretations* (New York, Harcourt, Brace & World, 1969), 58. Reprinted by permission of Harcourt, Brace & World.

Barton J. Bernstein, of Stanford University, and Allen J. Matusow, of Rice University, are historians of modern America.

SAMUEL P. HAYS

The Politics of Reform in
Municipal Government in the Progressive Era
[1964]

In order to achieve a more complete understanding of social
change in the progressive era, historians must now undertake a deeper
analysis of the practices of economic, political, and social groups.
Political ideology alone is no longer satisfactory evidence to describe
social patterns because generalizations based upon it, which tend to
divide political groups into the moral and the immoral, the rational
and the irrational, the efficient and the inefficient, do not square with
political practice. Behind this contemporary rhetoric concerning the
nature of reform lay patterns of political behavior which were at
variance with it. Since an extensive gap separated ideology and practice, we can no longer take the former as an accurate description of
the latter, but must reconstruct social behavior from other types of
evidence.

Reform in urban government provides one of the most striking
examples of this problem of analysis. The demand for change in municipal affairs, whether in terms of over-all reform, such as the commission and city-manager plans, or of more piecemeal modifications,
such as the development of city-wide school boards, deeply involved
reform ideology. Reformers loudly proclaimed a new structure of
municipal government as more moral, more rational, and more efficient and, because it was so, self-evidently more desirable. But precisely because of this emphasis, there seemed to be no need to analyze

From *Pacific Northwest Quarterly,* 55 (October 1964), 157–69. Reprinted
with permission of the author and *Pacific Northwest Quarterly.* Only a portion of article appears here, and footnotes have been omitted.

Samuel P. Hays, whose contribution to the history of recent America
is discussed in the introduction to Wiebe's *The Search for Order* (112–17),
teaches history at the University of Pittsburgh.

the political forces behind change. Because the goals of reform were good, its causes were obvious; rather than being the product of particular people and particular ideas in particular situations, they were deeply imbedded in the universal impulses and truths of "progress." Consequently, historians have rarely tried to determine precisely who the municipal reformers were or what they did, but instead have relied on reform ideology as an accurate description of reform practice.

The reform ideology which became the basis of historical analysis is well known. It appears in classic form in Lincoln Steffens' *Shame of the Cities*. The urban political struggle of the Progressive Era, so the argument goes, involved a conflict between public impulses for "good government" against a corrupt alliance of "machine politicians" and "special interests."

During the rapid urbanization of the late 19th century, the latter had been free to aggrandize themselves, especially through franchise grants, at the expense of the public. Their power lay primarily in their ability to manipulate the political process, by bribery and corruption, for their own ends. Against such arrangements there gradually arose a public protest, a demand by the public for honest government, for officials who would act for the public rather than for themselves. To accomplish their goals, reformers sought basic modifications in the political system, both in the structure of government and in the manner of selecting public officials. These changes, successful in city after city, enabled the "public interest" to triumph.

Recently, George Mowry, Alfred Chandler, Jr., and Richard Hofstadter have modified this analysis by emphasizing the fact that the impulse for reform did not come from the working class. This might have been suspected from the rather strained efforts of National Municipal League writers in the "Era of Reform" to go out of their way to demonstrate working-class support for commission and city-manager governments. We now know that they clutched at straws, and often erroneously, in order to prove to themselves as well to the public that municipal reform was a mass movement.

The Mowry-Chandler-Hofstadter writings have further modified older views by asserting that reform in general and municipal reform in particular sprang from a distinctively middle-class movement. This has now become the prevailing view. Its popularity is surprising not only because it is based upon faulty logic and extremely limited evidence, but also because it, too, emphasizes the analysis of ideology rather than practice and fails to contribute much to the understanding of who distinctively were involved in reform and why.

Ostensibly, the "middle-class" theory of reform is based upon a new type of behavioral evidence, the collective biography, in studies by Mowry of California Progressive party leaders, by Chandler of a nationwide group of that party's leading figures, and by Hofstadter of four professions—ministers, lawyers, teachers, editors. These studies demonstrate the middle-class nature of reform, but they fail to determine if reformers were distinctively middle class, specifically if they differed from their opponents. One study of 300 political leaders in the state of Iowa, for example, discovered that Progressive party, Old Guard, and Cummins Republicans were all substantially alike, the Progressives differing only in that they were slightly younger than the others and had less political experience. If its opponents were also middle class, then one cannot describe Progressive reform as a phenomenon, the special nature of which can be explained in terms of middle-class characteristics. One cannot explain the distinctive behavior of people in terms of characteristics which are not distinctive to them.

Hofstadter's evidence concerning professional men fails in yet another way to determine the peculiar characteristics of reformers. For he describes ministers, lawyers, teachers, and editors without determining who within these professions became reformers and who did not. Two analytical distinctions might be made. Ministers involved in municipal reform, it appears, came not from all segments of religion, but peculiarly from upper-class churches. They enjoyed the highest prestige and salaries in the religious community and had no reason to feel a loss of "status," as Hofstadter argues. Their role in reform arose from the class character of their religious organizations rather than from the mere fact of their occupation as ministers. Professional men involved in reform (many of whom—engineers, architects, and doctors—Hofstadter did not examine at all) seem to have come especially from the more advanced segments of their professions, from those who sought to apply their specialized knowledge to a wider range of public affairs. Their role in reform is related not to their attempt to defend earlier patterns of culture, but to the working out of the inner dynamics of professionalization in modern society.

The weakness of the "middle-class" theory of reform stems from the fact that it rests primarily upon ideological evidence, not on a thorough-going description of political practice. Although the studies of Mowry, Chandler, and Hofstadter ostensibly derive from behavioral evidence, they actually derive largely from the extensive ex-

pressions of middle-ground ideological position, of the reformers' own
descriptions of their contemporary society, and of their expressed fears
of both the lower and the upper classes, of the fright of being ground
between the millstones of labor and capital.

Such evidence, though it accurately portrays what people thought,
does not accurately describe what they did. The great majority of
Americans look upon themselves as "middle class" and subscribe to
a middle-ground ideology, even though in practice they belong to a
great variety of distinct social classes. Such ideologies are not rationalizations or deliberate attempts to deceive. They are natural phenomena of human behavior. But the historian should be especially
sensitive to their role so that he will not take evidence of political
ideology as an accurate representation of political practice.

In the following account I will summarize evidence in both secondary and primary works concerning the political practices in which
municipal reformers were involved. . . .

Available evidence indicates that the source of support for reform in municipal government did not come from the lower or middle
classes, but from the upper class. The leading business groups in
each city and professional men closely allied with them initiated and
dominated municipal movements. . . .

The movement for reform in municipal government, therefore,
constituted an attempt by upper-class, advanced professional, and
large business groups to take formal political power from the previously dominant lower- and middle-class elements so that they might
advance their own conceptions of desirable public policy. These two
groups came from entirely different urban worlds, and the political
system fashioned by one was no longer acceptable to the other.

Lower- and middle-class groups not only dominated the pre-
reform governments, but vigorously opposed reform. It is significant
that none of the occupational groups among them, for example, small
businessmen or white-collar workers, skilled or unskilled artisans,
had important representation in reform organizations thus far examined. . . .

Reformers in the progressive era and liberal historians since
then misread the nature of the movement to change municipal government because they concentrated upon dramatic and sensational episodes and ignored the analysis of more fundamental political structure,
of the persistent relationships of influence and power which grew
out of the community's social, ideological, economic, and cultural
activities. The reconstruction of these patterns of human relationships

and of the changes in them is the historian's most crucial task, for they constitute the central context of historical development. History consists not of erratic and spasmodic fluctuations, of a series of random thoughts and actions, but of patterns of activity and change in which people hold thoughts and actions in common and in which there are close connections between sequences of events. These contexts give rise to a structure of human relationships which pervade all areas of life; for the political historian the most important of these is the structure of the distribution of power and influence.

The structure of political relationships, however, cannot be adequately understood if we concentrate on evidence concerning ideology rather than practice. For it is becoming increasingly clear that ideological evidence is no safe guide to the understanding of practice, that what people thought and said about their society is not necessarily an accurate representation of what they did. The current task of the historian of the progressive era is to quit taking the reformers' own description of political practice at its face value and to utilize a wide variety of new types of evidence to reconstruct political practice in its own terms. This is not to argue that ideology is either important or unimportant. It is merely to state that ideological evidence is not appropriate to the discovery of the nature of political practice.

Only by maintaining this clear distinction can the historian successfully investigate the structure of political life in the progressive era. And only then can he begin to cope with the most fundamental problem of all: the relationship between political ideology and political practice. For each of these facets of political life must be understood in its own terms, through its own historical record. Each involves a distinct set of historical phenomena. The relationship between them for the progressive era is not now clear; it has not been investigated. But it cannot be explored until the conceptual distinction is made clear and evidence tapped which is pertinent to each. Because the nature of political practice has so long been distorted by the use of ideological evidence, the most pressing task is for its investigation through new types of evidence appropriate to it. The reconstruction of the movement for municipal reform can constitute a major step forward toward that goal.

GABRIEL KOLKO

The Triumph of Conservatism
[1963]

F OR MORE THAN FORTY YEARS there was a rough agreement about the nature and accomplishments of the progressive era. Any summary will partially caricature that consensus, so I will make my summary brief: In the years between the 1890s and the onset of World War I there occurred in many American cities, most states, and at the federal level a broad political movement whose purpose was to cope with the flaws of rapid industrialization and urbanization by democratizing the various American political systems and conferring upon these systems new powers of economic regulation. The entire process was far from easy and was of course never entirely completed, but in the end (by common consent, about 1916) American life was more humane, democratic, and the public interest better protected, than when the century opened. This synthesis of the progressive era was created by historians of intelligence and honesty, and from the earliest histories [1] into the 1960s this interpretive framework for the public events of the era seemed the right one into which to cast what they knew of these years. The synthesis relied heavily upon phrases such as social justice, democracy, and the "welfare state," and it arrayed a familiar group of progressive reformers—insurgent politicians, muckrakers, stray intellectuals, social workers, and one or two Presidents. It was invariably presented in a spirit of modest national self-congratulation at so much enlightenment and social progress.

The foregoing interpretative framework was not fundamentally disturbed by cumulative discoveries that progressive reformers had been somewhat reactionary in their preference for small-scale capitalism, in their subsurface fear

Gabriel Kolko, *The Triumph of Conservatism: A Reinterpretation of American History, 1900–1916* (New York, Free Press, 1963. Paper: Quadrangle).

[1] Good examples are Benjamin P. DeWitt, *The Progressive Movement* (New York, Macmillan, 1915) and Harold U. Faulkner, *The Quest for Social Justice, 1898–1914* (New York, Harper, 1931).

of cities, in their insensitivity to the plight of nonwhite and nonentrepreneurial groups.[2] Progressivism, historians in the 1950s were quite ready to admit, had been a more complex social movement than originally thought, with illiberal as well as liberal tendencies. But even after Hofstadter, its liberal aspects (meaning an emphasis upon social justice, humanitarianism, and public regulation of private enterprise), appeared to have overshadowed the more defensive reform reflexes of the middle class, such as prohibition, immigration restriction, Sunday-closing laws, eugenics, and so on. New information about who progressives were and what they wanted could usually be fitted into the old framework, the "People vs. the Interests" schema Arthur M. Schlesinger, Jr., once summarized in an oft-cited definition: "Liberalism in America has been ordinarily the movement on the part of the other sections of society to restrain the power of the business community." When new data could not easily be contained in the old bottles, such as Robert Wiebe's demonstration in his *Businessmen and Reform* (1962) that businessmen had often worked *for* progressive legislation, it was set aside in a "file for later use" category.[3] In writing and in teaching, the old periodization held firm into the 1960s, with its sharp break between the reform years and the decade of postwar conservatism. George Mowry proved in 1958, in *The Era of Theodore Roosevelt 1900–1912,*[4] that a gifted historian could absorb and use the new information about the shortcomings of progressives without abandoning the main outlines of the synthesis created by DeWitt and Faulkner many decades before.

Then in 1963 came Gabriel Kolko's *The Triumph of Conservatism,* which offered historians a way out of the complexities and inconsistencies which had been building up since the early 1950s. Kolko's synthesis was based on exten-

[2] See Richard Hofstadter, *The Age of Reform* (New York, Alfred A. Knopf, 1955); John Chamberlain, *Farewell to Reform* (New York, John Day, 1932); George Mowry, *The California Progressives* (Berkeley, University of California Press, 1951); and Dewey Grantham, Jr., "The Progressive Movement and the Negro," *South Atlantic Quarterly,* 54 (October 1955), 461–77.

[3] (Cambridge, Harvard University Press, 1962.)

[4] (New York, Harper & Row, 1958.)

sive new research and offered a new theoretical key to
American social and political developments in the early
twentieth century. Yet despite the strong appeal of a new, integrative interpretation of a period whose details had become
increasingly unmanageable under the old people vs. interests
dichotomy, Kolko's book ran into criticism. Since it was a
work of ambitious scope, it drew criticism of unusual volume
and thoughtfulness. In addition to the usual reviews, a session
at the December, 1966, American Historical Association convention in New York was devoted to an assessment of the
book. Critics questioned—among other things—the validity
of conclusions about progressivism drawn from such a
restricted area of its domain (federal regulatory legislation,
and not all of that), Kolko's tendency to find large business
interests agreed on the nature of a desired public policy when
much evidence shows them divided and irresolute, and his
unproven contention that the states harbored many radical
impulses.

Whatever may be the settled decision of students of
American history on the Kolko thesis, the book has already
had a salutary impact. Some of us had forgotten how many
groups invariably have access to governmental machinery,
and we had come close to the view that a law which in-
creases federal supervision of some economic process is
necessarily a gain for "the public" or some worthy but disadvantaged group. If Kolko has reminded us of nothing else,
he has reminded us that each expansion of federal activity
must be scrutinized carefully to locate its beneficiaries and
its initiators. The state may be used and has been used to
strengthen the position of the privileged, even in the midst
of "reform" eras. This reminder concentrates our attention
more upon Congress, the details of legislation, the economic
state of affected industries, and the details of administration
than upon elections, platforms, and political talk in all its
forms. Kolko also called into question the habit of emphasizing the difference between the New Freedom and the New
Nationalism, between Theodore Roosevelt, Taft, and Wilson,
and especially between the progressive period and the years
that followed. To him the solemn doctrinal quibbles in the
ranks of reformers were of little significance, and one need
not entirely agree with this position in order to agree that

blurring the divisions between progressives and between periods is a healthy corrective, given past writing on these matters. The progressive historians undoubtedly exaggerated the extent to which America teetered between sharply different social alternatives at the whim of an election.

Nonetheless, most historians today (so far as I can judge) still hold fast to an interpretation of the progressive period which emphasizes complexity, and they resist Kolko's theory that in the progressive era a group of large businessmen fastened "political capitalism" on American society. They await further study of individual laws,[5] and read the current evidence to mean that the regulated business interests won a few and lost a few. They point out that scholars had long been aware of the involvement of businessmen in all forms of progressive activities, naming books like Samuel P. Hays' *Conservation and the Gospel of Efficiency* as a recent and sophisticated example of the unravelling of the decisive influence of large resource users in the progressive conservation movement. As such studies accumulated, American historians had taken a position emphasizing the complexity of political life. Not only did reformers apparently come in many varieties, but the "business community" was so rent with commercial and ideological divisions that the phrase has no usefulness. They see Kolko's book as a step back toward an older Manichaeanism where big business was always on one side and the public good on the other.

This state of affairs may change: Kolko's book is still a lively issue in graduate schools, and its influence may have just begun. As it is, Kolko has made his mark on every historian of the twentieth century, even on those most cool to his interpretation. Scholars of "liberal" reform are unlikely ever again to give business archives and journals only a perfunctory search, and will no longer carelessly use phrases such as "protection of the public interest" to describe what was done to whom when government assumed greater control

[5] John Braeman's study of the Meat Packing Act somewhat contradicts Kolko (see Braeman, Robert Bremner, and Everett Walters (eds.), *Change and Continuity in Twentieth-Century America* (Columbus, Ohio State University Press, 1964); and Robert U. Harbeson disputes his interpretation of railroad regulation in "Railroads and Regulation, 1877–1916, Conspiracy or Public Interest?" *Journal of Economic History,* 27 (June 1967), 561–78.

over formerly private activities. Kolko, of course, contended for much more than that, and perhaps takes small comfort in such signs of the impact of his book.

Actually, Kolko's book points to the importance of work he declined to attempt in any systematic way, the close study of the policies of the federal regulatory agencies. Who benefitted when economic activities were subjected to forms of governmental control in the progressive era is a question which cannot be answered even by the most intense scrutiny of legislative activity, as important as that is. Most of the legislative enactments of that period, or any other, represent to a large extent the fewest possible clear decisions between claims of competing groups, reserving the really difficult decisions to some regulatory agency, or the courts. The fight, except in the cases of self-executing legislation such as the tariff or the income tax, was in its early rounds when the President signed a bill. From this perspective Kolko's book ends too soon, and we must welcome studies such as that of James Weinstein, in *The Corporate Ideal in the Liberal State: 1900–1918,* which pay close attention to the war period, a time when many of the tentative half-victories of the progressive era became consolidated.[6]

[6] (Boston, Beacon Press, 1968.) Another valuable study of the important postlegislative history of progressive regulatory efforts is G. Cullum Davis, "The Transformation of the Federal Trade Commission, 1914–1929," *Mississippi Valley Historical Review,* 49 (December 1962), 437–55.

CRITICAL COMMENTARIES

ROBERT H. WIEBE
[1964]

Gabriel Kolko has obscured the significance of his provocative book on progressivism by inflated claims to originality. The general interpretation, which he insists is so startlingly new, descends in a direct line from John Chamberlain and Matthew Josephson. Within this framework, Kolko has to a remarkable degree emphasized precisely the same findings and incidents, with some elaboration, familiar to any reader of Mowry, Link, Garraty, and other recent students of the period. Challenging a mythical "standard interpretation," he breathlessly announces that prominent progressives desired to conserve capitalism, that gentlemen's agreements existed between the executive and the house of Morgan, that businessmen initiated movements toward national regulation of the economy, that the federal government under Theodore Roosevelt and Woodrow Wilson was not an inert, soulless bureaucracy, and so forth. Only the sections on the dispersal of economic power early in the twentieth century fulfill the promise of originality. Although some of the data is commonplace and much of it does not prove the chaotic competition he posits, the whole constitutes a novel, intriguing argument.

Beneath the camouflage, Kolko's story is extremely simple. At the turn of the century, inefficiency and an expanding economy threatened the economic power of big businessmen. They turned to the federal government, which was staffed by utterly subservient men

From *Journal of American History*, 51 (June 1964), 121–22. Reprinted by permission of the Organization of American Historians.

Robert Wiebe teaches history at Northwestern University. His books are cited and discussed in other parts of this volume.

lacking ideas of their own and holding the same antidemocratic, capitalist values as the magnates. After experimenting with ways of using the government to secure their economic power, big businessmen eventually dictated the regulatory legislation of the New Freedom and established the basis for perpetual control over the economy.

Behind the interpretation lies one vital premise: that a handful of big businessmen monopolized national political power during the progressive era. Kolko does not assume that economic power automatically translated into political. That, according to his conclusions on economic decentralization, would have diffused political power. Instead, a small elite held *all* the cards, and "any administration had to represent the desires of big business." Despite a formidable apparatus of theory, Kolko never explains why or how this was so; he only alludes to a tight national consensus of capitalist values and an "Establishment" of socially homogeneous economic and political leaders as possible answers.

But if one accepts the indispensable premise, the rest, including his selection of primary sources, follows naturally. The progressive movement was in reality a few pieces of regulatory legislation. Individuals fall neatly into place; among innumerable examples, "Tobacco's man in the higher circles of government was Elihu Root," a slightly confused Louis Brandeis was "antilabor in fact as well as in principle," and an academician such as John R. Commons was a naive "totalitarian." The failures of business measures were inconsequential quirks of democracy, their successes "essential" victories. Differences among important participants were "rhetorical," similarities "ideological." Leaving his elite undefined, Kolko handles the business community like an accordion, expanding it in areas of agreement and contracting in areas of disagreement. Only once does he lose control of the technique and become hopelessly tangled explaining away conflicts over the formation of the Federal Reserve Act. Rarely, as in the story of the big packers and the Meat Inspection Act, does he ignore a mound of evidence his criteria required him to use. Kolko's volume, in other words, is a rigid, modern version of an important but recently slighted interpretation from the 1930s.

JAMES WEINSTEIN
[*1964*]

Those who are committed to the view that during the progressive era (1900–1916) and again during the New Deal, our large corporations suffered temporary eclipses of their political power, will be disturbed by Gabriel Kolko's *The Triumph of Conservatism.* For the idea, as expressed by Arthur M. Schlesinger, Jr., that "liberalism in America has been ordinarily the movement on the part of other sections to restrain the power of the business community" is here effectively and brilliantly challenged. If this book is taken as seriously as it should be, and if Kolko's findings are integrated with the approach and theses in the last sections of William Appleman Williams' *Contours of American History,* a new school of American historiography will emerge and those concerned with effecting humanist social change here will be given a powerful intellectual tool.

Kolko demonstrates that by the early 1900s, businessmen—especially the leaders of the large corporations and banking houses—looked to the federal government for protection and regulation. In turn, the leading politicians of the Republican, Democratic and Progressive parties, "in virtually all cases," resolved those problems on which popular agitation had focused *in the manner advocated by the representatives of the concerned business and financial interests.* Further, he argues convincingly that political intervention into the economy "was frequently merely a response to the demands of particular businessmen." . . .

Unfortunately, Kolko examines only the major economic reforms of the period and fails to examine the full range of social and political reforms. He deals almost exclusively with regulatory legislation and agencies, emphasizing the immediate, narrow motives of the

From *The Nation,* 198 (April 20, 1964), 398–400. Reprinted by permission of *The Nation.*
James Weinstein, author of books and articles on the history of progressivism and American socialism, was the editor of the journal *Studies on the Left* from 1960 to 1967.

businessmen involved. In so doing, he misses a great deal of the complexity of the business leaders he describes and of the progressive era—an era remembered as such precisely because of the different social forces which were in a constant state of tension and flux.

This narrowness of approach leads Kolko to begin his book with a chapter in which he argues that economic reform was motivated by the fact that most trusts were unsatisfactory: they did not capture an increasing portion of the market in their respective industries, and efficiency and profit levels did not rise above average. His point is not well taken . . . in seeking reforms businessmen were certainly interested—as Kolko maintains—in rationalizing the trust system and in stabilizing industrial conditions. But in the progressive era, as again in the 1930s, they were also concerned with the preservation of large-scale industrial capitalism itself. Marcus A. Hanna, steel magnate, powerful politician and first president of the National Civic Federation, made it clear in 1903 that it was his aim to establish a relation of mutual trust between the laborer and the employer," and thereby to "lay the foundation stone of a structure that will endure for all time." Not all businessmen were as far-sighted or grandiose as Hanna, but even as narrow-minded a man as Samuel Insull recognized by 1909 that it was only a matter of time before regulation of utilities would be brought about. Knowing this, Insull preferred to "help shape the right kind of regulation," rather than "to have the wrong kind forced upon" him.

Kolko, then, underestimates the impact of the anticorporation Left. He does not take into account the extent to which reform was motivated by the desire *to head off more radical action* at the hands of the Socialist Party or of neo-Populist progressives (under the leadership of such men as La Follette, Frank P. Walsh, Tom Johnson of Cleveland, Samuel Jones of Toledo, Frederick C. Howe, George L. Record, Lynn Frazier and others). The combination of these forces, had it occurred, could have meant much more severe regulation than that initiated by the businessmen. This was why Roosevelt told the leaders of the National Civic Federation that he wanted to see "radicalism prosper under conservative leadership" in such a manner "that the progressive people will not part company with the bulk of the moderates."

One reason for Kolko's minimization of the role of the Left in determining the character of the progressive era is his belief that "no socially or politically significant group tried to fashion an alternative means of organizing industrial technology in a fashion that permitted democratic control over centralized power, or participation in . . . decisions in the industrial process." It is true that the neo-Populists offered no comprehensive alternates, but functioned on an issue-to-issue basis. The Socialists were not, and did not view themselves as, immediate contenders for power. Nevertheless, both groups were concerned with democratic control of the industrial process, and both represented potential alternatives. . . .

The Socialist Party—a mass, popular force during that era—not only exerted constant pressure from the Left. It also served to train and give ideological direction to a host of future leaders of more immediately successful radical movements, such as the Nonpartisan League of North Dakota and Minnesota, and the Farmer-Labor parties of Washington, Minnesota and Illinois. During the progressive era, as Kolko has proven beyond doubt, it was business and financial leaders who shaped basic legislative and Executive policy, or at least defined the limits of reform. But as long as a radical opposition survived (at least until 1924), these men could not rest easy. Again in the nineteen thirties, the Great Depression raised the question of the survival of our system. Like the progressive era, the New Deal was a period of minor social reform, the limits of which were set out by the most sophisticated politicians and big-corporation liberals, with the explicit purpose of bringing the Left and the labor movement into a consensus under their leadership. The Socialists had understood this tactic and avoided its pitfalls during the progressive era, but during the New Deal the Left was absorbed in the consensus. The legacy of that second period was a liberal conformity in which the Left lost more and more of its influence and bargaining power until, after the Second World War, it disappeared entirely.

Kolko's book contributes greatly to a clarification of this historical process. Its limitations, though not unimportant, do not seriously reduce the value of the book or the magnitude of Kolko's accomplishment, which is very great. He helps us to understand the underlying nature of American liberalism, which means to understand American politics in this century.

DEWEY W. GRANTHAM, JR.
[*1964*]

Although the author of this interesting book chides his fellow historians for their failure to deal broadly with the progressive era, he himself has not given us an adequate synthesis. His primary concern is the relationship between politics and economics during the decade and a half before World War I. His thesis is that the significant phenomenon of the progressive period was not the political regulation of the economy but rather the control of politics by business. He contends that conservative solutions to the emerging problems of an industrial society were almost uniformly applied, resulting in a conservative triumph in the effort to preserve "the basic social and economic relations essential to a capitalistic society."

It is unquestionably true that by the turn of the century American businessmen had begun to sense the uses of federal regulation of the economy. For one thing, such regulation might deliver them from state controls of a more democratic and radical character. It might also serve as a method of rationalizing an economy that continued to be surprisingly fluid, decentralized, and competitive. It is at this point that Kolko's analysis is most suggestive and potentially most useful. He argues that contemporary analysts and later historians of the period misread the dominant tendencies of the economy, and in a series of case studies he attempts to demonstrate the failure of voluntary business efforts (through mergers and other kinds of combination) to bring "irresistible competitive trends" under control. The result was a growing resort to politics at the national level, first through informal understandings and détentes and eventually, during the Wilson administration, through formal legislation and administrative action. Ultimately, Kolko concludes, businessmen defined the limits of political intervention, "not merely because they were among the major initiators of federal intervention in the economy, but pri-

From *The South Atlantic Quarterly,* 63 (Summer 1964), 433–34. Reprinted by permission of Duke University Press.
Dewey Grantham teaches history at Vanderbilt University.

marily because no politically significant group during the progressive era really challenged their conception of political intervention."

In recent years other students of American progressivism, including Samuel P. Hays and Robert H. Wiebe, have shown that businessmen, so often the villains in the progressive rhetoric, were actually an important source of reform. But no earlier writer has advanced such a monolithic interpretation of the role of the major economic interests in the formulation and implementation of progressive measures as that set forth in this volume. In the reviewer's opinion the author has exaggerated both the extent of business unity and the conservatism of Theodore Roosevelt, Woodrow Wilson, and some other progressive leaders. Political intervention meant different things to different groups, and the meaning of the synthesis of economics and politics in Washington cannot really be determined until much more is known about the motives and aspirations of the various elements urging reform, including thousands of businessmen not immediately identified with large interests. There was undoubtedly a large entrepreneurial strain running through progressivism, and most Americans accepted the desirability of perpetuating their capitalistic society as axiomatic. But the business view of reform was a restricted one, lacking much of the democratic faith and moral fire of the representative middle-class progressive. Progressivism was more than a question of economics, and to suggest that the supremacy of political capitalism at the end of the era sums up the movement is to miss much of its spirit and accomplishment.

A session devoted to Kolko's book was held at the December 28, 1966, meeting of the American Historical Association in New York City. Critical commentaries were read by Professors Richard M. Abrams of the University of California, Berkeley, Gerald D. Nash of the University of New Mexico, and J. Joseph Huthmacher of Rutgers University. Mr. Kolko concluded with a rebuttal. I have edited each of these statements to conform to the spatial limits of this book (deleting all but two footnotes), and present them in print for the first time.

RICHARD M. ABRAMS

A Critique of the Kolko Thesis
[1966]

Mr. Kolko's book compels us to look beyond the reform rhetoric and legislative enactments of the progressive movement to both the roots of its most vital energy and to the fruit of its labors. The book is not the first to have done so, but few have done it with such impressive scholarly paraphernalia. Kolko's intensive research into primary sources lends seductive authority to what he has to say. The accent, however, must be on the seductiveness rather than on the authority with which Mr. Kolko writes, for his use of those sources leaves room for more than casual doubt about his care and objectivity. *The Triumph* is an important book, but at least as much because it is bound to beguile our eagerly cynical sophomores as because it suggests important modifications in our understanding of the nature of the progressive movement.

Kolko's data is sufficient to demonstrate (1) that many of the most powerful corporations and business groups participated in the

From a paper delivered at the meetings of the American Historical Association, December 28, 1966. Published with the permission of the author.

movement for Federal regulation; (2) that they did so partly because their various pools, consolidations, trusts, and trade associations had failed to produce "conditions of stability, predictability, and security" such as their giant investments required, and partly in the hope of forestalling or superceding disparate state regulations; (3) that some major business interests were probably able to turn to their advantage some of the measures ostensibly designed to constrain their power; and (4) (more generally) that business entrepreneurship in early 20th-century America (as in the 19th century) was not confined to the economic arena but continued to put government and politics to its service. We are made to see once more—as John Chamberlain in *Farewell to Reform* and Matthew Josephson in *The President Makers* long ago pointed out—that in establishing commissions to adjudicate conflicts that once had been resolved in the hurly burly of the market place, progressive reformers merely changed a predominantly economic conflict into a political one—i.e., shifted the scene of many of the principal economic conflicts from the price-and-market arena to the society's political agencies. This meant that problems such as farmers' and merchants' access to credit, the determination of railroad rate differentials, the constriction or enhancement of opportunities for corporate expansion, the allocation of market shares, the utilization of the nation's natural resources, and the like, were to be resolved no longer primarily by the price-and-market system or, alternatively, by the concerted arrangements of private economic interests, but in political councils wherein shifting political pressures tended to replace shifting economic advantages as determinants of the distribution of the rewards that the society had to offer. The politicization of economic policy-making, moreover, also meant that *insofar* as economic preponderance tends to be registered in the political scales, *insofar,* that is, as political power is a function of economic power, political decisions have tended to favor those business interests that already enjoyed ascendancy in their own particular sectors and in the economy as a whole.

Kolko actually does not make most of these points in precisely this way; rather his material makes them for him. What Kolko wishes to argue goes much beyond such points—and indeed beyond what his material can sustain. He argues not merely that many of the most powerful business groups—as well as farmers, unionists, civic reformers, and such—had a positive interest in regulation but that they constituted *the* most important promoters of regulation. He declares not merely that many financial leaders sought greater monopolistic power ("stability, predictability, etc.") than they had, but that in fact, contrary to most assumptions about the trusts, most industries suffered severely from excessive competition against which they sought relief from the Federal government. He contends not merely that the regulatory measures failed to alter the balance of industrial power but that the most powerful business groups *designed* them to buttress their already established (although troubled) competitive advantages. He asserts not merely that *many* of the predominant business groups frequently proved able to turn the regulatory commissions to their own advantage, but that the commissions "invariably" served their interests and were "invariably" designed to do so.

On the last point, Kolko offers no substantial evidence whatever. He asserts, for example, but nowhere demonstrates, that the Meat Inspection Act enhanced the power of the "Big Five"; he does show that it *could* have operated that way and we know from the conventional literature that in many ways it did. We know from other studies that at times the Federal Trade Commission did function on behalf of industry leaders, but if that were always the case someone forgot to inform big business spokesmen about it when they were smearing the FTC as a nest of Bolshevists within five years of its creation. The Federal Reserve System certainly has helped "the bankers," and indeed one would not care to deny that it was *designed* to help "the bankers." But nowhere does Kolko show us *which* bankers received and/or were intended to receive the greatest leverage, nor at whose expense in and out of the banking sector; he only wishes us to know that because it was designed "by and for bankers" it could not have been of much use to "the masses."

In each case, Kolko commits grave sins of omission. To note only one, he fails to mention that *many* sectors of the political economy had vital interests in each regulation proposed. He thus duplicates the kind of error of which he accuses more conventional historians who, for example, used to stress the role of "the farmers" in reform movements without noting that big and little businessmen, shippers and railroad managers, mine owners and operatives, and so on, all possessed and expressed an interest in some kind of regulation —each group hoping, to be sure, to shape the law to its own advantage. This is all the stranger, because early in the book Kolko aptly remarks that, despite all rhetoric, "it was never a question of regulation or no regulation, of state control or laissez faire . . . [but] rather . . . of what kind of regulation and by whom." [p. 4]

By focusing too exclusively on the role of the "big businessmen," he errs not only in suggesting that they were alone in the field, he also tends to fall prey to their defensive laments. It is surely remarkable how eagerly so militant an anticapitalist as he accepts the capitalists' tiresome pleas of impotence against charges of "monopoly"—as if Kolko has never heard of the distinction between open market and oligopolistic competition! But then it is scarcely worth pursuing the point because Kolko tosses it aside himself: "Whether there are a few or many companies does not change the basic control and decision-making power of *the institution of business* in relation to the other important classes of society, but only the detailed means by which that power is exercised and certain of the ends toward which it is directed" [p. 56; emphasis added].

Kolko frequently shifts the terms of the argument. To attempt to follow him is to embark on a tantalizing adventure in logic and semantics. At times it is hard to believe that the confusion is not deliberately contrived. The trouble, I suspect, is that Kolko finds it hard to concentrate on his subject; for the phenomenon he is dealing with was essentially a case of intracapitalistic rivalry, and to a militant anticapitalist it must seem like much ado about nothing.

One discovers Kolko's difficulty at the very beginning, where he attempts to explain some of his terms. For example, he defines "conservatism" as "an effort to preserve the basic social and economic relations essential to a capitalist society." With such a definition, one wonders why Kolko adopts his debunking style? No one outside of the hysterical right wing has ever imagined that anticapitalism triumphed in America, nor has any significant historian argued that the progressives were anticapitalist. Nearly everyone has agreed that (for better or worse) all the major reform movements in the country's history were designed to make "capitalism" more workable, and perhaps also more humane.

A random application of "conservatism" as Kolko defines it quickly demonstrates the sterility of the definition. "The Bureau of Corporations Bill [of 1903]," he writes on p. 71, "passed with conservative support and was motivated by conservative intentions." Translation: The Bureau of Corporations was designed to preserve the basic social and economic relations essential to a capitalist society, and a lot of procapitalists supported it. In a literal sense, no one can fault the statement. But no one either then or since ever contended otherwise. Sheer logic (to say nothing of the historical evidence) suggests that the earnest controversy over the Bureau must have focused on some vital point of contemporary concern that Kolko has managed to overlook. Indeed, it is typical of Kolko's assertions that if one translates them literally they break down into truisms; and like all truisms, they simply miss the point. His oversights, of course, are understandable when one considers that Kolko has clearly begun with the premise that any change short of overturning "capitalist society" is no change worth talking about. Nothing much, then, has ever happened in America, and all the controversies highlighted by "most historians" (a frequent pejorative) have all been sham battles designed to fool "the masses."

But this is only to introduce the problem. Unfortunately, there is room here for only one substantial illustration of Kolko's technique. I come to it literally by letting the book fall open at random.

On p. 161, Kolko is working on his point that Federal regulation served to protect big business from popular legislation. He writes: "Big businessmen feared democracy, especially on the local and state levels where the masses might truly exercise their will, and they successfully turned to the federal government for protection." We will disregard for present purposes the compound nonsense of the middle clause. The half-truth of the rest of the sentence can hardly be news to "most historians," though Kolko presents it as a revelation. Certainly, *some* businessmen sought at different times and places state *and* federal agencies which might serve as buffers, even as many reformers sought intelligent and nonpartisan public supervision of corporations through the same such agencies.

After leading the paragraph with the above sentence, Kolko quotes at length from an editorial in *Bankers' Magazine* for April 1901, which argues that if businessmen organized they could "control the ballot," and legislatures and government executives would have to "listen to the demands of organized business interests as against the demands of other groups." There is no doubt about the plutocratic intent of the editorial (although it evidences little "fear of democracy"). But it is more important that we see how Kolko fails to discern the historical context of the editorial. It was, after all, precisely at this time that the business community was beginning to mobilize—under Mark Hanna's tutelage—in order to displace the professional politicians and boodlers from leadership in the political parties. Kolko takes care to include the following sentence of the editorial: "The business man, whether alone or in combination with other business men, seeks to shape politics and government in a way conducive to his own prosperity." But he chooses to omit the very next sentence: "When business men were single units, each working out his own success regardless of others in desperate competition, the men who controlled the political organizations were supreme." Unless one wishes to identify "the masses" with the politicos, one can see that the editorial is not really concerned with the Demos at all.

Kolko's next sentence gives us no trouble: "Nor did the values of the *Bankers' Magazine* represent an isolated phenomenon, even if these values were never expressed quite as systematically." But what follows seems a non sequitur: "Roosevelt's view of the dangerous, potentially irresponsible character of the masses, and the need to channelize them along controllable lines, was expressed by many others as well." His example of the "many others" turns out to be Charles S. Mellen, the egregious president of the New Haven Railroad, who in 1904 told the Hartford Board of Trade: " '. . . the day has gone by . . . when a corporation can be handled successfully in defiance of the public will, even though that will be unreasonable and wrong. A public must be led, but not driven, and I prefer to go with it and shape or modify . . . its opinion, rather than be swept from my bearings with loss to myself and the interests in my charge.' " Kolko then concludes the paragraph with how William Dudley Foulke, "a leading civil service reformer in this period, indicated that popular government and parties were the source of spoils, and that the aim of civil service reform, which Roosevelt so notably advanced, was to mitigate this evil of democracy."

There are so many things wrong with the paragraph that it is hard to know where to begin and still keep within our space limitations. Shall we observe the remarkable example of the "guilt-by-association" technique in the last sentence (Foulke = antidemocratic civil service reformer; Roosevelt = civil service reformer; *ergo,* Roosevelt = antidemocratic)? Shall we note that there is nothing on the pages Kolko cites from Foulke's memoirs (3, 257–58) to suggest the elitism of civil service reform (except perhaps for a disparaging general reference to Andrew Jackson's administration)? Should we wonder why Kolko points out Roosevelt's anxieties concerning "the dangerous, potentially irresponsible character of the masses" without ever mentioning his frequently expressed objections to the dangerous and downright irresponsible character of many business men and corporations? Each of these points could take up pages. The paragraph is characteristic of the book in that it elicits a kind of "run-on" criticism, without a satisfying beginning or end. For our purposes here, it will have to suffice to consider Kolko's references to Mellen and "the masses."

If Kolko had been looking for an expression of Charles Mellen's proclivity for elitist prerogatives, he could have found far better than what he comes up with here. Indeed, here Mellen appears to be saying merely what one might expect from someone whose interests depended in some measure on the public's good will. The statement itself seems quite innocuous. What is it, then, that bugs Kolko? As with much of the book, here one has to readjust one's bearings to see a thing the way Kolko sees it. The crux is that Kolko would have us understand Mellen to mean that public opinion (and "the masses"?) must be *manipulated* ("shaped," "modified") so that he and men like him may not be "swept from his bearings." Perhaps for an era as familiar as ours is with "news manipulation," "opinion making," "brainwashing," and the like, Mellen's remarks may have an insidious sound. Yet, if we can subdue our modern technopsychological sensitivities, we should be able to distinguish between persuasion, influence, and cajolery, and the dishonesty implied by "manipulation." How else should a public will or opinion be formed if it should have no leaders or shapers or modifiers? Mellen may well have been an arrogant fool, but in pleading before the public the case for his corporate interests, he was probably no more wilfully dishonest than is Kolko in pleading what he chooses to believe are the interests of the masses.

And who or what are "the masses"? I must confess a certain embarrassment in seeing the phrase used so naively after decades of disputation had presumably rendered its meaning and utility into nothingness. At any rate, in Kolko's scheme "the masses" are quite evidently the victims of all the evil perpetrated by the cynical big businessmen and their progressive dupes. The phrase seems to encompass all of society except for those associated in some commanding way with "the institutions of business." It might perhaps be a shorthand for antibusiness interests, but the hazard of equating "the masses" with "antibusiness interests" is exemplified in Kolko's treatment of Roosevelt. T.R., he says, feared "the unthinking masses" (the irony is Kolko's) and sought to save business from stirring into action "a formal democracy [that was] potentially capable of really operating as a democracy." [p. 160] Of course, Roosevelt never concealed his fear of the potential destructiveness of what *he* would have regarded as a *maddened* or *misguided* democracy. It would be helpful, though, if Kolko gave us an idea of just how a democracy is supposed to operate when, according to *his* lights, it "really operates." Presumably, everything would be "just fine" for "the masses." Suppose then that the masses were "farmers," and "workers," and "intellectuals," and "students," and "office workers," and "professionals." Were these groups supposed to be united on what was good, but were thwarted by the contrary organized might of "big business" in alliance with "big government"? Are we to assume, for example, that if men such as Mellen did not "manipulate" their opinions, all these diverse groups would have had some kind of spontaneous (and pure?) opinion of their own on "good," "justice," and "right" that all of them could have agreed on?

The historical evidence seems overwhelmingly against it. Yet I would not be surprised if Kolko would answer, "Yes." For he seems to operate in that world of surrealistic logic that has become popular in recent years. "In the last analysis," writes Herbert Marcuse, the surrealists' metaphysician,

the question of what are true and false needs must be answered by the individuals themselves, but only in the last analysis; that is, if and when they are free to give their own answer. As long as they are kept incapable of being autonomous, as long as they are indoctrinated and manipulated (down to their very instincts), their answer to this question cannot be taken as their own.

There is, of course, a sense in which the statement is perfectly true. If we could all agree on what constituted indoctrination and manipulation, and who was manipulating whom and for what, we might agree on the meaning of individual autonomy, and on the proper distinction between true and false needs.

In the "last analysis," Kolko has written a book for the faithful, a well researched tract for our own times, rather than a serious history of the progressive era.

GERALD D. NASH

A Critique of the Kolko Thesis
[*1966*]

Professor Kolko's interesting volume provides a provocative stimulus not only for discussion of progressivism, but of major trends in government's relation to business in twentieth-century America. Perhaps the major question about his book is this: Has Kolko achieved his own avowed aim of providing us with a convincing new interpretation of the progressive era? Is his concept of the growth of a political capitalism in the United States valid? The many merits of his book, its freshness and frequent originality, are bound to make critics reluctant to voice doubts concerning its content and conclusions. Yet, even those who admit the many virtues of the volume may still wonder whether *The Triumph of Conservatism* really does present a new framework for analysis of the progressive era. In fact, they may speculate whether its main theme—postulating the growth of a political capitalism in America—is valid.

At least four questions of this thesis are relevant. First, does Professor Kolko's terminology obscure his thesis? Secondly, has he torn his evidence—as well as his main hypothesis—out of a broader context? Third, are some of his assumptions [such as his distinction between federal and state policies] warranted by available evidence? Finally, how valid is his proposal for alternatives to what might have been, or to the type of economic democracy which he wished had developed in America?

First let us turn to Professor Kolko's imprecise terminology which partly obscures his theme. He refers frequently to "the masses." [pp. 161–163] Who precisely comprise this group? And what, exactly, are what he calls "their genuine desires?" Moreover, which people

From a paper delivered at the meetings of the American Historical Association, December 28, 1966. Copyright © Gerald D. Nash. Published by permission.

comprise the mythical "public"? [p. 282] Even more unclear is his use of phrases such as "public opinion," and "public interest." [p. 252]

In emphasizing—and criticizing—what he considers the inordinate or preponderant influence of business leaders in shaping policy during the progressive era, Professor Kolko is much concerned with divergence from what he loosely calls "the public interest." This abstract ideal, which constitutes the basis for his condemnation of political capitalism—or business influence on federal policy—is a term that has aroused much scholarly debate and discussion. An effort to define the phrase "public interest," has kept a whole generation of political scientists fully occupied. Thirty years ago Pendleton Herring forcefully argued that "public interest" was a semantic term whose meaning was "vague and elusive." . . . To be sure, there are special interests such as business interests, farm interests, labor interests, and others, but who represents the ambiguous public? In his effort to introduce stark realism into the study of government-business relations during the progressive era, therefore, Professor Kolko at the same time introduces undefined concepts which vitiate the force of his main thesis.

This leads us to the second question about Professor Kolko's main theme. Does he distort the context within which business interests operated to influence public policy? His emphasis on business as the only or major influence on public policy neglects not only divisions within the business community itself, but the wide range of other pressure groups whose impact was no less important. In this book Professor Kolko sloughs over many of the issues of public policy in which business pressures played a minor role. Moreover, with this exclusive emphasis, Kolko largely ignores the broader institutional framework of the American political system in which special interests have access to policy making organs of various levels of government. These weaknesses in the Kolko thesis deserve closer examination.

Various historians such as Robert Wiebe have shown that during the progressive era the business community was rent with divisions. These were far more common than the carefully selected examples of business unity which Professor Kolko discusses in his book. Yet, the lack of harmony was there and is apparent to any student familiar with the diversity of issues that arose in government-business relations during this period.

A specific illustration of this point can be made in regard to contemporary controversies over tariffs in the three decades after 1890. In fact, conspicuously missing from Kolko's volume is any extended discussion concerning the disputes among businessmen surrounding tariffs. One looks in vain in the body of the work, or in the index, for extended analysis of this issue. Yet it stirred strong passions among contemporaries. Historians of a later generation thus can hardly afford to ignore it. Such discussion may be missing from Professor Kolko's book because much of the history of tariffs since 1890 simply does not substantiate his main thesis. Who was it who said: "The mother of Trusts is the customs tariff bill"? Was it Sockless Jerry Simpson or some other Populist radical crusader? Or was it Grover Cleveland, or a spokesman for low-tariff Democrats? Or was it Oscar Underwood or a member of the Southern coalition in Congress? No, it was none other than George O. Havemeyer, president of the American Sugar Refining Company which controlled ninety percent of the sugar refining facilities in the United States. As head of the frequently criticized sinister Sugar Trust, Havemeyer made this oft-quoted statement in 1899 before the United States Industrial Commission to buttress his arguments against high sugar duties.

But, alas, despite the fact that he had a near monopoly in the industry he was unable to persuade protection minded Congressmen to take his advice. Unfortunately, opinion within the sugar industry was widely divided over the wisdom of a sugar tariff, with opinions usually related directly to the self-interest of particular producers. Thus Claus Spreckels agreed with Havemeyer that the sugar tariff placed a tax on American consumers which he estimated to amount to about one hundred thirty-four million dollars annually. Competing beet sugar manufacturers, such as T. G. Palmer, thought the burden on purchasers to be only half as great. Some refiners were much in favor of tariff duties on sugar, as Charles B. Warren of the Michigan Sugar Company revealed clearly in his testimony of 1909 before the House Ways and Means Committee. In the case of sugar, therefore, even the largest refiner found himself unable to influence federal policy that affected his industry. His example indicates that major interest groups within a particular industry were often unable to incorporate their proposals in federal legislation, illustrating the reverse of Professor Kolko's main contention.

A similar example can be found in the oil industry at the opening of this century. In discussing the Bureau of Corporation's investigation of Standard Oil Company activities in Kansas during 1905 Professor Kolko gives the impression that this was largely guided by corporate interests. Moreover, he is silent on the origins of this inquiry and neglects to discuss the influence of other interest groups which were responsible for federal action. Most important, perhaps, were the independent oil producers, organized in the Kansas Oil Producers' Association. In 1905 they were greatly angered over Standard's inability to provide pipeline service for the increasing flood of petroleum which they produced. From 932,000 bbls. in 1903, their total jumped to 4,250,000 bbls. two years later. Since the Standard Oil Company owned most pipelines and storage facilities in Kansas, the independents were dependent on it for marketing outlets.

Whether Standard Oil was responsible for any wrongdoing in this situation is questionable. The company simply did not act rapidly enough in building new storage and pipeline facilities for handling the unexpected flood of additional petroleum. Perhaps it was a case of inefficiency or miscalculation rather than of intended skullduggery. Nevertheless, the independents began an antimonopoly campaign in 1905. In the Kansas state legislature that year they secured passage of a bill for the construction of a state owned refinery to provide competition for Standard. The lawmakers there also enacted other bills to declare pipelines common carriers, a maximum rate tariff bill, and an antidiscrimination statute. And, in addition, Congressman Phillip P. Campbell of Kansas introduced a resolution in the House assigning the Bureau of Corporations the task of investigating Standard's activities in Kansas. Such were the origins of the Bureau's inquiry developing in a context very different from that sketched by Professor Kolko. Not only does he neglect even to mention the important influence of the Kansas independent oil producers in securing the federal investigation, but he is also silent in regard to the remedial legislation which they secured within the state of Kansas.

The distorted context within which Professor Kolko seeks to interpret the progressive era is also reflected by the very narrow range of interest groups which he chooses to consider. Has he mistaken the trees for the forest? Has he made a big leap from a highly selected— and relatively small body of evidence—to develop a broad theory about the federal government's role in the economy? And does this big leap lead into an abyss? In the book he focuses exclusively on selected business groups who were important architects of a limited number of federal laws. At the same time he ignores or dismisses a wide range of other interests. Using precisely the same conceptual framework that Professor Kolko has developed in this volume, he— or someone else—could easily demonstrate that in any given sphere of public policy, pressure groups which were most directly affected by it played an important, and often crucial, role in shaping legislative or administrative action. Certainly this would buttress his contention that business groups shaped selected federal policies that bore closely on their particular economic welfare. But it would undermine his broad general thesis that business interests shaped the entire range of public policy.

One could write a whole series of books to illustrate this weakness in Kolko's analysis. We could have a volume on "The Triumph of American Labor Reform," showing how organized labor was able to have virtually every one of its demands incorporated in federal and state policies during this period. Was not the La Follette Seamen's Act of 1913 primarily due to the influence of Andrew Furuseth? We could also have a volume on "The Triumph of the American Farmer," demonstrating how almost every one of the demands of organized farm organizations between 1890 and 1921 was achieved in federal and state laws. After all, John Hicks in *The Populist Revolt* illustrated this theme more than thirty-five years ago. We could have many other volumes each indicating how particular pressure groups exercized a predominant influence in shaping public policy which related to their special interests.[1] But this still would not prove Professor Kolko's general theory based on analysis of one interest group only, that it—and no other—dominated the entire range of federal action during the Progressive Era, and that indeed, it set the pattern for the age.

In fact, the process whereby special pressure groups influenced the formulation of public policies was not unique to business. The structure of the American institutional and political system allowed a great variety of interest groups to channel their demands for public action through a large number of political and administrative officials at various levels of government. To focus on only one segment in this broad spectrum of interest groups is to tear it out of context, to mistake a vignette for the larger picture. Thus, we can question Professor Kolko's logic in selecting a number of instances in which business groups did play an important role in policy formation, and then deducing from this small and unrepresentative sample a broad theory about the whole spectrum of government's relations to the economy. . . .

[1] An alternate theory of cooperative capitalism is discussed in Gerald D. Nash, *United States Oil Policy 1890–1964: Business and Government in Twentieth Century America* (Pittsburgh, University of Pittsburgh Press, 1968).

In short, Kolko's analysis ignores not only the divisions within particular business groups, but neglects to consider the relevance of other pressure groups who also had a vital part in shaping public policies—although not in instances cited in Mr. Kolko's book. To demonstrate the importance of a few select business groups in one narrow sphere of public policy is certainly a contribution. But to relate that influence to the entire range of public action and to the interpretation of an entire period, leads to a largely unsubstantiated theory.

A third major criticism of Professor Kolko's stimulating volume can be directed towards some of his broad assumptions—especially his clear distinction between the nature of state and federal economic policies. "Big businessmen feared democracy," writes Professor Kolko, [p. 161] "especially on the local and state levels where the masses might truly exercise their will, and they successfully turned to the federal government for protection." Ignoring for the moment the semantic problem of just exactly who comprised "the masses" or the determination of precisely just what policies constituted their supposed true will, this artificial distinction between federal and state policies introduces an unwarranted fiction into American history which has little basis in fact. The process whereby interest groups worked through political institutions to influence the course of public policy was no different in the states than at other levels of government. Many volumes which discuss state policies of this era in detail, including those of Professors Huthmacher, Abrams, Sam Hays, Nash, Roy Lubove, Robert S. Maxwell, George Mowry, James H. Timberlake, Winston Flint, and others, contain sufficient evidence to indicate that policymakers on the local level had no monopoly on virtue, and that the process of policy formulation there was similar to that in Washington.

This brings us to a fourth question. Implicit throughout Professor Kolko's book is his bitter disappointment with—and condemnation of—the system of government-business relations which developed in twentieth-century America. That the structure had many imperfections, that it produced injustices, few historians would deny. Whatever was, was not necessarily right. But such severe negative criticism invites constructive proposals concerning other possible courses of action—or, as Professor Kolko phrases it, with what might have been. After 344 pages of indictment, however, Kolko comes up with no positive or realistic alternatives. As he concludes:

"Perhaps industrialization would not have permitted democratic control and direct participation in the work process under any circumstances. All one can do is point to the large extent to which the concentration of industry in this period had nothing to do with considerations of efficient technology, and that no effort whatsoever was made to democratize the work situation and industrial control—much less . . . to make decentralization or workers' control possible."

Perhaps. But is such a view realistic? Since 1900 has there been any highly industrialized nation in the world in which the process of industrialization was undertaken as a democratic mass movement? Certainly not Soviet Russia, nor Great Britain, nor France or any other important power. In every instance, a small and highly skilled group of entrepreneurs and managers provided the impetus for shaping many governmental policies which were deemed conducive to industrialization. Where a managerial group did not appear—or where political institutions were too inflexible to adjust to the needs of an industrial economy, as in Spain, Latin America, or the American South—the process of industrialization was seriously retarded. Perhaps it was the genius of the American political system that its flexibility permitted thousands of interest groups to work for change and adjustment in response to the emerging needs of a technological society.

To conclude, Professor Kolko has written a book that deserves the attention of every serious student of twentieth-century America. Whether he has achieved his prime aim—to provide us with a new synthetic theory for interpretation of the progressive era—is open to question. Vagueness of key terms, a distortion of the context within which interest groups in the United States operated, and unsubstantiated assumptions about distinctions between state and federal policies, vitiate his major thesis. And one would still want to know, after reading his very stimulating book: Why should the influence of corporate interests on federal policies be interpreted as constituting the essence of the progressive movement when the bulk of progressive reform legislation was enacted in the states and dealt with social and political reforms much more than with economic reforms? But if Professor Kolko has not supplied us with a new middle-range synthesis to interpret the Progressive Era he has provided much new and provocative evidence that should lead to reexamination of many well-worn cliches about that period. His emphasis on the desire of businessmen to achieve stabilization of competition could well result in a reassessment of the merger and trust movement of that era from other than a moral condemnation along paths blazed by Professor Chandler. And the book provides much important evidence to illustrate the direct relationship between select business interests and federal officials.

J. JOSEPH HUTHMACHER

A Critique of the Kolko Thesis
[1966]

Since I am not an economic historian, I will gladly defer to others for discussion of the more purely economic underpinnings of the thesis that Professor Kolko develops in his book, *The Triumph of Conservatism.* . . .

However, I think I do qualify as a member of that school of historians which in recent times has devoted its efforts to complicating —not to say confusing—our historical literature regarding the causes, nature, and meaning of the so-called progressive era, by emphasizing the complexity of the combinations of forces, factors, population elements, groups and organizations, individuals, and motives that were involved in the making of that era. . . .

Professor Kolko has performed a service on behalf of the obfuscationist school I have just referred to—and has provided us with material for still another convention session on the progressive era— by calling attention, in greater detail and with much greater zeal than has been mustered before, to the role that business, and particularly big business played, in order to serve its own ends, in instigating and/or promoting certain economic regulatory measures that were enacted on the federal level during the first two decades of this century. In doing so he helps throw still another ingredient into the bubbly melting pot of progressive era scholarship, and he reminds us again that not all of the so-called reform enactments of that era issued

From a paper read at the meetings of the American Historical Association, December 28, 1966. Published by permission of the author.

exclusively from such pure, disinterested, or humanitarian motives as has sometimes been supposed. He reminds us that business interests commonly deemed conservative had a hand in molding the progressive years.

But while I, as a member of the obfuscationist school gladly welcome the additional piece that Professor Kolko has helped hand us to be fit into our multiple causation jigsaw puzzle, I regret that he shows so little inclination to join our group. He declines to view the selfishly-motivated conservative business influence at work in the progressive era as merely one of several or many competing influences. He declines to regard its handiwork, as reflected in the federal regulatory measures he has examined, as only one aspect of the progressive era's legislative record—one that must be weighed against other components of that record. No; his approach is much simpler. He finds the selfishly-motivated conservative business influence to be the almost exclusively predominating one; and he regards its manifestations, as embodied in the federal regulatory measures he has dealt with, as constituting the be-all and end-all of American legislative activity between 1900 and 1916. On the basis of all this, he regards those years not as a period of mixed, faltering, but at least partial progress toward a better America; but rather as the period that witnessed the "triumph of conservatism." The conclusion is, that from the point of view of anyone really interested in creating a more humane and liberal society, the misnamed progressive era was a tremendous "flop."

I realize that the summation of Kolko's work that I have just given may be open to challenge, and that I may be accused of setting up a straw man. For at certain places in his book he does seem to limit the applicability of his analysis and conclusions relatively narrowly to federal legislation affecting business. Occasionally he refers to other types of progressive legislative causes and to state-level agitation and activity. And on p. 279 he even writes that "Progressive politics is complex when studied in all of its aspects. . . ."

But unless gross misreading of the book has misled me, the modest and moderate statements of the sort I have just mentioned are vastly outnumbered and overshadowed by those of a much more expansive and inclusive type, whose net effect is to subsume the meaning and significance of the entire progressive era into Kolko's devastating critique. . . . I will not catalogue the many specific statements of this latter type that I have in mind. I will only remind you that on p. 9 of his Introduction the author writes: "In this study I shall attempt to treat the *progressive era* as an *interrelated* and, I hope, explicable *whole*. . . ." [Italics mine]. But this is several pages after he has already told us: ". . . I contend that the period from 1900 until the United States' intervention in the war, labeled the progressive era by virtually all historians, was really an era of conservatism." And in what follows that Introduction, I find little effort on the author's part to really explore in breadth and depth the whole complex variety of interrelationships among men, groups, motives, and forces that were operative in America during the years 1900–1916, or to discriminate among the myriad measures and results that flowed from those interrelationships.

In Kolko's view, apparently, the only interrelationships that counted were those that existed between the business and political elites—the establishment, he calls it. The only measures that counted were those instigated or molded by business to serve its own self-interested purposes. And the only result that counted was the way in which that establishment and those measures fastened the grip of a political capitalism—dominated by a virtual plutocracy—on the whole American economy, on the nation's politics, and on the country's civilization for at least the century to come. To Kolko, these phenomena constituted "the essential character" of progressivism.

Here is one level on which I think Professor Kolko's work is open to question. For it assumes that the pieces of federal business regulatory legislation that he deals with in detail in his book make up the most important—indeed, the crucial—aspect of the progressive era record. I am troubled by his failure to push his investigation further, and in other directions, before arriving at his sweeping conclusions. What about other types of congressional enactments in these years: the measures submitting the income tax and direct election of Senators amendments for ratification, for example; or the federal child labor act, the Seamen's Act, the Adamson Act, the federal employees' workmen's compensation act, rural credits legislation—all of which represented significant federal departures in the direction of creating a welfare state? And on the level of state government, which during the progressive era remained the focal point of agitation for social welfare and labor legislation—the variety and volume of such enactments was, in my estimation, truly impressive and significant. Professor Kolko himself refers, at p. 163, to "state efforts to implement economic and social welfare laws of every type." I cannot agree with his conclusion that those efforts were "short-circuited" and rendered meaningless and inconsequential by the "seamy side" of national progressivism on which he dwells. No; before he can convince me that "the history of the United States from Theodore Roosevelt through Woodrow Wilson is consistently conservative"—as he asserts in another of his more expansive passages—he will have to convince me that business was just as much the initiator of, or just as much in favor of, and just as successful in having its way in the case of the kinds of legislation I have referred to, as it seems to have been in the case of federal banking and business regulatory legislation. Thus far he has not attempted to do so. And from what we know about the nature of the struggle for social welfare and labor legislation in places like New York State and Massachusetts, I doubt very much that he can do so.

To restate my own position, it is that in the realm of welfare state legislation, and particularly on the state level—where Kolko acknowledges that there existed "the radical potential of mass grievances and aspiration—of genuine progressivism"—the nonbusiness reformers carried off a great many prizes during the years we are concerned with. Their achievements in these respects constitute much more the essential character and meaning of the progressive era, in my estimation, than does the aspect of progressivism explored by Professor Kolko in his study of federal legislation regulating business and banking. Those achievements established the basis of the modern American welfare state, and I think they justify our retaining the appellation "progressive era" for the period 1900–1916, and justify our viewing it as a period of significant advance toward creating a more equitable American society. Certainly they should be enough to prevent our relabeling that period the triumphal era of conservatism.

Or are they? Most probably not, in Professor Kolko's estimation, and here I would like to move on to another level of discussion concerning the work we have under review. For I think it is clear that, to Kolko, the basic and fundamental defect marring the progressive era —and adding up to nothing less than what he calls the betrayal of liberalism—was its "lack of a truly radical, articulated alternative economic and political program capable of synthesizing political democracy with industrial reality." (Elsewhere he speaks favorably of "democratic control and direct participation in the work process"; of democratizing "the work situation and industrial control"; and of industrial "decentralization or workers' control"). Now, I'm not sure what specific system or "ism"—if any—Kolko has in mind here as his ideal, for he states that "such a program was never formulated in this period either in America or Europe."

Be that as it may, however, I'm certainly willing to agree with him that no such far-reaching transformation as that he refers to came about in America during the progressive era, or was even articulated by any socially or politically significant group. For certainly the non-business reformers who were responsible for the advances in the kinds of social welfare and labor legislation I mentioned earlier—i.e., the middle-class social justice crusaders, organized labor, the farm lobby organizations, the political machine spokesmen for the industrial working class—were not out to overthrow the inherited American system of values. Like the major political parties and leaders of the time, they were—to use Kolko's words—"conservative in the sense that they believed in the basic value of capitalist social relations—of some variation of the status quo." In this broader sense, then, it is true that even the progressive era social welfare and labor reformers were conservative, of course, in comparison with the revolutionary radical movements that some countries have experienced, and that some American historians have envisioned. That is to say, viewed from the worldwide perspective, the reforms of the progressive era took place within the broad and general conservative framework that has been the framework of all of American history. It would be surprising to me were the case otherwise.

It seems to me that Professor Kolko treats his period in a vacuum, therefore, when he asserts that "there was nothing inevitable or predetermined in the peculiar character given to industrialism in America." The boundaries *were* there, set by America's experiential, ideological, and cultural heritage—Louis Hartz, Clinton Rossiter, Oscar Handlin, and others have told us why and how—just as Russia's heritage set limits to what we might expect to develop in that country as industrialism transformed her economy. Preeminent in America's heritage was the pervasive attachment to private ownership and the exploitive economy that gripped not only the business elements and the middle classes, but farmers and the industrial workers as well. That attachment makes it entirely understandable why proposals for the kind of "participatory democracy in industry," idealized by Professor Kolko were never seriously set forth or supported in the progressive era. And it seems to me that if one is to be realistic and historically minded, the record of America's reformers and of her reform epochs must be evaluated in terms of the possible, with due account being taken of the overall boundaries imposed by her culture. An author who does not do so enters into the realm of speculation, wishful thinking, and philosophy, or moralizing, agitation, and propaganda—which is his prerogative, of course. One is always free to regret that America is America because she is America. But I'm not sure that preoccupation with such regrets is conducive to best understanding or explicating the whys and hows of American history.

Given all this, then, I think it only natural that reform in industrial America should be boundaried by the kinds of piecemeal reforms that have gone into the making of our modern welfare state. They have brought about a considerable variation in the overall status quo, Professor Kolko's other book notwithstanding, and insofar as the roots of many of them reach back to the progressive era, that period properly looms large in the history of the development of modern liberalism—American style. That era was characterized by a paucity of revolutionary alternatives to the status quo, as Professor Kolko laments in the last sentence of his book, to be sure. But there was no vacuum—the country's cultural heritage took care of that—and within the framework set by that heritage there took place a complex inter-mingling of conflicting interests, motives, programs, and results. And while the exponents of political capitalism on whom Kolko concen-trates won some innings, the nonbusiness reformers had theirs, too. The game was called off because of darkness caused by war clouds, but it would be resumed at a later date, and it still goes on today.

Out of that interplay, to move on to another area of discussion, has emerged not only our welfare state—which, as I have suggested, was about as extreme a type of liberal society we were apt to create, given our heritage as we entered the twentieth century—but also a good deal of the sort of political capitalism whose early course Profes-sor Kolko charts. The Business Establishment advocates of economic rationalization and stabilization seem to have achieved their goals to a considerable degree. Has capitalism thereby been made more so-cially responsible? I sympathize with Professor Kolko's observation that it would take him another volume to discuss that question. But I would like to raise the question for possible consideration here—since I think it is very important. And I would also like to suggest an affirmative answer.

For if America were more or less bound by her cultural heritage to remain wed to private ownership and exploitative economy, as I think she was, then it does seem to me that the proponents of what we are here calling "political capitalism" have played a more con-structive role, on the whole, in evolving a better American society than have the proponents of "true, unfettered competition." For "true, unfettered competition" often degenerated into cut-throat competition of a sort that hurt consumers and workers just as much, if not more, than it hurt the competitors themselves. . . .

To recapitulate then:

(1) A vast and apparently unbridgable gap exists between the "tabula rasa," or "clean slate," attitude with which Professor Kolko approaches the years 1900–1916, on the one hand, and the "cultural determinist" approach that I have emphasized. As a result of this difference, his view of the progressive era is dominated by his fascination with its failure to develop radically revolutionary programs of participatory democracy in industry; from my point of view, it would have been very surprising indeed had such programs received any serious articulation or support.

(2) As a result of the paucity of truly radical alternatives to the status quo that characterized the Progressive Era—alternatives that alone would satisfy Kolko's criteria of liberalism—he underestimates the significance of the somewhat-less-than-radical alterations that the welfare-state-oriented reform accomplishments of the progressive era did bring about in the status quo; he neglects the importance of the nonbusiness reformers who engineered those alterations; and he slights the question of whether political capitalism was more conducive than "true, unfettered capitalism" to the creation of a better society.

(3) Instead, he dwells almost exclusively on the machinations of the exponents of "political capitalism," excludes from adequate consideration the role and accomplishments of nonbusiness reformers, and thereby overinflates the significance of political capitalism's victories.

(4) All this does not detract from the service Professor Kolko has performed in forcefully calling our attention once again to the role that the exponents of political capitalism did play in the progressive era. In this respect he has made an important—though certainly not entirely original—contribution to our growing understanding of the complexity of that period. But the limitations imposed by his basic approach have distorted his perception of the essential character of the era, it seems to me, and have prevented him from giving us a satisfactory and all-encompassing treatment of the progressive era as an interrelated and explicable whole. That task has yet to be accomplished.

GABRIEL KOLKO

Response
[1966]

Since I am interested in a descriptive social and economic theory of modern industrial society, and America in particular, I decided to examine several critical theoretical problems in the empirical context of the formative American experience between the years 1877 and 1916. I was, above all, concerned with the nature of American economic development in its political setting and the functional economic origins of political bureaucracies. Briefly, I maintained that there was no decisive technological imperative for the existing economic organization, and that the instabilities of the economy and the unique problems of banking, big business, and railroads required political intervention on a Federal level to create economic and social stability. The industries to be regulated often initiated these reforms and an important portion of them invariably controlled the regulatory agencies. Various groups advocating reforms, for whatever their reasons, associated diverse rhetoric with such measures, which began first in the 1880s in the railroad sector, but both the intentions and consequences of what we call progressivism were limited to the solution of specific industrial problems rather than alteration of the existing distribution of wealth and power in American society.

I also indicated that the national character of the economy, and the fear or distaste of local and state reforms, made Federal regulation imperative and the only means of introducing stability into the economy, especially in railroads, banking, and such specialized industries as meat packing. Political power in our society, I suggested, responded to power and influence in the hands of businessmen who had more leverage over politics, given the consensual nature of social and political priorities in America, than over their own business

From a paper read at the meetings of the American Historical Association, December 28, 1966. Published by permission of the author.

affairs—and they were quick to use it to solve business problems. . . .

There is no question that I deliberately obscured divisions in the business community, for I was concerned less with the lack of harmony than with who succeeded, their relative importance rather than their numbers. There were many business opinions on any given legislative proposal, and when this disunity was too great, as in the case of tariffs or insurance regulation, it meant a general ineffectuality. I dealt only with reform movements that obtained their goals in some measure, especially in critical areas we most associate with the period —those at the so-called commanding heights of the economy. I could not consider every opinion or event of the period on the Federal level, but only those that have preoccupied most historians because of the obvious significance of the problems, the general and valid assumption being that the comprehensive control of the banking or railroad sectors is of somewhat greater consequence to the entire fabric of the economy than an eight-hour day for railroad workers (which, parenthetically, I did discuss in my *Railroads and Regulation*). If all one does is to look at diversity and disagreement within the ranks of business and reformers, then the basically amoebic description of the phenomenon cannot be stopped until we have reached a point of absurd reductionism and considered everyone. The critical question is: "What are the major positions and who wins, and why?" The motives of the losers, or those who created pressures that others redirected toward their own ends, are far less crucial, despite the fact that this has preoccupied historians somewhat more than I felt desirable. The issues for me were which legislation counted and the distribution of actual power in society, and not that every sector obtained at least some relatively minor concession. In brief, it was a question of who succeeded and not who failed in attaining their main objectives. Business was not just another interest group, but it defined the essential preconditions and functions of the larger American social order, and it was the security and continuity of business as an institution that was accounted for, first of all, by the reform movements that began after the Civil War and culminated in progressivism.

This analysis is based on a functional view of American reform, on the consequences of legislation rather than the motives of all reformers, motives I thought paramount mainly among those who were to be regulated and who had power. Social theory, muckrakers, or intellectuals did not influence the important businessmen, and they most certainly did not aspire to have these intellectuals regulate them. They preferred that their own lawyers and direct representatives play that role, and the majority of key regulatory and commission executives were in fact drawn from these elements. With the exception of an important group in the National Civic Federation, big businessmen were not for state or Federal social welfare laws, but these cost them very little and they usually articulated their political power only when they desired something for themselves. But such welfare measures did not change the structure of power and wealth where implemented, and such business opposition to them as there was soon became largely rhetorical. But they often favored a privately defined company welfare program as part of a rationalized welfare capitalism, one that neutralized the threat of unionism. If big and small businessmen split on these and other issues of the role of the Federal government in the economy, they invariably favored government intervention, within a conservative framework, in those specific instances when it was to their advantage.

On this there was near unanimity, and the fact that most nonbusiness groups ultimately shared this consensus does not alter the fact that reform led to class ends and the satisfaction of class needs, for the phenomenon of mass consent to a society based on the superiority of a relatively small elite is a familiar event in the 20th century. It is elite opinion, not mass attitudes or, more usually in the case of those who refuse to share them, apathy that moved policy and society, however interesting and numerous the others may be. And it is not merely conflict in society that defines whether the fundamental hegemony of business in American life is challenged, but the level and purpose of such conflict as may exist. That the Federal government associated the welfare of society with the welfare of regulated industry is reflected in the personnel and management of the Federal regulatory agencies in this period, and when key bureaucrats were not pliable they were, as in the case of Harvey Wiley, unceremoniously fired. There was no sustained clash between any Federal government agency in existence or created during this period and the industry it regulated, and political scientists have produced a vast and sophisticated literature on the extent and significance of the phenomenon after the First World War, one which merely corroborates my general theme on political regulation as an adjunct to industrial control.

In developing my interpretation I slighted the nature and motives of local and state reform, against which I suggested Federal regulation was a shield. There were complexities in this area, revealed in recent years by Samuel Hays and James Weinstein, among others, that show many local reformers as conservative and even venal in their *intentions*. And there were also urban reformers and Populists seeking changes we commonly regard as liberal in impulse. But whether or not motives very much like those behind Federal regulation stimulated state and local reforms, nationally oriented big business groups certainly considered their lack of uniformity as seriously troublesome in its consequences, and suitable Federal legislation as a necessary rationalizing force.

Historians have, to a remarkable extent, interpreted the progressive era as a problem of intellectual and economic history, and they graphically illustrate the difficulties in projecting the sometimes valuable insights of contemporary muckrakers and scholars on the structure of their times, as if they perceived it with a higher sensitivity than men of affairs. But correlation is not causation, and the agitation and observations of these writers had no more influence on the course of reality or business policy than, as Irvin Wyllie has shown, Social Darwinism had on the predatory conduct and thought of late 19th century businessmen, who like their later peers had no time to read books and magazines. Muckraking was no longer important after 1912, when most progressive Federal legislation was enacted, but beyond this is the question of the significance of reform that, while perhaps liberal in the eyes of its advocates, was conservative in consequence and essentially identical in principle to business-sponsored measures. That these nonbusiness reform elements created pressure for action strikes me as being of less consequence than the fact that they merely served to reinforce less disinterested groups who should be the primary object of our attention. For in the progressive era it was elite opinion and needs, not intelligence or irrationality, that directed policy. . . .

I should like to suggest certain of the lines which would have to be examined within the framework of the analysis I have advanced, subjects ignored for too long because of the basic assumptions that have kept us from asking the proper questions. The first requirement will be that we look much more closely at movements in recent American history that have succeeded rather than those that have failed. It is a minor scandal that we have many more detailed studies of the history, structure, and social composition of that boring and impotent phenomenon, the American Communist Party, than the somewhat more consequential Republican Party, and we have examined alleged authoritarian tendencies among farmers and workers, who had neither much power nor success, far more closely than among men who defined the rules of the game and could implement their biases. There is not one good study of the important progressive and civil liberties, much less civil rights, even though these problems impinge in the most obvious way on the very quality and purpose of American reform and offer us important new insights on why the Red Scare had the endorsement of the vast majority of prewar insurgents and progressives. And we know nothing of the theory of party organization during the progressive era, when the authoritarian control of one national convention led to a split directed by a former President who had managed two earlier party conventions in much the same way. Did these men really consider themselves involved in a crusade for democracy and the welfare state? And if not, what then? In brief, what were the formal and operational political and legal assumptions of the progressives?

In *The Triumph of Conservatism* I exaggerated the extent to which new centers of economic power were created independently of older Eastern wealth, a problem I reconsider in detail in a paper on the social basis of success in American history in *The Critical Spirit: Essays in Honor of Herbert Marcuse*.[1] Suffice it to say, the vital role of Eastern wealth, and a reappraisal of the relationship of the Eastern social elites to the entrepreneurs in new industries as well as reform politics needs a much more careful examination to determine if, as Hofstadter implies, there was in fact a class basis for social reform *from above*. The extent to which Federal legislative conflicts must be understood as competition between regions organized on cooperative lines, seeking preferences not so much for individual capitalists as for regional economies, ought to be tested more thoroughly as a topic, for it might reveal much of the interclass nature of what we call reform movements, movements that in many instances simply reflected the desire of such alliances to use political weapons against one another, but always, ultimately, for private ends.

A more naturalistic view of recent American history will also compel us to discard conventional periodizations of the post–Civil War era, and to stress much more emphatically the significant elements of continuity. Railroad regulation is surely the best single example of what we now call progressivism, and I began my book on the subject with the year 1877. The only differences between the 1880s and 1900s were in the nature of the economic problems that had to be confronted in the wake of the chaos of the industrial merger movement of 1897–1901 and in the magnitude of economic growth,

[1] K. H. Wolff and B. Moore (eds), *The Critical Spirit: Essays in Honor of Herbert Marcuse* (Boston, Beacon Press, 1968).

but the responses were the same. The period 1900–1916 will have to be reexamined much more closely, above all, for its continuity with the generally regarded conservative 1920s, both from the viewpoint of contemporary definitions and for the extent of interlocking personalities and ideals, all of which can be measured much more precisely. Henry May has correctly observed that the participants of the 1920s regarded it as a decade of revolution and progress, but there can certainly be no doubt that Harding and Coolidge time and time again evoked the Republican tradition of Roosevelt and in many respects exceeded it in fact, even as trust busters initiated 132 cases in 1921–1928 as opposed to forty-four in 1901–1908 and ninety-six in 1913–1920 (none of them, so far as I can tell, of any consequence to the larger contours of the economy). Perhaps more than any other figure, we ought to study the personality and career of Herbert Hoover, whose engineering perception and passionate Wilsonianism made him one of the most symbolic links in the continuity not merely between the progressive era and the 1920s, but in the whole of the first half of this century. It was Hoover, after all, who was called upon to define food policy after both wars, who as Secretary of Commerce and then as President attempted to realize the Wilsonian world dream in its ambiguous dimensions, and who was relied upon by Truman to streamline a giant Federal bureaucracy. The concepts of consensus, bipartisanship, or monolithic hegemony, whichever you prefer, all assume this larger common agreement and force us to discard the liberal-conservative dichotomy and decide whether it was one or the other or perhaps as I have tried to suggest, even conservatism wrapped in liberal rhetoric. The only way this can be done is by confronting the phenomenon of power and purpose in American history as something to be studied explicitly, hopefully in its larger political, economic, and international context. To do so, however, one must accept the realistic terms of the debate as having value even before its final outcome can be known. If such an approach unquestionably raises as many new issues as it can solve at this time, ultimately it will help move the writing of recent American history toward a closer approximation of reality.

ROBERT H. WIEBE

The Search for Order, 1877-1920
[1967]

THE AGE OF REFORM had offered the first major review of the progressive era since John Chamberlain's *Farewell to Reform* (1932), and while it was not entirely incompatible with the old liberal interpretation, it both arose out of and strongly contributed to a deepening sense that progressivism could no longer be described as a people's uprising for democracy and justice. Kolko's *The Triumph of Conservatism* offered the first entirely new way of looking at the period since the liberal interpretation first began to seem too restrictive. But those who read the monographic literature and attended professional meetings knew there was another general interpretation of progressivism being formulated. Beginning in the late 1950s, younger scholars—raised in an America of large, impersonal organizations and affected much more directly by science than by the ideal of political or economic democracy—began to point out how much of the talk and action of the progressive forebears of the modern world had been concerned with promoting efficiency and the rule of experts. Books such as Samuel P. Hays' *Conservation and the Gospel of Efficiency* and Samuel Haber's *Efficiency and Uplift: Scientific Management in the Progressive Era* brought this dimension of progressivism, which had long been noticed but never much emphasized, to the foreground.[1]

This enlarged understanding of the progressive interest in efficient organization and functioning was eventually to point the way to a new imperative framework within which

Robert H. Wiebe, *The Search for Order, 1877–1920* (New York, Hill and Wang, 1967. Paper: Hill and Wang).
[1] Hays (Cambridge, Harvard University Press, 1959); Haber, (Chicago, University of Chicago Press, 1964). Benjamin DeWitt's pioneering book, *The Progressive Movement* (New York, Macmillan, 1915) had devoted one chapter (out of sixteen) to "Efficiency," but for forty years the concept was not seriously explored by scholars. The importance of functional organization in the reform era did not escape Hofstadter, who discussed it at some length in *The Age of Reform.*

to view the prewar period, and one which, unlike that offered by Kolko, encompassed the activities of progressivism at all levels and in all forms—local and state as well as national, civic reform and prohibition and settlement work as well as economic regulation, professional men from engineering, law, medicine, and social work as well as the larger businessmen. A leading figure here was Samuel P. Hays of the University of Pittsburgh. Hays' book on conservation (1959) revealed him as a scholar attuned to the interest-group struggles behind a movement which had always been misleadingly pictured as a simple confrontation between business interests on the one hand and the public interest (essentially, preservation) on the other. In a series of articles which appeared between 1960 and 1965, Hays urged a fundamental reorientation in the theory and practice of "political" history.[2] These articles had an incalculable influence, and their chief impact was upon those interested in the progressive era, since most of Hays' examples of both new questions and new answers were drawn from the late nineteenth and early twentieth centuries.

Hays, as so many other postwar historians, had been strongly influenced by the social sciences—in particular, by sociology. He urged that historians shift their attention from the episodic and formal aspects of human behavior to the underlying trends and social processes by which society operated, and he called for the study of groups and their interaction rather than of individuals and their ideas. He went on to offer evidence which suggested that the progressive movement, if scrutinized for the actual group interests it brought into conflict and the changes in social structure it brought about, begins to appear as an effort by upper middle class businessmen and professionals to construct a more centralized and efficient society. These men shared the reform impulse with groups somewhat lower on the social scale who represented traditional small-town values and fought to preserve them by prohibition laws, antitrust agitation, and so on. Hays, in an essay published in 1967 entitled "Political Parties

---

[2] See "History as Human Behavior," *Iowa Journal of History,* 58 (July 1960), 193–206; "The Politics of Municipal Reform in the Progressive Era," *Pacific Northwest Quarterly,* 55 (October 1964), 157–69; "The Social Analysis of American Political History, 1880–1920," *Political Science Quarterly,* 80 (September 1965), 373–94.

and the Community-Society Continuum," [3] suggested an interpretive framework which might accommodate the vast
store of somewhat contradictory data recovered by historians
from the progressive era. He saw the United States (roughly
1890–1920) as a society making the transition, in Ferdinand
Tonnies' words, from "Community" (Gemeinschaft) to "Society" (Gesellschaft), a transition in which local, personal
relations were replaced, through technological change, by a
national system of bureaucratic, routinized, relatively impersonal relations in a society where power flowed increasingly from local elites to be centralized in the hands of
a new elite whose claim to power rested upon expertise rather
than reputation. This framework, Hays argued, allows us to
understand how some men became reformers in order to
rationalize a somewhat chaotic, inefficient society, yet found
themselves rubbing shoulders in the various municipal, state,
and national reform campaigns with men and women whose
goals were quite the opposite—to defend the life-style and
values of the small-town culture which felt itself drained of
talent, respect, and power by the rise of the new business–
government bureaucratic order.

   Although Hays' argument was much fuller than I have
been able to suggest here, he had offered a series of essay-
length suggestions for understanding the progressive era, but
had not yet published a comprehensive synthesis. That synthesis came with Robert Wiebe's publication of *The Search
for Order* in 1967. Wiebe had earlier [4] studied the relation
between reform and the various elements of American business, and while he found businessmen favorably inclined
toward a number of "reform" measures (most notably, federal regulation of railroads and banking), he, unlike Kolko,
was unwilling to draw conclusions about the progressive im-

---

[3] In William Nisbet Chambers and Walter Dean Burnam (eds.),
The American Party Systems (New York, Oxford University
Press, 1967). Another historian who led the way in describing
progressivism as on the whole a conservative effort to find solutions to the disorder of the late nineteenth century through the
rhetoric of class unity and institutions of social control was Row-
land Berthoff, in his article "The American Social Order, A Conservative Hypothesis," *American Historical Review,* 65 (April
1960), 495–514.
[4] *Businessmen and Reform: A Study of the Progressive Movement*
(Cambridge, Harvard University Press, 1962).

pulse after his own examination of what businessmen had thought and done in those years. He sensed something broader happening in America in that period than just some businessmen learning to use the state to solve their economic problems. Like many in this generation of historians,[5] Wiebe acquainted himself with currents of thought in modern sociology. One recognizes especially the influence of Max Weber, with his absorbing interest in bureaucratization as the key to the modernization process. Whatever the precise influences, Wiebe produced in 1967 an interpretive history of the progressive era which integrated a wealth of detail into the community-society framework.

The Search for Order emphasized the systematizing effects of modern technology: a society of isolated communities and local elites giving way to a nationalized system based on a growing specialization of function, bureaucratic relations, organized interest groups, and a guiding elite of technical and professional managers in business and government. The transition was neither smooth nor complete by 1920, but for Wiebe the dynamics of the shift are another version of the story of reform. Members of a "new middle class" of

[5] Many examples come to mind of historians, most of them under forty, who have lately exploited the general perspective of sociology (an interest in social structure and processes, replacing the traditional interest in political narrative and individual portraiture), some of its concepts, and occasionally even a more quantified methodology. In addition to Hofstadter and Hays, one might mention David J. Rothman, *Politics and Power: The United States Senate, 1869–1901* (Cambridge, Harvard University Press, 1966): Lynn Marshall, "The Strange Stillbirth of the Whig Party," *American Historical Review,* 72 (January 1967), 445–68; and Stephan Thernstrom, *Poverty and Progress: Social Mobility in a Nineteenth-Century City* (Cambridge, Harvard University Press, 1964). The field of urban history has reflected the influence of the social sciences more extensively than any other, although the experience of urban historians suggests that history and the social sciences are not easily crossbred. See Eric Lampard, "American Historians and the Study of Urbanization," *American Historical Review,* 67 (October 1961), 49–61, and Charles N. Glaab, "The Historian and the American City: A Bibliographic Survey," in Philip Hauser and Leo F. Schnore, *The Study of Urbanization* (New York, John Wiley, 1965). Political science and psychology are strongly influential in the recent work of David Donald; see Donald, *Charles Sumner and the Coming of the Civil War* (New York, Alfred A. Knopf, 1960), and *The Politics of Reconstruction, 1863–1867* (Baton Rouge, Louisiana State University Press, 1965).

rising professionals and businessmen became reformers in order to erect the bureaucratic institutions necessary to impose predictability and order upon economic political operations which were now more efficient and more extended but also necessarily more delicate and intolerant of irregularity. Men from the older communities became reformers—but of quite a different sort—in order to defend, as best they could without fully understanding the threat, the life of "island communities" in the rural hinterland and in the ethnic ghettoes of the cities.

The Search for Order was a masterly achievement on many counts. Three generations of historians had furrowed the period with familiar questions and familiar disputes. Wiebe brought to every development of these years a fresh appraisal, and there is nothing more difficult in the craft of history. The employment of any interpretive framework both illuminates and confines, but Wiebe maintained a deft touch in his integrative efforts. His conceptual scheme succeeded time and again, as in the chapter on progressive thought (Chapter 6), in bringing into relief the common qualities of a series of events whose relation to similar and/or merely contemporaneous evidence had earlier been missed. As was to be expected, a number of matters gave Wiebe some organizational difficulties which he did not entirely solve. The book contains discussions of some themes (notably foreign policy), events, and men which do not seem easily digested by his conceptual apparatus. His transitions are not always clear. The style, frequently both incisive and elegant, is also sometimes obscure and even awkward. The impressionistic technique gives the book a readability and charm which in many ways enhances its impact, but some have registered their preference for more rigorous documentation.

One might wonder, moreover, if Wiebe has not been so impressed with the bureaucratic style of pioneering social groups that he seriously underplayed the passionate, Protestant-evangelical element in that generation, a matter of substance as well as style. Efficiency was indeed a conjuring word for progressives, but so was conscience, and so was crusade. Another quality of the book which might have attracted more attention was the weight Wiebe gave to the psychological costs of the transition to society. Hofstadter came under much criticism for what some thought an inadequate degree of attention to the real economic hardships and injustices which faced American society in this period. Wiebe, despite his sensitivity to the conflict of economic groups, appears also to stress the *anxieties* ("identity crisis," "confused loyalties") of indignant, politicized groups at the expense, some might argue, of an adequate appreciation of more *material* maladjustments and strains. Perhaps Wiebe, too, will be called a conservative. Actually, all four—Hofstadter, Kolko, Hays, and Wiebe—describe progressivism as a conservative movement. In Hofstadter's version, distinctly conservative people appear to be engaged in strenuous activities which did more to resolve their own inner tensions than the problems of the disadvantaged. The other three, it seems to me, describe progressivism as essentially a conservative counterrevolution—but with an important difference of attitude. The reassertion of social control over the disorderly tendencies of the nineteenth century was seen by Kolko as directed against a promising local radicalism, and by Hays (note that his interest has been primarily in urban reform) as against a collection of local communities of a distinctly democratic cast for whom he seems to have some sympathies. For Wiebe the counterrevolution was directed against a local system which had simply outlived its time for which he displays no nostalgia or admiration which I could detect.

These criticisms will seem more weighty to some than to others. With every deficiency of the book exposed, it is an invaluable and unique contribution. No one can read Wiebe's final chapter, with its summary of recent social changes and its brilliant intuition that the progressive institutional accomplishment might yet be turned either to the uses of freedom or order, without being visited by the conviction that Wiebe has perceived as well as any living historian where America had been and where she was going. Wiebe has demonstrated the enormous explanatory power of what must be the central dynamic of the period, the transition from community to society, and has done so with imagination and brilliance. It takes little prophetic insight to predict that this book will have a boundless influence on the teaching and writing of recent American history.

CRITICAL COMMENTARIES

SAMUEL P. HAYS

[1968]

The Search for Order was published in 1967, and when the present volume was compiled all the reviews of Wiebe's book were not yet in, and there had been no other published discussion. The calendar, not the intrinsic importance of the book, accounts for the relative brevity of the following critical commentaries.

Mr. Wiebe's book provides the outlines of a simple but potentially extensive conceptual framework that will have a major impact on the context of American history between 1877 and 1920. Many will recognize his views as a variation of the community-society or local-cosmopolitan typology, well known in sociology but clearly applicable to historical description. Preurban, industrial social organization, so Wiebe's argument goes, rested on community, in which the focal point was a set of face-to-face primary group relationships through which life was understood, values generated, and economic and political institutions developed. But urban, industrial society created a new set of relationships, above and beyond community, linking people over far broader geographical areas. The scope of human thought expanded, understanding of reality came through impersonal media rather than personal contact, and organized group action joined

From *American Historical Review,* 73 (April 1968), 1248–249. Reprinted with permission of the American Historical Association.

Samuel P. Hays has been identified earlier in this volume, and his remarks on *The Search for Order* are therefore of special interest.

specialists over wide areas rather than only those within a limited geographical community.

Social change in modern America, Wiebe argues, involved the decline of community and the rise of society. The protest movements of the late nineteenth century, for example, were rooted in the defense of community, and the reform movements of the early twentieth century involved attempts to work out the new forms of more cosmopolitan social organization. As implied in the book's title, the forces of modern society eroded community, setting loose human relationships from older roots and creating an often disorderly, mobile, undirected set of social forces, while the drive to shape new social forces constituted an attempt to bring order and direction into this chaos through organization and system.

The strongest part of the work lies in the author's description of the new, more cosmopolitan human relationships that grew with urban industrialism. He provides, for example, striking illustrations of the process of rationalization on linkages among people. But most important is his description of the "new middle class" as the root of reform movements in the early twentieth century. Convincingly he argues that this source was not the "old middle class," the independent proprietor of the past, but the new group of professionals and organizational representatives who were constructing new systems, ordering life with large, rather than parochial, perspectives, and seeking to manipulate factors beyond community. In this context, reform was not the irrational expression of an attempt to regain a lost status, but a conscious and reasoned effort to shape institutions according to the values of the new social order.

Wiebe has difficulty with the ethnocultural components of community, which generate one form of expression of defense; he stresses only the evangelical Protestant values of community and the links between these and agrarian protest. Yet the small community of the German and the Irish, of the Catholic and Lutheran, highly antievangelical, intensely antiprohibitionist, and anti-Sabbatarian were as much an expression of the values of the small community as were those in the evangelical Protestant tradition. The ethnocultural conflicts of the last three decades of the nineteenth century were, in fact, conflicts between two sets of tradition-oriented systems of value, each rooted in the personal relationships of the community. Moreover, he misses entirely the powerful force of community within the city, the decentralization of urban life in the last half of the nineteenth century into an ever-increasing number of subunits, each with relatively autonomous institutions and each with a separate political voice in urban government. These prevailed until the reform movements of the twentieth century.

Wiebe's argument is often partially developed, often tentative and incomplete. Facts covered in conventional treatments are artificially squeezed into the pages of the book, often quite removed from the general argument, and give rise to a disjoined flow of thought. The writing is, moreover, often kaleidoscopic and impressionistic rather than systematic. Despite all this, the outlines of the major argument came through clearly, to provide one of the freshest forms of conceptual reorientation to appear on the modern American history scene in years.

WALTER T. K. NUGENT

[1967]

[*The Search for Order*] is the best book now in print on the history of the United States from Reconstruction through World War I. There is much here that has been bandied about at conventions for the past couple of years, and urged as research topics for a few years before that, but which has never before been put between two covers in a coherent and attractive fashion. There is much here, too, that is the author's own. Robert Wiebe has brought off a synthesis of unusual distinction and much originality.

The general theme is the breakdown of the isolation of people and communities prevailing in the latter part of the nineteenth century and the replacement of this isolation by institutional and *processual* centralization in nearly every aspect of life. The old "ethical" values

From *The Journal of American History,* 54, 2 (September 1967), 429–30. Reprinted by permission of the Organization of American Historians.
     Walter T. K. Nugent, whose views have appeared earlier, teaches history at Indiana University.

were being replaced after 1900 by "bureaucratic" ones, for example. Though the "bureaucratic" trend was by no means over with by 1920, it had become the well-established key to the future. The reviewer doubts that "bureaucratic" is the most appropriate word for what happened. But the overriding trend of the period, whatever its right name, is the one which Wiebe has identified as "bureaucratization." It was a trend involving an increase in communications, voluntary associations, and intergroup relations; and it continued until the elements were present that could be welded together quickly on demand, as demonstrated, the author says, by Wilson's domestic-mobilization schemes of World War I.

The book is mainly descriptive and does not achieve (or attempt to achieve) more than a low level of generalization. Analysis is seldom explicit, but description is almost always interesting. There is not much explanation of why the bureaucratic trend and its sub-trends took place, except a set of vague social-psychological suggestions and, more often, the juxtaposition of rarely related phenomena (often in very thought-provoking impressionistic ways) to form a "pattern." For example, anti-monopoly and a "preoccupation with purity and unity" expressed "community self-determination" [pp. 52, 56]; these underlay anti-alien feeling; temperance, Jim Crow, and the mushrooming of voluntary associations such as the Knights of Labor, Bellamy clubs, and farmers' alliances (what about lodges and benevolent associations?). Likewise, in chapter six, the documentation for the shift from "ethical idealism" to "bureaucratic" values is impressive, though the reasons for the shift are not very clear. The technique produces its plausibilities, however, as when the author severely criticizes Roosevelt-Wilson foreign policy on the ground that statesmen failed to extend increased communication and bureaucratization beyond the boundaries of the United States, with the result that "America's first ventures into foreign policy showed an unmistakable immaturity." [p. 254]

The suggestiveness of this idea, and many others in the book, is considerable indeed. Despite the author's reliance on descriptive and impressionistic techniques, which he handles unusually well, the fact that this is the first book to present a unified intelligible overview of the half century before 1920 makes it required reading for anyone interested in modern America, or for that matter in the modern world. Since the book so abounds with information and is written very gracefully, that reading requirement is a very light burden.

ROBERT F. DURDEN
[*1967*]

Professor Wiebe starts this provocative study from the premise that nineteenth-century American society consisted of "island communities" and that poor communication limited interaction among the islands while it also scattered the power to form opinion and to enact public policy. Each community's affairs were handled informally since local autonomy continued to be the essence of American democracy. By the 1870s, he argues, community autonomy was badly eroded even though the illusion of authority lasted on. In the 1880s and especially the 1890s, however, citizens struggled in vain to defend the independence of the communities only to lose confidence finally in the old system and old ways.

Early in this century, then, in the progressive era, Professor Wiebe sees an alternative system emerging. The "regulative, hierarchical needs of urban-industrial life" gave rise to a new scheme of things in which government possessed for greater power, authority became more centralized, and men sorted themselves out more by occupation than by community. With applications in foreign as well as domestic affairs, this was "America's initial experiment in bureaucratic order, an experiment that was still in process as the nation passed through the First World War." [p. xiv]

In addition to his forthright, clear thesis, Professor Wiebe has also graced his study with considerable literary appeal. He writes wittily and well. For example, in an early chapter on "The Distended Society" of the late nineteenth century, he concludes that because of a "lack of anything that made better sense of their world, people everywhere weighed, counted, and measured it." [p. 43]

Unfortunately, *The Search for Order* offers no documentation

From *Journal of Southern History*, 33, 3 (August 1967), 420–21. Copyright 1967 by the Southern Historical Association. Reprinted by permission of the Managing Editor.
Robert F. Durden teaches history at Duke University.

at all for its numerous and original insights and interpretations. "Champions of the community," an "urban elite," "prominent citizens," or "certain magnates"—these and other similarly vague and unspecified persons or groups leave one hungry for the evidence on which an elaborate superstructure of interpretation and many striking generalizations have been built. The bibliographical essay fails to compensate for the missing documentation, for it is limited to the secondary, interpretative literature, and no manuscript or other primary sources are indicated. In short, the thesis is striking, impressive, and pushed far with logic and clarity. Yet the reader is all too often left to wonder just how or why Professor Wiebe arrived at his ideas.

Professor David Donald, the editor of the series, hails this as "not merely the standard book in its field, but the take-off book—the book . . . that will shape the pattern of future research and writing on the whole broad era from 1877 to 1920." [p. ix] Maybe so, but if so, many historians will be swallowing a great deal on faith.

AUGUST MEIER

Negro Thought
in America, 1880-1915
[1963]

GREAT HOPES had been raised among American Negroes after emancipation, and they were not entirely dashed by the end of Reconstruction in 1877. Relations between the races remained (in retrospect) relatively cordial and rational for a period after Reconstruction, and while the Negro did not advance as quickly as he hoped, he was at least struggling chiefly against the impersonal forces of poverty and economic and political inexperience, not yet against any systematic white opposition to his aspirations for a more equal status. But beginning in the late 1880s and more noticeably in the 1890s there occurred a sharp increase in white racism. Race relations deteriorated, and in state after state whites withdrew such civil rights as they had accorded to blacks since the War and built a structure of laws and practices which left the Negro disenfranchised, segregated from public facilities, with his education neglected and economic and social opportunities virtually closed off. The Jim Crow system of legal discrimination was complete in North and South by about 1905, and with it had come not peace but a higher level of tension, with race riots in New York City in 1900, in Springfield, Ohio, in 1906, in Springfield, Illinois, in 1908, and elsewhere. In Rayford Logan's words: "The last decade of the nineteenth century and the opening of the twentieth century marked the nadir of the Negro's status in American society." [1]

Since this deterioration in the situation of blacks was brought about by whites, the causes of it must be sought within white society, and historians have turned their attention to this with good result.[2] As for the Negro, his role was

August Meier, *Negro Thought in America, 1880–1915; Racial Ideologies in the Age of Booker T. Washington* (Ann Arbor, University of Michigan Press, 1963. Paper: University of Michigan Press).

[1] Rayford Logan, *The Negro in American Life and Thought: The Nadir, 1877–1901* (New York, Dial Press, 1954) 52.

[2] See C. Vann Woodward, *The Strange Career of Jim Crow* (New York, Oxford University Press, 1955) and John Higham, *Strangers in the Land* (New Brunswick, Rutgers University Press, 1955).

to devise some response. The main outlines of that response have always been clear: in 1895, at the Cotton States and International Exposition in Atlanta, Negro educator Booker T. Washington of Tuskegee Institute outlined a path of accommodation for the Negro, stressing gradualism, voluntary social separation, Negro self-help, and industrial and agricultural education. Most Negroes, it seemed, agreed with Washington that sheer survival, let alone progress, required something like Washington's program. Whites were totally dominant and most of them were in a dangerous frame of mind, and the only path for blacks seemed to be a strenuous effort to elevate themselves by their own mastery of agricultural and mechanical skills, combined with a tacit understanding that full social and political equality, while not renounced in principle, would in practice be deferred to the distant future when blacks had proven themselves fit and desirable citizens.

A few younger, Northern black intellectuals, we have always known, rejected the "Bookerite" philosophy, and insisted that some measure of militant protest was better designed to resume the Negro's advance toward full citizenship than Washington's spirit of acquiescence. W. E. B. Du Bois published a stirring attack on Washington in 1903 in his *Souls of Black Folk,* and he and other black intellectuals and professional men formed the Niagara Movement in 1905 and joined with liberal whites to found the NAACP in 1909. Their friction with the Washington group increased until and beyond Washington's death in 1915.

But this was just the framework. Many questions remained, and as the civil rights movement began to make its broad impact on black and white society, increasing numbers of historians turned their attention to the gaps in our knowledge of the Negro past. The Washington–Du Bois dispute was clearly a classic moment in American Negro history, with blacks debating the right strategy and tactics for a subordinate minority in a racist society, a debate in which the stakes seemed to be the very survival of a race. What exactly had been Washington's appeal, and how had he become so influential? To what extent did he—or Du Bois or William Monroe Trotter or Frederick Douglass—speak for the majority of blacks at the turn of the century?

The shelf of volumes on black history began to expand in the late 1950s. In addition to Rayford Logan's work (already cited), there was the brief biography of Washington by Samuel Spencer in 1955, two fine biographies of Du Bois in 1959 and 1960, and a useful collection of essays on Washington in 1962.[3] But the most comprehensive treatment of this period in Negro history came from August Meir in 1963. Meier surveyed a thirty-five-year period in a sensitive blend of intellectual and institutional history, and revealed for the first time the variety of attitudes among the large group of articulate Negroes who lived through what was in some respects the most trying era in the black past. Meier resurrected black thinkers who had fallen into oblivion, but he also wrote informed and perceptive essays on two principle American black politicians and intellectuals, Washington and Du Bois, essays that will command attention however much is written on these men. In his book we find themes familiar to any contemporary: the proper balance of accommodation and protest; of assimilation and separatism; "liberal" versus vocational education; the appeal and proper limits of racial pride and solidarity; the relative advantages of the political as against the economic ladder to Negro advancement. We learn that more alternatives were perceived and explored by blacks in the harsh years of the late nineteenth and early twentieth centuries than we had thought, and that the strain of protest ran deeper than those familiar with Washington's pervasive influence had ever imagined. Meier found more opinions, more nuances between opinions, and more shifting opinions than many readers find easily manageable, and despite his efforts at institutional history, he could not get much beyond the intellectual history of articulate blacks. But his book remains an indispensable survey of the

[3] Samuel Spencer, Jr., *Booker T. Washington* (Boston, Little, Brown, 1955); Francis L. Broderick, *W. E. B. Du Bois,* (Palo Alto, Stanford University Press, 1959); Elliott Rudwick, *W. E. B. Du Bois* (Philadelphia, University of Pennsylvania Press, 1960); Hugh Hawkins (ed.), *Booker T. Washington and His Critics* (Boston, D. C. Heath, 1962). See also Louis R. Harlan, *The Negro in American History* (Washington, D.C., Service Center for Teachers, 1965); Donald J. Calista, "Booker T. Washington: Another Look," *Journal of Negro Education,* 49 (October 1964), 240–55; and Louis R. Harlan, "Booker T. Washington and the White Man's Burden," *American Historical Review,* 71 (January 1966), 441–67.

best political and social thought among a group of Americans whose story, now that it is being told, not only provides Negro Americans with a part of the lost record of their race but retrieves for whites an important if unflattering portion of their own.

CRITICAL COMMENTARIES

LESLIE H. FISHEL, JR.
[1965]

Meier has immersed himself in the sources and has acquainted himself with Negro leaders of the past as few scholars have done. He brings to his work a dispassion which belies his deep personal commitment to equal rights.

His book, whittled down from a massive dissertation and smoothed into publishable form, makes a decisive double-cut into virtually untrod prairie. There have been few meritorious studies of the Negro after Reconstruction, when the white man settled into the pattern of racial separation which is only now being reshaped. Mr. Meier's study approaches this earlier period from a particular point of view—the Negro's rationale—but it manages to go a long way toward filling in the gaps in our knowledge of the Negro's various responses to the dominant white pattern.

The second swath which the book makes in this virgin area pivots on the author's particular point of view. Few historians have concentrated on what the Negro thought in the post-Reconstruction era or how he rationalized his actions and his reactions to life in white America. Because the Negro had only a handful of leaders conscious of the need to spell out their rationale, much of Meier's evidence comes from Negro newspaper editorials, church publications, and occasional correspondence. The result is a virile grass-roots philoso-

From *Wisconsin Magazine of History,* 48 (Spring 1965), 238–39. Reprinted with permission of *Wisconsin Magazine of History.*
    Leslie Fishel was for ten years the Director of the State Historical Society of Wisconsin, and is now President of Heidelberg College, Tiffin, Ohio.

phy, not always coherent, often contradictory, and rarely without protest.

The word "protest" comes closest to defining the unifying thread during these years from 1880 to the first World War, since almost all Negro leaders were protesting in one form or another. Even Booker T. Washington, whose public statements were generally phrased in a "conciliatory tone," worked secretly against disfranchisement and segregation. The very agencies of self-help which flourished in this period—businessmen's leagues, farmers' conferences, and labor unions —were protesting the segregated nature of society.

Underlying the variegated forms of protest was a driving force with a built-in contradiction. Race nationalism or, in Meier's phrase, "race solidarity," was a hard-core concept with a pumpkin-pie periphery. Virtually all Negroes were loyal to their race, but at some point they had to choose between segregating themselves or working for integration. Forced into separate institutions, they felt at home; comforted by the hospitality and a sense of accomplishment, their desire for protest dulled. At what point does the Negro school become a desirable end in itself? At what point the Negro insurance company, the Negro church or fraternal order? These questions are not easily answered, and not confronted once but continually. Pre–World War I Negroes faced them daily and Meier's heading for the final section of his book suggests the dilemma of "The Divided Mind of the Negro, 1895–1915."

Meier's subject matter contains a number of inherent difficulties which even he is unable to overcome completely. He is forced into great detail because of the lack of secondary sources, particularly in biography. Men and women of merit who, for their place in Negro affairs, deserve a biographical treatment, have none. Equally troublesome is the fuzziness of a central theme in Negro history: Is it truly a history of the Negro or a history with emphasis on the Negro? Because of Meier's catholic approach, this question is germane and one which he never fully resolves for himself. I would guess that his point of departure would be the second rather than the first question, but the point is somewhat obscured. The author confronts still another dilemma in his efforts to tag various individuals and schools of thought within the Negro group for purposes of identification and discussion. This is not a new historiographic problem, not even in Negro history where contemporaries were free with their labels. The more specific Meier gets, the less meaning his own distinctions have. For example, using Kelly Miller's phrase, "Radicals and Conservatives," as a chapter heading in the book's final division, Meier runs athwart the large number of Negro leaders who were one or the other at various times and occasionally even simultaneously. A prime example, which he cites, was the Chicago attorney, S. Laing Williams, who had depended upon Booker T. Washington for a political appointment and who, with his wife, was ideologically close to Washington. Yet Williams was an officer in the local branch of the NAACP from its inception. The use of the terms "radicals and conservatives" is further muddled, since "The radical Negroes were chiefly 'radical' on the race question, and most of them remained 'conservative' in their broader economic and social outlook." [p. 184]

These are, I repeat, difficulties inherent in the subject matter. If there is an author's flaw here it is Meier's inclination to de-emphasize, but not omit, historical progression in favor of analysis in terms of the times. The Booker T. Washington school might be more clearly delineated when seen in relation to pre–1890 and post–1920 race relations than in terms of the kaleidoscopic strands of thought which interweaved with Washingtonian conceptualizations. To be specific, R. R. Morton and F. D. Patterson, Washington's successors at Tuskegee, are sounder baseboards with which to compare Washington and his supporters than are W. E. B. Du Bois and William Monroe Trotter. I suggest this only because I think Meier's emphasis on contemporary analysis, comprehensive as it is, lacks the clarity which a slightly different emphasis might bring.

These are the reflections of one who admires the book and respects its author. It is an important breakthrough in the field of Negro history by an able, perceptive, and forceful scholar.

GEORGE B. TINDALL
[1964]

This book significantly illuminates the complex themes of racial ideologies in that dismal period of Negro history bounded at one end of Reconstruction and at the other by the death of Booker T. Washington, the Great Migration, and the emergence of the New Negro. No brief summary can do justice to the diversity of information presented by Professor Meier, much of it new. He not only explores the expressed thoughts of articulate Negroes but pursues general trends through their institutional expressions: the convention movement, churches, schools, fraternal societies, and self-help groups. There is an effort throughout to relate trends in racial ideologies to broader trends in the social thought and forces of the day. . . .

One is struck repeatedly by the paradoxes, or seeming paradoxes, of Negro thought and social action: Washington, the theoretical embodiment of accommodation, shrewdly ambiguous about ultimate ends, surreptitiously engaged in attacks on disfranchisement and segregation, eschewing politics but a powerful politician in his own right; W. E. B. Du Bois, the incarnation of protest but "the epitome of the paradoxes in American Negro thought," scholar and prophet, mystic and materialist, integrationist and advocate of racial solidarity, giving priority at different times to political rights and economic co-operation, "an equalitarian who apparently believed in innate racial differences; a Marxist who was fundamentally a middle-class intellectual." Most of the paradoxes arose from the dual identity of Negroes as both Negroes and Americans, and from their development of race pride and

From *Journal of Southern History,* 30 (May 1964), 236–37. Copyright 1967 by the Southern Historical Association. Reprinted by permission of the Managing Editor.

George B. Tindall, of the University of North Carolina, recently published *The Emergence of the Modern South: 1913–1945* (Baton Rouge, Louisiana State University Press, 1969).

separate institutions without abandoning the goals of civil rights and integration.

Negro ideologies of the period were basically responses to the persistent decline in Negro status and they leave the reader with a sense of floundering helplessness, of Negroes talking mostly to one another, vainly seeking an exit from the wilderness of segregation and proscription. Yet in the end a central theme begins to emerge. Out of their very separation, American Negroes had painfully evolved a nascent sense of solidarity, self-help, and self-realization that issued into the New Negro movement of the 1920s. The convergence of ideologies is strikingly illustrated in two events of 1916: the Amenia Conference and the choice of a former Washingtonian (or "Booker-ite"), James Weldon Johnson, as national organizer for the NAACP.

In the course of his research the author has brought to light a number of previously unexplored Negro manuscripts and publications. The style, unfortunately, is somewhat stiff, but the mood is consistently one of scholarly detachment and dispassionate analysis. The book is an important contribution to the understanding of American Negro history. More than that, it has cleared the path and pointed the way for the next steps toward examination of the New Negro and civil rights movements.

TOM KAHN
[1964]

August Meier is a rare combination of academician and activist. He helped found Baltimore's Civic Interest Group and participated in its direct action projects. He is as comfortable writing for *New Politics* as for *The Journal of Negro History.*

From *New Politics,* 3 (Winter 1964), 123–24. Reprinted by permission of the author and *New Politics.*

Tom Kahn is Executive Director of the League for Industrial Democracy, and a free-lance journalist.

This volume derives from Meier's doctoral dissertation at Columbia, a scholarly and detailed study of "racial ideologies in the Age of Booker T. Washington." This age is aptly named, for Washington so dominated the thought and political direction of his contemporaries that even his opposition made its way only gradually out from under his far-cast shadow, and then never quite freed itself from the ambivalences he symbolized.

But, as Meier perceptively shows, it was less the man who dominated the age than the reverse. Washington was the product of the New South, of Social Darwinism, of petty bourgeois values toward work, money and morality that molded American life in those years. Moreover, Washington's stress on self-help, racial solidarity and independent economic up-life have always struck responsive chords in the Negro community, especially in times of discouragement. And that, to put it mildly, is what the period of 1880–1915 was. Lynchings reached their peak, segregation and disfranchisement were secured by law and violence, and the North, with few exceptions, succumbed to a virulent racist psychology.

Not surprisingly, therefore, the essentially conservative Bookerite nationalism had deep roots in the attitude of the Negro masses and was especially articulated by a new entrepreneurial class which serviced the Negro community exclusively. Agitation for political and civil equality came primarily in this period from educated Negroes who had cultural ties with whites or were dependent on white customers. Interestingly, assimilation and protest tended to go hand in hand —a suggestive contrast with today, when the social base of protest having shifted, militance seems more often linked with nationalism.

But the rich diversity of detail which Meier presents discourages easy generalization. No sharp split developed between tne Bookerites and anti-Bookerites until 1900, and meanwhile, many of the "Talented Tenth"—editors, educators, ministers, lawyers, etc.—shuttled between the two poles, with some sacrifice to consistency. Shifts in personal allegiances were largely in response to the enormous power Washington wielded over political appointments for Negroes and other philanthropic funds for Negro education—a power unprecedented and never since duplicated.

How much the educated class articulates the views of the masses is a problem inherent in intellectual history. In the case of the Negro's intellectual history, in this period, the problem is exacerbated by the degradation of the masses. Still by interweaving the threads of Negro thought with the rise of separatist and mutual aid institutions,

Meier builds a good case for the proposition that aspects of Washington's philosophy spoke to the felt needs of betrayed Americans. . . .

There was, of course, ideological debate, and Meier's discussion of the trend toward pro-labor economic radicalism on the part of Negro militants is especially interesting. Indeed, ideological differences seem to have been expressed with more sophistication than at present. But the language is in the classical style of the elite, and the words seem spoken in a vacuum. But that's what happens when they are filtered through masses in motion.

CHARLES WALKER THOMAS
[1964]

Here indeed is a medley of historical and sociological emphases: now the author holds forth as historian; now, as a sociologist. Professor Meier's cultural history parades a plethora of detail on all sides of a controversy. Before the reader pronounces this work markedly objective, however, he should assess its recurrent emphases that constitute a veritable refrain, consider its proportion, reflect upon the apparent conclusions the author comes to just short of making explicit, and examine the backdrop of the period's political history which must illumine at every turn the development of Negro thought. This reviewer submits that one must be something of a social philosopher to effect properly insightful value judgments as he courses through Meier's book.

The principal thesis of the work is the insistence that ambivalence has characterized the Negro's stance regarding integration into American life on the one hand and self-segregation on the other. Even prior to the Reconstruction a very real ideological conflict was

From *Journal of Negro History*, 49 (October 1964), 278–80. Reprinted with permission of *The Journal of Negro History*.

Charles Walker Thomas is Dean of the District of Columbia College, Washington, D.C., and a member of the editorial board of *The Journal of Negro History*.

evident among the articulate Negroes. Perhaps the author as historian might have developed more fully what alternatives to self-segregation and accommodationist thought and action really existed. Meier makes passing reference to the hostility of the white world as a cause of Negroes' withdrawal into self-segregation. Such causal hostility needs to be explored in detail to make it clear what choices were in fact available to Negroes intent upon functioning in the South, where agitation or overt protest was virtually proscribed.

For survival's sake, Negroes, particularly in the South, were forced to turn to their own resources to help themselves. Propelling them toward racial solidarity, their efforts, the author suggests, help to effect self-segregation. And this is, ironically, the antithesis of what Meier asserts is Negroes' persistent, ultimate aim: their assimilation into the main stream of American society. Moreover, emphasis upon self-help was congenial to the mood and temper of the last century with its stress upon individualism and self-realization.

Posing an ethnic ambivalence in Negro thought, a strong current of protest in the interest of civil rights and political equality was kept active by vigorous assimilationist advocates like Frederick Douglass, Charles W. Chestnutt, and Monroe Trotter.

Booker T. Washington, as the central figure of enormous power, dominates the work. Himself the epitome of the dualism in Negro thought, as delineated by Meier, never confused his immediate objectives and his ultimate goals. His public utterances and his undercover maneuvering were often poles apart. The author observes that "although Washington held to full citizenship rights and integration as his objective, he masked this goal beneath an approach that satisfied influential elements that were either indifferent or hostile to its fulfillment." [p. 116] Without hammering home the point, Meier supplies the key to any valid appraisal of Washington's contribution in noting that "Washington appealed to the highest sentiments and motives of the whites and brushed over their prejudices and injustices in an attempt to create the favorable sentiment without which Negro progress was doomed." [p. 106]

This history, nevertheless, provides no flattering portrait of Booker Washington. Always the consummate politician, deft in maneuver in human relations, he is pictured as a virtual dictator maintaining a position of control over much Northern and Southern philanthropy and political preferment.

The celebrated feud between Washington and Du Bois as well as much anti-Washington feeling was engendered, the reader concludes, more from jealousy over Booker Washington's control of funds than from conflicting educational ideologies. Certainly Meier does not try to explain away the cleavage between the advocates of industrial training and those of liberal arts education, but he does hold that the self-improvement emphasis was so insistent that many leaders were ideologically closer to Washington than is popularly believed. Even Du Bois and Washington were for a time in practical agreement, but Du Bois could not abide the latter's strangle hold control of funds.

A large number of Washington's followers were, according to Meier, opportunists hoping for financial aid or political favors. John Hope, the author states, was unique among Southern educators: he refused to genuflect to Washington.

Meier's exploration of Du Bois' dualism—his fostering race pride and self-improvement and his thrust toward assimilation into the main stream of American life is one of the best parts of the book. For Du Bois the salvation of the race lay in the education and leadership involvement of the "Talented Tenth." Further, the author provides a fresh insight in detailing, as he does, Du Bois' "early tendencies toward an accommodating view point." He is nonetheless credited with expressing more effectively than any of his contemporaries the protest element in Negro thought.

Meier is certainly a cautious scholar. This reviewer wonders whether the author is one step short of making a value judgment when he observes: ". . . one must note the compensatory and psychological role the Negro history movement played—no matter what the larger view of its supporters. . . . For it gave dignity in the face of insults and provided arguments for equality in the face of assertions of inferiority. . . . The movement was chiefly significant as part of the complex of ideas that included self-help, race pride, and solidarity." [pp. 263f] Is there a suggestion of the pejorative here? And does Meier intend to put advocates of the study of Negro history on the defensive?

This scholarly treatment is iconoclastic. Familiar luminaries, appropriately denuded, are made to stand in the harsh light of sycophancy and political opportunism.

All in all, the book presents a dismal outlook. But this is not unusual for cultural history in a world in which the incidence of social and political evil is what it is in ours. One bright note of hope, however, should not be overlooked: the recognition accorded the emergence of the NAACP, "the most effective organization yet established for the agitation of Negro rights."

EUGENE D. GENOVESE
[1967]

Before World War II and immediately after, an irrepressible band of Negro historians, occasionally joined by a white historian, usually a radical, strove to restore to the Negro a sense of his past and to bring to all Americans a sense of the Negro's contribution to our national life. Until a few years ago works on Negro history were shunned by publishers as unmarketable; today, publishers complain that they cannot get enough books to publish, and scholarly journals vie with one another for manuscripts. This victory has been bought at a price. In order to offset stereotyped notions of Negro passivity, historians have tended to dramatize the heroic moments; in order to force attention to the Negro's place in our national history, they have slid into some sweeping exaggerations. Most of the older scholars tried to keep on guard against a romantic view, but there has been a growing danger of an oscillation from a reactionary and ignorant view of the Negro, or no view at all, to a romantic and one-dimensional view. Thus the ideologically conservative portrait of every slave a Sambo has given way to the ideologically liberal portrait of every slave a potential Nat Turner.

August Meier has been in many ways emotionally and intellectually tied to the older, heroic school of Negro history; but strong doses of skepticism and a noticeable aversion to dogmatism temper his passionate commitment to racial justice and equality and, together with his impressive learning, place him in the front rank of his field. . . .

Meier's *Negro Thought in America* (first published in 1963 and

From *The Nation,* 204 (June 12, 1967), 758–61. Reprinted with permission of *The Nation.*

Eugene Genovese, the young historian whose *The Political Economy of Slavery* (New York, Alfred A. Knopf, 1965) won him recognition as one of the country's leading scholars in Negro and Southern history, teaches history at the University of Rochester.

now appearing in paperback) . . . [is not] a simple book, for its beauty lies in the clarity with which so many complexities and subtle nuances are explored. . . .

Meier focuses on the articulate Negroes and accepts some distortion, for, as he observes, these would tend to be the prominent and socially privileged. To compensate somewhat, he searches institutional as well as intellectual developments in order to get some clues to the state of mind of the masses. Perhaps his most important contribution is the demonstration of a persistent duality in Negro life between integrationism and separatism and especially his probing examination of the specific forms and consequences of this duality. Meier points out that the integrationist tendency has generally prevailed during periods of upsurge, optimism and white dependence on Negro support—as, for example, during the war for Southern Independence and immediately thereafter—whereas the separatist (Black Nationalist, Black Power) tendency has generally prevailed during periods of defeat and disillusionment and the flight of white allies.

This integrationist-separatist antagonism has rarely expressed itself in pure form; usually both elements, although in different proportions, have intruded themselves into movements and even individuals. Cutting across this antagonism has been the division between the leaders and the led. The generalization laid down by Meier for Reconstruction will, with proper application, serve for other occasions: "While the masses were primarily interested in landownership, the elite leaders, who had achieved some sort of economic security, were first and foremost interested in political and civil rights." Throughout the history of the Negro in America the emphasis on economic advance has been closely related to separatism and has been a working-class as well as a petty-bourgeois demand. Philosophies of racial exclusiveness and institutional separatism have formed part of a broader complex of ideas that has included racial pride and solidarity. In the age of Booker T. Washington, as well as before and since, Negroes have had to fight for integration, while creating separate organizations. "They appeared to be creating a segregated movement in itself, to be fostering the very thing they were attacking." Much of Meier's book is devoted to a searching examination of this paradoxical duality.

The clarity with which Meier presents this duality renders strange his assessment of Booker T. Washington. He insists on cluttering up an incisive discussion with dark suggestions that Washington's preponderance somehow does not indicate that he reflected the "aspirations" of the black masses and that he was "power" motivated. "Aspirations" is a loaded word. The point, as Meier's account shows, is that Washington spoke for and to the possibilities for the Southern black masses in a period of retreat and defeat. As for "power," Meier's embarrassed discussion provides enough reason to forget it. Washington was human and convinced of his own superior wisdom; the fact remains that he did the best he could for his embattled people. Perhaps the best part of Meier's discussion is his demonstration of the use to which Washington's philosophy was put: in the South it spelled accommodation; in the North a doctrine of self-help and go-it-alone for a people without substantial allies who nonetheless had the wherewithal to assume a defiant stance.

One of Meier's most significant findings concerns the decline in Washington's power, which roughly coincided with the formation of the NAACP. By the time he died, most of his power had disappeared. As his political position with the Republican Party slipped and his control of patronage dwindled, his enemies finally saw their chance. The subsequent changes opened the way for a more militant movement, but proved less extensive than appears on the surface. Northern Negro acceptance of Washington's leadership had never meant acquiescence in his accommodationist philosophy, which had been designed for a difficult Southern setting. Southern Negro acceptance of Washington's leadership had meant such acquiescence because no alternative had presented itself or was to present itself for a long time after his death. The integrationists spoke for a new Negro middle class that aspired to assimilation but was itself rising on an expanding Negro market and had the most to gain from an espousal of racial pride and solidarity. The Northern Negro politicians especially had to walk a tightrope, and part of Du Bois' status rests on his having grasped, so much better and earlier than most, that Negroes somehow had to integrate and separate at the same time.

Meier's account of the years 1880 to 1915 could in most respects be extended into our own day. New problems have arisen to complicate the old, but all or at least most of the old remain, for they have arisen from the paradox of the Negro in America, within which he is nothing if not an American, and still has never been permitted to become fully an American either. Meier's praise of the pragmatic streak in Negro thought is therefore hard to take: "There is something pragmatic about the ideologies of American Negroes. They will take the path that seems most likely to eliminate or at least minimize the discrimination involved in the American race system." Reflecting on how far back the Negro remains, we may question the wisdom of this pragmatism. Short-run tactical approaches have their place but their only real virtue lies in their supposed ability to deliver victory. The failure of black America to develop a long-range ideology and strategy of liberation has cost it dearly and, if the present signs of reaction are not deceptive, may soon take another heavy toll. Meier underestimates the savage emasculation wrought by slavery, paternalism and persistent violence. It will take much more than shrewd tactics, limited gains and heroic moments to bring the black masses that *élan*, self-discipline and political cohesion without which their liberation is unlikely.

It would be unfair to Meier's remarkable effort to press this argument further, but I do wish he had pondered more carefully the words he quotes from the Southern Negro political and religious leader, Bishop Henry M. Turner: "A man who loves a country that hates him is a human dog and not a man." This sentence ought to be taken neither as an understandable but reckless outburst nor as a moral judgment on a too often apathetic people, for it contains in embryo an understanding of the terrible effect wrought by centuries of slavery and a glimpse of the harsh work needed to exorcize it.

ERNEST R. MAY

~~~~~~

The World War and
American Isolation
[1959]

ARTHUR S. LINK

~~~~~~

Wilson the Diplomatist
[1957]

I HAVE THE STRONG IMPRESSION, which some learned specialist in the American Civil War would probably challenge, that more first-rate intellectual and polemical talent has been engaged in trying to explain why America became involved in the First World War than in any other war in our history. Woodrow Wilson addressed himself to the question in his War Message on the night of April 2, 1917, and the discussion goes on undiminished today. From the beginning, the question of *why* we decided for war was blended with judgments as to whether we should have done so at all, or in the manner we did. The record of Wilsonian diplomacy, 1914–1917, has attracted scholars of strong moral and political convictions, and with almost no exceptions they thought it proper to take sides—to talk of faults, mistakes, even crimes, and also of wise and provident leadership. To Wilson and those of his advisors who wrote later on, the issues were relatively simple. The Germans asked for war, and deserved defeat. A generation of scholars in the 1920s and 1930s, revisionists like Hartley Grattan, Walter Millis, and Charles Tansill, also thought the issues simple.[1] Wilson and his government had been unneutral from the beginning, largely in order to protect America's growing economic stake in an Allied victory, and had shaped pro-Allied maritime policies which left Germany no choice but submarine interdiction.

Ernest R. May, *The World War and American Isolation, 1914–1917* (Cambridge, Harvard University Press, 1959. Paper: Quadrangle Books). Arthur S. Link, *Wilson the Diplomatist* (Baltimore, Johns Hopkins University Press, 1957. Paper: Quadrangle Books).
[1] This literature is reviewed in Richard Leopold, "The Problem of American Intervention, 1917: An Historical Retrospect," *World Politics*, II (1950), 405–25, and Daniel Smith, "National Interest and American Intervention, 1917," *Journal of American History*, 52 (June 1965), 5–24. Some leading revisionist histories were: C. Hartley Grattan, *Why We Fought* (New York, Vanguard, 1929); Walter Millis, *Road to War, 1914–1917* (Boston, Houghton Mifflin, 1935); and Charles C. Tansill, *America Goes to War* (Boston, Little, Brown, 1938).

But Wilson was not without scholarly defenders. In the 1930s the Yale historian Charles Seymour found the Germans unreasonable and Wilson generally temperate, committed to the victory of neither side, and operating within the limits of international law insofar as it was then clarified.[2] Seymour's work was impressive, but when, after the Second World War, most scholars interested in the decision of 1917 rejected the revisionist critique of Wilsonian diplomacy it was not because they had accepted Seymour's defense. Wilson was due for a new round of criticism, but from a different angle. The events of the 1940s had led scholars interested in American foreign relations to ask if perhaps the ineffectuality of our foreign policies—which post–World War II intellectuals were even more willing to grant than the worried men of the 1920s and 1930s—might not be rooted less in specific errors than in a moralistic national habit of thought. These scholars, like everyone else believers in collective security, criticized not an "unneutral" eagerness to intervene but a style of thought which employed American power too late and for the wrong reasons. To George Kennan, Hans Morgenthau, Robert Osgood, and others, it appeared that Wilson's mistake had been not so much entering the war but entering it for idealistic rather than realistic purposes.[3] As they saw it, foreign policy required a realistic appraisal of the requirements of national security; national security in the twentieth century was potentially at stake in developments in other parts of the world, given the economic and military realities of modern industrial life; therefore American policymakers must be willing to employ limited force abroad for limited, specific, and plausible ends. But Wilson, as they saw it, had searched the international scene not for American national interests and how they might be protected, but for the commands of international law and human rights. When these brought him to the edge of a conflict which some of

[2] See *American Diplomacy During the World War* (Baltimore, Johns Hopkins University Press, 1934), and *American Neutrality, 1914–1917* (New Haven, Yale University Press, 1935).
[3] George Kennan, *American Diplomacy, 1900–1950* (Chicago, University of Chicago Press, 1950); Morgenthau, *In Defense of the National Interest* (New York, Alfred A. Knopf, 1951); Robert E. Osgood, *Ideals and Self-Interest in America's Foreign Relations* (Chicago, University of Chicago Press, 1953).

his advisors urged him to enter for quite sensible reasons, he asked for war in idealistic language which set unreasonable goals and insured disillusionment and reaction.

These books largely set the terms in which the argument over American entry would henceforth be carried on—realism or idealism. Had our first sustained adventure in world politics been based primarily on an irrelevant and dangerous type of Presbyterian moralism? The realist school, writers such as Kennan, Morgenthau, and Osgood, argued that it had. Library shelves also held all those old books urging the economic interpretation, as well as Seymour's classic exposition of the "submarine" argument, and these views naturally remained a part of the ongoing discussion. But a group of new scholars who joined the issue in the later 1950s took up principally the challenge of the realists, and argued that Wilson and his advisors had a reasonably sophisticated and tenacious understanding of America's stake in the survival of the Atlantic democracies, and that the President's decision to go to war was based substantially on realistic grounds, whatever the language he chose to use before the public. The principal books in this last burst of scholarly activity were Edward H. Buehrig's *Woodrow Wilson and the Balance of Power,* Arthur Link's *Wilson the Diplomatist,* and Ernest May's *The World War and American Isolation, 1914–1917.*[4] The argument over the balance of realism and idealism in Wilsonian preentry diplomacy, which has been ably summarized by Daniel Smith [5] in a *Journal of American History* article in 1965, has produced roughly equal bodies of evidence for both positions, and has come temporarily to something like a standoff.

The Link and May books command attention for many reasons, quite apart from their arguments (which are not identical) that Wilson acted out of realistic as well as idealistic assumptions and motives. Link, the Princeton historian

[4] Buehrig (Bloomington, Indiana University Press, 1955); Link (Baltimore, Johns Hopkins University Press, 1957); May (Cambridge, Harvard University Press, 1959). For an interesting discussion of the issue, see Arthur S. Link, "The Higher Realism of Woodrow Wilson," *Journal of Presbyterian History,* 41 (March 1963), 1–3; reprinted in Arthur S. Link (ed.), *Woodrow Wilson: A Profile* (New York, Hill and Wang, 1968).
[5] Smith, "National Interest," *op. cit.*

who shortly after the war had commenced a monumental biography of Wilson (volumes have appeared in 1947, 1956, 1960, 1964, and 1965) naturally speaks with special authority. Wilson had other biographers, but none with access to such a full range of private and newly opened governmental manuscript materials, and none with such intellectual gifts.[6] Link's *Wilson the Diplomatist* previewed the position he would take on Wilson's diplomacy when the biography reached the war period. His interpretation was closest to that of Seymour, in finding the war to have been thrust upon a reluctant President whose choices had been inexorably narrowed by circumstances. Link brought to this interpretation an erudition, open-mindedness, and subtlety far surpassing that of any previous scholarly defender of the President. And one notices in *Wilson the Diplomatist* another quality which had been notably lacking in all that had been written on this subject previously (with the one exception of Kennan), a pervading sense of fatalism, of an absence of feasible alternatives, of a gifted and not inflexible President who was unable to bend the complex energies of wartime societies toward any end but the one he ultimately accepted.

This spirit is, if anything, more evident in May's *The* *World War and American Isolation*. The book treats politics and diplomacy in three nations, and exhibits a striking absence of censure or condemnation. The leading statesmen attempted to formulate sane policies in a setting of domestic political pressures which May is at some pains to describe, and the reader cannot fail to be impressed with the mismatch between the resources available to Wilson, Grey, and Bethmann, as against the popular passions, military ambitions, and political fears of those who would enlarge and prolong the war. May has written elsewhere that he thinks the time for condemnation has passed and that the historian must now describe how a thing happened rather than search out the fools and criminals. "The deeper streams in current historical thinking," he wrote in 1960, "run less after praise and blame than in search of understanding and sympathy." [7] In the end, May found little for which Wilson could be

[6] Link, like Wilson, is a Presbyterian and a Southerner.
[7] Ernest May, *American Intervention: 1917 and 1941* (Washington, Service Center for Teachers of History, 1960), 19.

faulted. At each step, Wilson's decision had been virtually the only one possible, given the political, military, and mental world in which he exercised the limited powers of his office.

These books have been deservedly praised in many places, Link's especially for the subtlety and intelligence of his argument, May's especially for its grasp of relevant detail, its multinational perspective, and its full account of the political setting of policy making. They have not, of course, satisfied everyone. Readers of the following critical comments will note important questions of a methodological nature, for example the possibility that May's inability to use British foreign office records made the passages devoted to Britain highly tentative, or that his attention to American domestic pressures was inadequate. But the central question must be, Is their sympathy for Wilson justified? May's comment about sympathy and understanding raises a matter the philosophers are welcome to continue to fail to settle, but to many it will surely seem (especially if the critical spirit of the 1960s persists) to be questionable philosophy wrapped around a resourceful conservatism, a nice product of a decade when American thought lacked a cutting edge. A more radical thinker is sure things could have been different, and indignant that they were not. If one finds that "whatever was, was right," one will naturally be suspected of having arrived at that conclusion not because the evidence is clear that men had no real choices, but because the scholar in question has lost his capacity, if he ever had it, for indignation and imagination.

The question of whether these two books and others of their school are flawed because their authors are conservative has been raised only infrequently,[8] but it ought to be more openly discussed if those engaged in historical debate are to bring under some control the factors of contemporary mood and personal bias that have accounted for those discouraging cycles of interpretation which keep pedants busy but weary the reading public. It is best to see this as an historical question, not properly addressed by searching the social views of any scholar. We have retrospect; let us use it. Were there better courses of action? Were there real opportunities to

[8] See William Appleman Williams, "The Acquitting Judge," *Studies on the Left,* 3 (1963), 94–99.

adopt them? Has the evidence to answer this question been massed and weighed before reaching judgment, or has indulgence shortened the argument, blunted the inquiry, and exonerated the decision-makers?

The books under discussion may well withstand such tests. May, especially, probed hard at each point of decision. No reader has properly used either book until he probes equally hard. This, it should be warned, will require more reading. It may also lead to different conclusions. The reader may, for example, share my own feeling that both authors actually describe for us a Wilson who was deeply confused (which is completely understandable), who could derive no firm guidance from international law, his own or his country's principles, or any matured philosophy of foreign relations, and who therefore let himself be guided chiefly by an astute political feel for what would most unite and least divide his party and country. The reader may conclude that Wilson's response to the Gore-McLemore proposals, to cite an example, was inexcusably rigid, and wonder why it was not called as much in these volumes. Or he may share the authors' sense of the limits within which Wilson operated, exculpate the President from having failed in any important way to work consistently for peace and the national interest, and still feel that the larger American system which so constrained the President should itself be given a more searching examination. These are, obviously, some of my own thoughts upon rereading these books, and that they raise such difficult and fundamental questions is a sure sign that one deals with authors of intellectual depth and sensitivity, and with events of the highest importance.

ERNEST R. MAY
The World War and
American Isolation: 1914-1917
[1959]

CRITICAL COMMENTARIES

RICHARD W. LEOPOLD
[1959]

In this sound and sophisticated study Professor May has given depth and meaning to American involvement in 1917 by analyzing the interplay of diplomacy and domestic forces in the United States, Great Britain, and Germany. Bringing to bear a firm command of printed materials in several languages, an intelligent use of American manuscripts and captured records from the Wilhelmstrasse, and a thorough understanding of the basic issues, he has written the most broadgauged account yet available of the high-level decisions reached in Washington, London, and Berlin.

From *Mississippi Valley Historical Review,* 46, 1 (September 1959), 333–35. Reprinted by permission of the Organizaton of American Historians.
Richard W. Leopold, one of the leading diplomatic historians in America, teaches history at Northwestern University.

Although the British side is the least well developed and although shuttling the reader between three capitals makes for some repetition, the tragic story of how the triumph of the immoderates in Europe compelled a hesitant United States to intervene clearly emerges. In England, Grey succeeded in maintaining American good will during the crucial months before the submarine brought the Wilson administration into conflict with the Reich. After mid-1915 Grey steadily lost ground to the advocates of ruthless economic warfare who spurned the peace efforts of the American President. In Germany, Bethmann Hollweg managed for two years to restrain his critics, civilian and military; but he was unable to co-operate with Wilson in a negotiated peace, the one step that could have kept America out of the struggle. When the Balkan victories late in 1916 freed divisions to guard the Dutch and Danish frontiers, and when the number of U-boats in service gave color to the exaggerated claims of the admirals, the Chancellor could not—it would be better to say he did not try to—prevent unrestricted operations. In the United States, Wilson wavered at the outset, grew steadily in comprehension, combined patience with firmness, and sought tenaciously to mediate. But by March 1917, he reluctantly decided that disunity at home and disrespect abroad posed greater dangers than a war that promised to bring about the type of peace which, he felt, alone could make the world free.

The author has no ax to grind or reputations to redeem. He believes American involvement was inescapable, not the result of insidious propaganda, personal greed, or diplomatic ineptitude. He finds little fault with Wilson's broad policies and cannot see how the executive could have chosen another course. He denies that the United States took up arms because its security was in immediate peril; he does not hesitate to argue that a pacifistic President actually defended that "creature called prestige." For Wilson in 1917, the submarine was a very real issue; it threatened his cherished rule of law and the rights of humanity.

Quite apart from these conclusions, scholars will find in Mr. May's pages a satisfying handling of many topics inadequately dealt with in the past. His discussion of Bethmann Hollweg's troubles with the Reichstag is the best in English. His parallel account of the Chancellor's clash with the military is unsurpassed down to March, 1916; after that date the treatment in Karl E. Birnbaum's *Peace Moves and U-Boat Warfare* (1958) is fuller. Because the Foreign Office archives are still closed the author has to be more cautious when he turns his attention to London, but again his summary is the most discriminating yet published. One can only regret that he did not seek more aggressively access to the private papers of certain British leaders, for their letters and memoranda would have thrown important light on events after the *Sussex* crisis. Mr. May's judgments on Wilson's course of action are shrewd and informed, and he makes some interesting observations about the meaning of the House-Grey agreement and the alternative of limited war in April 1917, to full belligerency. His twenty-eight page bibliographical essay, while necessarily brief in its evaluations, is surprisingly complete in its listings.

A few criticisms are in order. There is a disconcerting absence of specific dates in the text, an omission the footnotes rarely remedy. The contrast between Grey and the immoderates is probably overdrawn, and the contention that by December 1916, England was able to withstand any economic pressure from the United States will certainly elicit dissent. The interplay of diplomacy and politics is not consistently worked out for the United States; in places the description of the American scene is woefully thin. One may question whether there is sufficient consideration of isolation as a policy to justify its inclusion in the title, and the index fails to unlock the rich materials that precede it. There are also the inevitable slips—such as referring to the sinking of the *Sussex* and describing Borah as a pacifist. Yet, on balance, these shortcomings are far offset by the many valuable features of a book which, for the topics it discusses, is not likely to be superseded until the Anglo-French archives are opened and until Arthur S. Link's life and times of Wilson moves to 1917.

RICHARD L. WATSON, JR.
[1959]

Ernest R. May's excellent book, the title of which is, however, never clearly explained, provides a reassessment of American involvement in World War I by examining the issues of neutral rights and

From *American Historical Review,* 64 (July 1959), 973–75. Reprinted with permission of the American Historical Association.
Richard Watson teaches history at Duke University.

Wilson's peace proposals through the eyes of the American, British, and German governments. Similar to Seymour and Link in his interpretation and in his rejection of the revisionism of the 1920s (the word propaganda, for example, is rarely mentioned), May adds new dimensions particularly in providing a concise description of the development of German policy. An exhaustive bibliographical essay testifies to the multiarchival nature of the research.

May believes that "questions of American policy became key issues in domestic struggles for power" in Britain and Germany. In Britain the issue was the extent of the "blockade" and the importance of Anglo-American friendship. In Germany the theme was Bethmann-Hollweg's struggle against a combination of individuals and groups over the use of the submarine. In the United States, according to May, "the drama was less a factional struggle than a contest within one man's conscience." May shows that American policy favored the Allies, but that this favoritism resulted not from conscious unneutrality but from what Wilson and his advisers considered the interests of the United States. Although Link has suggested that United States relations with Britain deteriorated to a point where an outright break was conceivable in 1916, May believes that only if the Germans had cooperated more with Wilson's peace efforts could the tie with Britain have been broken.

In January 1917, however, Ludendorff and Hindenburg compelled Bethmann to agree to unrestricted submarine warfare. Even then, May insists in agreement with Link, Wilson did not consider war inevitable. He was not convinced that United States intervention was necessary for an Allied victory. (May, in a unique analysis, even questions whether an American economic embargo would have been disastrous to the Allies.) At the same time, Wilson believed that acquiescing in the German decree would mean sacrificing "American prestige and moral influence" in making the peace. After several weeks of soul searching and observation, Wilson concluded that war was the only possible alternative. May insists that Wilson's decisions concerning the submarine were not a "tragedy of errors" but were consciously formulated in accordance with what he believed to be American interests. These interests were not the bankers and munitions makers of the revisionists but foreign trade, Wilson's concern for which William Diamond has already so well described. In the last analysis, according to May, peace between the United States and Britain was preserved because they shared "a community of beliefs," something that was lacking between the United States and Germany. May's defense of

Wilson, although convincing to this reviewer, might be less so to one with a different frame of reference.

May writes succinctly, and his conclusions are clearly stated in frequent summaries. He skillfully shows the interrelationships between politics and diplomacy. He faced a difficult problem of organization, however, and at times his topical solution leads to confusion. For example, the armed ship scheme of early 1916 and the mediation proposals of the same period are described chapters apart, and the extent to which the one impinged on the other is difficult to grasp. Treating each country separately, moreover, likewise leads to confusion. In a chapter on Germany, for example, one reads that the "burden of choice between war and peace" lay upon Germany; in reading about Wilson, one learns that his was the decision for war; yet in the rhetoric of the book's final paragraph May asserts that United States involvement was inevitable. In short, the book could have been somewhat improved by a greater attention to chronology.

L. W. MARTIN
[1960]

Despite its title this useful book is likely to find a place on the shelf devoted to European diplomacy. Though the treatment of Wilson is thorough and thoughtful, it does not fundamentally remold the accepted interpretations. Such fresh sidelights as are cast by Mr. May come chiefly from his method of marshaling the alternatives which might have lain before the policy makers at each critical juncture. It is, however, in the many chapters devoted to German policy that this method yields its richest returns. This is the first adequate work on German policy toward America as a neutral to be based on

From *Political Science Quarterly,* 86, 2 (June 1960), 305–06. Reprinted by permission of the *Political Science Quarterly.*
    Laurence W. Martin, a young scholar who recently published a study of Wilson and the British Left, teaches at the Massachusetts Institute of Technology.

extensive use of German archives. The author's sources and method make possible a deeper understanding of the debate on national policy which raged in Germany, a controversy which turned on a question of great interest today; namely, the proper place of military action in national strategy. Moreover the particular focus of the debate, then as now, was the problem of harnessing a new and potent weapon to the service of national interests. While the parallels are limited, modern students of these dilemmas will find the German experience both illuminating and depressing.

Most suggestive, perhaps, is the extent to which lack of consensus on national purposes prevented civilian leaders from establishing the well-defined aims which alone could provide standards for judging the expediency of military measures. Thus, if military leaders were unreasonable and partisan, political leaders failed to offer obvious goals to which the military could have loyally subordinated their efforts. There is also food for thought in the realization that, in Germany and Britain alike, public opinion was consistently marshaled in support of the "military" alternative at each stage of the debate.

In a work such as this which attaches much importance to public opinion and the press, the references to individual papers and to sources like the *Literary Digest* and *Enemy Press Supplement,* frequently combined in the same note, leave the reader uncertain of the extent to which the press has been explored. It is perhaps surprising to find no reference in text, notes or bibliography to the *New Republic,* a journal supposed to have caught Wilson's attention, especially in regard to neutrality. The style of the book is sometimes made awkward by the interpolation of phrases of a purple tint, and the numerous character sketches are not always integrated with the story unfolded. The case for elevating the reputation of Bethmann Hollweg is well made. But the evidence given for translating Falkenhayn, for example, from being "quiet, ascetic and energetic" [p. 95] to being "artless and impotent" [p. 277] is not convincing. Some will also think it harsh to Lloyd George to devote the final paragraph of the book to equating him with Carson, Tirpitz, Bassermann and Ludendorff. If these reservations are justified at all, however, they do not seriously detract from a generally readable and very welcome work of scholarship.

ARTHUR S. LINK
Wilson the Diplomatist
[1957]

CRITICAL COMMENTARIES

ERNEST R. MAY
[1958]

Arthur S. Link's *Wilson the Diplomatist* . . . is certain eventually to be superseded by successive volumes of Link's magisterial biography of Wilson. It does, however, have a value quite apart from its temporary utility as a forecast of the chef-d'oeuvre. When compared with the first volume of the biography, published in 1947, with Link's contribution to the New American Nation Series (*Woodrow Wilson and the Progressive Era*), printed in 1954, and with the second volume of the biography, which appeared in 1956, it indicates the progress of Link's thought about Wilson.

Wilson: The Road to the White House was coldly and detachedly critical. In the New American Nation volume, which extended to the presidential years, there began to appear a more favorable ap-

From *Mississippi Valley Historical Review,* 44, 4 (March 1958), 759–61. Reprinted by permission of the Organizaton of American Historians.
  Ernest R. May, whose scholarly work has been somewhat discussed earlier, has recently been named Dean of the Faculty, Harvard University.

praisal of Wilson. One obtained more sense, at any rate, of the forces that limited the President's initiative and of the complexity of his problems. The man who emerged had greater moral vigor and more capacity for leadership. In the second volume of the biography, *Wilson: The New Freedom,* these traits came more sharply into view. Although Link was still ruthlessly critical whenever the President's ideals and acts were at variance, the total image seemed somehow deeper, more sympathetic, more understanding—more a Rembrandt than a Goya.

In *Wilson the Diplomatist* this development continues. The essays deal with Wilson's neutrality diplomacy, his decision for war, the development of his peace program, and the struggles at Versailles and after. In them Link is less critical of the President's neutrality and peace policies than he appeared to be in the New American Nation volume, and Wilson seems more a prisoner of circumstances, himself nobler in thought and more realistic in diplomacy. The earlier book had no real explanation of the President's decision to opt for war instead of armed neutrality. In *Wilson the Diplomatist,* on the other hand, an eloquent chapter demonstrates that no other choice was possible if the President were to strive for the ideal peace that he envisioned. Dealing with the war and the treaty, which were not touched in the earlier book, Link seems equally sympathetic. He is not quite prepared to praise the Versailles treaty as R. G. McCallum did in *Public Opinion and the Last Peace,* but he writes: "for Woodrow Wilson the Paris Peace Conference was more a time of heroic striving and impressive achievement than of failure." Though granting that Wilson underestimated home opposition, Link finds it understandable that the President should have erred and that he should have fought as he did. The one reticence in *Wilson the Diplomatist* has to do with Wilson's refusal to compromise when the treaty battle was all but lost. Although Link suggests explicit alternatives, he is still hesitant to pass judgment.

Taken as part of the corpus of Link's writings, *Wilson the Diplomatist* may have an unintended permanence. It shows a mind working on the themes and materials that absorb it; it is printed evidence of thought in progress. It draws, of course, upon almost incredibly comprehensive research. The indications of Link's increasing sympathy for his subject are not evidences of declining rigor in critical scholarship or of any slackening in his determination to be detached, objective, and judicious. They are rather signs of the real truth in the vinegared adage, *tout comprendre c'est tout pardonner.*

Anyone who has read the incisive account of Woodrow Wilson's Mexican policy that appears in the second volume of Professor Link's massive Wilsonian biography will turn to this little volume of lectures with keen expectancy. Here, turning aside momentarily from the detailed narrative of the biography, Professor Link has so far anticipated the findings of his forthcoming volumes as to give us an analysis and interpretation of Wilson's diplomacy in relation to the European war and the peace settlements. He has embarked on the admittedly perilous experiment of doing this in small compass, presenting conclusions without being able to display his full range of evidence, and summarizing from details for which the student or the skeptic will have to go elsewhere.

The result is partly successful, partly doubtful. There is one excellent, initial chapter on Wilson's character, equipment and habits as a diplomat. When the book moves on to the complicated and (to Europeans particularly) baffling story of Wilsonian neutralism during the years of 1914–1917, one feels instantly that the process of simplification abundantly justifies itself; Wilson's motives, difficulties and responses emerge with notable clarity. One may feel that not quite enough, perhaps, is allowed for the insidious appeal to Wilson of the role of mediator—a role which neutrality encouraged and belligerency inevitably destroyed—but in general this is the most convincing and illuminating defence of his policy that is to be found, even though to some British readers it may come as a shock to discover how coolly the administration contemplated war with Britain in 1916.

However, when Mr. Link goes on to deal with Wilson's peace-making, doubts arise. Not, one need hardly say, about his mastery of the material in detail, but certainly about his understanding of the

From *The Economist*, 186 (February 8, 1958), 480. Reprinted by permission of *The Economist*.

European world into which his story moves and, even more seriously, about his grasp of the truly tragic dimensions of the Wilsonian failure. Here Mr. Link appears to have nothing fresh to say; worse still he appears to accept uncritically the useless frame of reference within which, since 1919, the Wilsonophiles have chosen to work. What does it mean to excuse Wilson's failure at Versailles on the ground of his no longer having "any power of coercion over Britain and France?" Were these not allies in fact if not in name? Can the illusion of American innocence, to which Wilson was such a victim, really survive what we now know of the realities of international life in 1919?

At the bottom, the true nature of the Wilsonian tragedy, both at Paris and back home, seems to have eluded Mr. Link. It was not that Wilson was a good man, representing an idealistic country, who was defeated by bad men and cynics. He was much more than this. He was a Promethean figure who thought he could transcend human and national limitations, taking his country and his world with him; the measure of his fall was pre-eminently the measure of his pride.

JOHN HIGHAM

~~~~~~

Strangers in the Land
[1955]

THE SALIENT CHARACTERISTIC of the early 1950s in America
was a narrow, repressive spirit, an anxiety that America
was allowing too many heretical ideas and life styles and
that her Anglo-Protestant-capitalistic core was again in the
direst peril. One of the very few beneficial results of this spell
of cultural and intellectual reaction was the stimulus it gave
to scholars like John Higham to study and record the history
of earlier such periods of cultural fright. *Strangers in the
Land* is not the first study of native-American fear of aliens
and their ways. Ray Allen Billington's *The Protestant Crusade: 1800–1860* told a major portion of the story of the
cultural self-defense of the white Protestant middle classes,
and before Higham's book other scholars had also paid some
attention to segments of post–Civil War nativism, such as
fundamentalism, prohibition, the second Ku Klux Klan, and
the Red Scare of 1919–1920.[1] But *Strangers in the Land* had

John Higham, *Strangers in the Land: Patterns of American Nativism, 1860–1925* (New Brunswick, Rutgers University Press,
1955. Paper: Atheneum).
[1] Billington, *The Protestant Crusade 1800–1860: A Study of the
Origins of American Nativism* (New York, Macmillan, 1938);
other early monographs were Charles Mertz, *The Dry Decade*
(New York, Doubleday, 1931), Norman K. Furniss, *The Funda-
mentalist Controversy, 1918–1931* (New Haven, Yale University
Press, 1954); John M. Mecklin, *The Ku Klux Klan: A Study of
the American Mind* (New York, Macmillan, 1924); and Robert
K. Murray, *The Red Scare: A Study in National Hysteria* (Minneapolis, University of Minnesota Press, 1955). There were other
monographic studies, of course, but little of it was first-rate, and
no one had brought it together in any systematic way. Two of the
most perceptive essay-length overviews were the chapter on the
origins of the Klan spirit in Frank Tannenbaum's *Darker Phases
of the South* (New York, Macmillan, 1924), and John M. Blum's
"Nativism, Anti-Radicalism, and the Foreign Scare, 1917–1920,"
Midwest Journal, 3 (Winter 1950–1951), 46–53, a broader study
than the title suggests. Higham had sketched some of his own
views in "The Origins of Immigration Restriction, 1882–1897: A
Social Analysis," *Mississippi Valley Historical Review,* 39 (June
1952), 77–88.

a scope and comprehensiveness no other work could offer. Higham described the rise of antiforeign sentiments after the Civil War to a temporary crest in the 1890s, the ebb of nativism in the optimistic years between 1898 and 1910, the beginnings of another shift toward reaction in national mood in the closing years of the progressive era, the effect of World War I on native-American opinion, and the culmination of postwar nativism in the immigration restriction acts of 1921 and 1924. Higham's intention was to write what would chiefly be a history of ideas, but he wisely paid considerable attention to the social determinants of the shift in public opinion from the openness of the 1860s to the racism and restrictionism of the 1920s. And the social setting of the rise of modern nativism had a magnificent sweep: waves of reform, the new immigration, the expanding influence of the Catholic Church, the entire complex of changes brought by industrialism. Finally, Higham was not content simply to chart the patterns of native-American prejudices, but developed a rough theory to explain its ebb and flow. He saw a clear correlation between the rise of nativism and crises of national confidence, which he thought related primarily to the business cycle.

That theory—which is of course much more persuasive in the book than in my brief summary—was not entirely convincing to a number of readers, among them the Harvard historian and specialist in American immigrant history, Oscar Handlin.[2] Both Handlin and the sociologist Nathan Glazer think Higham failed to recognize that he was dealing with an historic shift in American values away from egalitarianism toward a set of values more permeated with racism and conservatism, rather than with just another cycle (or two cycles) in the long, pulsating history of American nativism. A group of developments unique to modern America, they suggest, accounts for the details of Higham's story far better than do economic cycles. These comments remind us that historians and social scientists are still quite far from understanding the sources of prejudice. But a much more penetrating discussion of the book and the problems with which

---

[2] Handlin published another critical discussion of the cycle theory in an article, "Reconsidering the Populists," *Agricultural History,* 39 (April 1965), 68–74; see also Handlin, "How United States Anti-Semitism Really Began," *Commentary,* 11 (1951), 541–55.

it deals came from Higham himself, in an article in *The Catholic Historical Review* in 1958 (partially reprinted below).[3]

In that article Higham noted that the approach to nativism employed by himself and others had been to regard it as a problem in the history of ideas and, more specifically, as a matter of group irrationality. This approach, he now felt, resulted from and confirmed in practice a tendency to underestimate the objective conditions which gave rise to nativism and other ethnic conflict. Ethnic groups had real differences, not merely anxieties about contrasting life styles. Jostled together in occupational, residential, and political competition, the rising power and prestige of one group threatened the actual or potential interests of another. These objective conflicts and tensions were structured into American society, and were necessarily slighted by any approach to the study of nativism which treated it as a problem in mass irrationality.

Higham's discussion was candid and deeply perceptive. Notice that *Strangers in the Land* had been conceived and researched in the late 1940s and early 1950s. Liberal historians, as all liberal intellectuals, had reacted to that period of conservatism in a number of fairly uniform ways, among them development of strong scholarly interests in, and disapproval of, mass movements leading to social conflict and heightened tensions. Many of them also developed a sense that group differences and group conflict in the American past had been either less extensive than had been thought, or based more on subjective than objective concerns. Higham's article in *The Catholic Historical Review* identifies him as one who moved intellectually into the 1960s well ahead of most of his contemporaries. *Real* group differences and conflicts now seemed to him more important than his own or others' earlier writing had allowed. Nativism has undoubtedly been both irrational and deplorable in most of its manifestations, but the discovery of its roots in social relations involving power, preferment, and prestige revealed the limitations in approaching it as if it were only a mental

[3] John Higham, "Another Look at Nativism," *The Catholic Historical Review,* 44 (July 1958), 147–58.

problem for some very intolerant people. From this perspective, although Higham does not say so explicitly, history written from the earlier point of view was conservative history, i.e., it described for us an America whose social structure contained no serious, deeply rooted flaws and whose social problems were rather largely in the minds of her lamentably parochial and prejudiced middle and lower classes of Northern European stock. The new perspective, with its greater emphasis upon ethnic economic and political competition, will probably lead to better history. That remains to be decided. But it is quite clear that it will be a more radical history in its implications, and it bears a strong resemblance to other intellectual developments of the 1960s, among them the rise of nationalism and social criticism in the American black community.

Neither my own thoughts, nor Higham's comments in 1958, have the effect—let alone the intention—of dismissing the contribution of *Strangers in the Land*. It remains a unique and valuable synthesis of unparalleled scope. One is hard pressed to think of another single book which tells us so much about so many things—the conflict-laden final decades of the nineteenth century, the progressive movement, wartime attitudes and tensions, the Red Scare, the triumph of the restriction movement in the 1920s. It brings welcome illumination to elements more central to the American experience than the much-studied principles of the Declaration of Independence, elements such as racism, ethnic conflict, and the resort to repression in war and in times of high political stress. The book is a chapter in the history of the WASPs, a long, important chapter which our culture has had some tendency to ignore.[4] It is a most instructive book. As

[4] A growing number of talented scholars have expanded our understanding of nativist movements since Higham published his book. Some of these efforts should not be missed by those whose tastes incline them toward the darker side of American life: Stanley Coben, "A Study in Nativism: The American Red Scare of 1919–1920," *Political Science Quarterly,* 79 (March 1964), 52–75, an effort to explain the period through social psychology, while never losing sight of the acute social problems that eroded the good sense of so many people. There are splendid syntheses of the nativist currents of the 1920s in William E. Leuchtenburg's *The Perils of Prosperity, 1914–1932* (Chicago, University of Chicago Press,

this is still a white man's country, I think it will not be a best-seller.

1958), Chapters 4–12, and David Burner, *The Politics of Provincialism* (New York, Alfred A. Knopf, 1968), Chapter 3. William Preston, Jr., *Aliens and Dissenters: Federal Suppression of Radicals, 1903–1933* (Cambridge, Harvard University Press, 1963), is a depressing book, but not nearly so depressing as Leonard Dinnerstein's meticulous study, *The Leo Frank Case* (New York, Columbia University Press, 1968). Very unfavorable to the reputation of certain early liberals is Roger Daniels, *The Politics of Prejudice: The Anti-Japanese Movement in California and the Struggle for Japanese Exclusion* (Berkeley, University of California Press, 1962). A good example of the continuing inability of scholars to explain prejudice is an inconclusive article by Paul L. Murphy, "Sources and Nature of Intolerance in the 1920s," *Journal of American History*, 51 (June 1964), 60–76. The above is the merest sampling of a growing literature on the lot of ethnic minorities in America, and one may note that it, like Higham's book, excludes Negro–white relations, a subject for which "nativism" is hardly an adequate word.

CRITICAL COMMENTARIES

OSCAR HANDLIN
[1956]

In historical retrospect, the transformation of American immigration policy after the First World War will, no doubt, seem one of the decisive changes in the life of the nation. The consequences were momentous; and the complete reversal of popular attitudes reflected a long chain of historical developments. So long as the issues were still alive, it was difficult to assess the causes of the new departure. We have heretofore had only occasional and fragmentary contributions to the understanding of this most important event.

Professor Higham's study is the first serious historical account of the whole movement to restrict immigration. It is a thoughtful work, carefully put together and based upon the use of a wide range of sources. Its judgment is generally dispassionate and sound. It is well written and will add substantially to our knowledge of many phases of the history of the United States in the half-century after 1875. It is a good beginning to a revaluation of the whole movement it describes.

The subject is important and fresh enough, however, to justify some mention of the deficiencies of this excellent work. On some points of detail the author has gone seriously astray. It is surprising, for instance, that he should misunderstand the character and overlook the importance of the Dillingham Commission. [p. 189] Again, Professor Higham has not fully grasped the relationship of organized labor to the movement for immigration restriction; and the inability to use

From *Political Science Quarterly,* 71 (September 1956), 453–54. Reprinted with permission of the *Political Science Quarterly.*
Oscar Handlin teaches history at Harvard.

immigrant sources occasionally distorts his account. [pp. 45, 160, 188]

More important, he labors under the burden of an untenable thesis, one not really germane to his purpose, and yet that nevertheless too often intrudes, to the distortion of his views on significant points. He believes that nativism was a constant in American history, a kind of subterranean stream making its presence felt in "cycles" or "rhythms." In depressions, it burst into the open; in times of prosperity, it sank again beneath the surface.

This simplistic view is a source of constant difficulty. It simply does not fit the facts of the case Professor Higham honestly presents. To square the interpretation with events he is driven to treat deeply-held attitudes as if they could be turned on and off by monthly fluctuations in the stock market. Thus, anti-Catholicism faded after 1900, revived after 1907, "shrank like a pricked balloon" in 1915, was reinflated in 1920 and disappeared after 1924. [pp. 175, 200] A more realistic view would find a steady development of that sentiment for sixty years after 1880, with a peak between 1924 and 1928. Similarly I cannot find that the alternations of depressions and recovery had much to do with the consistent growth of sentiment in favor of immigration restriction between 1890 and 1924.

In any case, all this is not really relevant to the story. The restrictionist movement stands decisively apart from all earlier nativism. No significant group of Americans before 1880 conceived of an end to European immigration as a serious possibility. Thereafter growing numbers of them did. Economic changes had little direct relevance to this profound shift in sentiment. The transformation was rather due to the injection of a completely new ideological element, racism. Professor Higham has many interesting things to say about the influence of racism; fortunately, they are not altogether obscured by his theory of cycles and rhythms.

DAVID A. SHANNON
[*1956*]

Hansen, Handlin, Wittke, and others have given us excellent histories of immigration; now with John Higham's book we have a first-class history of opposition to immigration and immigrants. This is a major book, wide in its scope, thorough in its research, and objective and judicious in its treatment, on a theme that has long deserved a comprehensive account. Another general work in this field will not be needed for a long time.

After a quick review of early nineteenth-century nativism, Mr. Higham describes the rise of nativism in the 1880s and its decline in the late 1890s, the various efforts at immigration restriction, the political battles over literacy tests for immigrants, World War I nationalism and its effect on immigrants, the Red Scare of 1919–1920, and the Ku Klux Klan. The sixth chapter, "Toward Racism: The History of an Idea," is a model of intellectual history that strikes a good balance between the history of ideas and external forces that affect ideas and their reception. The eighth chapter, on nativism during the war and east European revolutions, is perhaps the most exciting reading in the book.

Throughout the book Mr. Higham emphasizes the various strains or sources of nativism, such as anti-Catholicism, anti-Semitism, antiradicalism, and economic competition in the labor market. He makes clear that nativism had stimulus from some reformers and radicals as well as from the right. This is a contribution, for we are too often prone to read into the past the tolerance toward immigrants and the antinationalism that have only relatively recently become part of the liberal creed.

Mr. Higham explains the sometimes startling ebbs and flows of

From *Journal of Economic History,* 16 (March 1956), 85–86. Reprinted with permission of the author and the *Journal of Economic History.*

David A. Shannon, whose principal interest is in the history of American socialism, is now Dean of the Faculty of Arts and Sciences, the University of Virginia.

nativist sentiments by relating them to such matters as the business cycle, the nature and volume of immagination, and war. But he has done more: he has obviously read widely in the literature of sociology, social psychology, and cultural anthropology, seeking an explanation of the waxing and waning of public prejudice. One can not but feel, however, that social scientists have fallen short of what historians may reasonably expect of them in the area of xenophobia. Cycles of nativism are here explained largely in terms of "confidence." Phrases such as "historic confidence" and "structure of national confidence" are common in this book. One might summarize the explanation in this oversimplified fashion: intensity of nativist sentiment and activity is in inverse ratio to the degree of public confidence. This explanation is, I think, satisfactory in a rough way, but it is not very precise or scientific. What exactly, is national or social confidence? How does one measure it? And to push the inquiry back further, how does one explain the fluctuating tides of confidence? On this point the author is not at fault. He sought in all quarters an explanation for his narrative, something a less able and conscientious historian might have ignored. He did all a historian can do as a historian. But the behavioral scientists did not furnish him enough that is scientific.

But Mr. Higham has furnished us with an excellent book. He has used a remarkable range of sources, including several manuscript collections in unexpected places, and he has told his story well.

NATHAN GLAZER
[1956]

John Higham's book deals with the background of one of the most important decisions in American history—the decision, made thirty-five years ago, to limit immigrants to this country to a relatively small and carefully selected number. Mr. Higham has done an impres-

From *Commentary,* 21 (June 1956), 587–89. Reprinted from *Commentary,* by permission; Copyright © 1956 by the American Jewish Committee.

Nathan Glazer teaches sociology at the University of California, Berkeley.

sive job. He has studied an enormous volume of letters, newspapers, organizational records, monographs, and has extracted from them a clear and convincing account of the major shifts in public opinion which made possible the reversal of an immigration policy that had been in effect for a hundred years. His book is to my mind a major contribution to American history.

The story Mr. Higham relates was not, I think, generally known even to historians before he undertook to tell it. *Strangers in the Land* opens in the 1860s on an America which has been absorbing great numbers of immigrants for decades, and in which the dominant social and economic, as well as intellectual elements take it for granted that this is the natural and proper course for the country. It is a period when economic self-interest and democratic ideology combine to support the historic policy of the open gate. There had been, in the 1850s, an outbreak of "nativism," generally based on Protestant resentment of heavy Irish Catholic immigration, but it had never become more than sporadic and local, and left no mark on legislation: In the country as a whole, during the 1870s and 1880s, there was hardly any feeling that immigration posed a problem for the nation.

But, Mr. Higham goes on to show, beginning in the late 1880s, American opinion, as reflected in organized groups and in regional sentiment, underwent a transformation that was complete by 1914. The labor unions had originally opposed only the immigration of contract laborers but by 1896 the American Federation of Labor had followed Gompers in his hostility to immigration, and American workers continued to stand against free immigration until the restriction movement finally triumphed.

Even progressives and Socialists, with their strong democratic orientation, were eventually to support immigration restriction. In 1916, the *New Republic* declared: ". . . the new democracy of today cannot permit . . . social ills to be aggravated by excessive immigration." In 1918, a quota scheme which was relatively liberal gained the backing of such people as Norman Hapgood, Robert F. Park, James Harvey Robinson, Oswald Harrison Villard, and Lillian Wald.

Of the various regions in the country, the South and West, because they had always been anxious to increase their population, had consistently favored free immigration. As late as 1903, the representatives of these two sections in Congress voted against the literacy test whose main purpose was to restrict immigration. But in 1907, both sections swung around and came out for restriction.

If we turn to the region that has the best right to be considered the home of a distinctively American culture and intellectual tradition, New England, we find a shift among leading intellectuals around the turn of the century from democratic egalitarianism to an exclusive and restrictive racism. True, a rather benign feeling in favor of the Anglo-Saxon race had long been part of the New England temper. But this was really a romantic regard for one's ancestors, and was not inconsistent in the minds of those who held it with the belief that one of the virtues of the Anglo-Saxon race was its assimilative power. Toward the end of the century, however, this kind of feeling about race was replaced by "scientific" notions stemming from physical anthropology and biology, and those who now spoke of the Anglo-Saxon race began to suggest the need to exclude "lower" races.

Thus by 1905–1906, the South, the West, the native-born working class, and the upper-class intellectuals had become especially strong supporters of immigration restriction. But Mr. Higham tells us that "it also received support in public opinion, and whenever restriction came to a vote in Congress it rolled up overwhelming majorities. . . ." From this point on, it was only "strategically situated minorities" who prevented the sentiment from being translated into law. Two such minorities were particularly influential: big business, which wanted cheap and plentiful labor even more than it feared foreign agitators, and lobbied vigorously through the National Association of Manufacturers and other organizations to maintain free immigration; and the immigrant groups themselves, led mainly by the Jews. The leaders of both parties, also, conscious of the importance of the vote of the foreign-born and their children, were wary about supporting immigration restriction. But in the end the demand for it became too strong for the opposition, and the gates were closed in the early twenties.

This is the main outline of Mr. Higham's story. He shows us *how* the gates came to be closed, but what he barely touches on— though he provides all the material to permit us to speculate on our own—is why one section after another, one social and intellectual and economic element after another, should have swung over to restriction. The only large thesis he suggests is that in times of economic crisis the opponents of free immigration waxed strong, while in times of prosperity their strength waned.

Restriction, Mr. Higham intimates, was successful after the First World War in large part because of the severe economic crisis —though an increase in nativist feeling arising from the war also helped. During the war, both parties had joined in denouncing hyphenated Americanism, in proclaiming "100-per-centism," and in insisting on the forced abandonment of foreign traits; a strong residue of this anti-foreign bias persisted after the war was over. Then came the Bolshevik revolution, and the exaggerated fear of foreign radicals that accompanied it. There was also the racism of Madison Grant and Lothrop Stoddard, for a brief moment enjoying some success in American intellectual life. Finally, there was the Ku Klux Klan, capitalizing on the strong suspicion of foreigners, radicals, and Catholics in small-town America. But one gets the impression from Mr. Higham's account that dominating this combination of factors, and lending power to each, was the economic crisis.

Yet I do not feel that this goes far enough. My own belief, based on Mr. Higham's book, is that what we had in the twenties was not only another wave of nativism—even if more persistent, complex, and successful than the others—but one reflection among many of a fundamental change that had taken place in the point of view of the American people.

The defenders of free immigration in the early twenties could argue quite effectively that immigration had greatly aided America economically and politically, and could still do so. This argument was completely in line with that clear and simple pursuit of self-interest, unhampered by traditional considerations (it was always a moot point anyhow what was traditional in America), that had been so striking a characteristic of 19th-century America. Farmers were happy to leave their farms and city-dwellers their houses purely for the sake of commercial advantage. By the same token, to bring in willing workers of other ethnic groups seemed a self-evident benefit: hardly anyone worried over the consequent loss of America's "traditional" ethnic homogeneity. But other countries, like Australia, with almost as much open land to be developed, had sacrificed a measure of wealth and political power for cultural and ethnic homogeneity.

Around 1900 America too, it seems to me, began to sacrifice economic self-interest for certain of the values that have always been associated with a fixed and stable society, and which involve such matters as status, traditional culture, and the like. It was about this time, for example, that in the South the last efforts to work together politically with the Negroes were abandoned and a policy of strict segregation was adopted, despite the real economic and political disadvantages of Jim Crow. The South had decided that Jim Crow was worth more than wealth and political power.

The rest of the country seems to have made a similar decision. Scarcely aware of what it had done, it tried to explain its feeling against foreigners in whatever terms were available—they were radicals, they were of inferior races, they could not be absorbed, and what not. But these complaints and rationalizations only served to conceal the basic fact that America no longer wanted to endure the violent and uncontrolled change that a full commitment to the principles of liberal capitalism demanded. To my mind, the end of free immigration was a reflection of this change, showing itself as a desire to maintain America as it was, regardless of economic or political advantage.

Any discussion of the "change of mind" of a nation is, of course, perilous. Yet, in effect, the subject of Mr. Higham's book is such a change of mind. He has done a remarkably good and stimulating job in recording the change. One hopes that, in some future book, he will go further in considering its full meaning.

JOHN HIGHAM

Another Look at Nativism
[1958]

In this article, Higham performs a rare and valuable service by reconsidering his own book in the light of its critical reception and his own further investigations.

My assignment . . . is probably not as treacherous as it appears to me to be; yet I embark upon it with acute trepidation. To deliver a paper on a subject *after* having written a book about it invites a

From *The Catholic Historical Review,* 44 (July 1958), 147–58. Reprinted with permission from *The Catholic Historical Review.*
    Higham is chairman of the Program in American Culture, University of Michigan.

kind of double jeopardy. There is, to be sure, an easy way out. I might sum up, more persuasively if possible, the story that is already copyrighted, with, perhaps, a special effort to lay low the critics. But they have been too indulgent for that, and anyway reiteration seldom sheds much light. Another possible way of proceeding is to flatter oneself that others may wish to go further in more or less the same direction that the author has taken, and to point out to them some parts of the terrain which he has only sketchily mapped and which they might well fill in. This strategem meets the need for innovation half-way while safeguarding the author's intellectual capital. Any activity that may result, however, is more likely to be trivial than significant. Moreover, to make such a summons requires a presumptuous self-assurance that is not always becoming.

Shall I, then, fall back upon a perilous, third alternative? Shall I acknowledge the expectation and hope, which historians are supposed to cherish, that new research will depart from present conclusions in the very act of appropriating them? Shall I confess that nativism now looks less adequate as a vehicle for studying the struggles of nationalities in America, than my earlier report of it, and other reports, might indicate? I am nerved to do so by the reflection that historical inquiry does not advance so much by reversal and disavowal as it does by a widening of focus. At its best it achieves a fruitful tension between perspectives that do not cancel, but rather complement one another.

In some such spirit, I propose that research on the conflicts associated with foreign elements in American society should take a new line. The nativist theme, as defined and developed to date, is imaginatively exhausted. Scholars who would do more than fill in the outlines of existing knowledge must make a fresh start from premises rather different from those that have shaped the studies of the last twenty years. To explain what I mean will require some consideration of the literature on nativism that is now extant, and it will be convenient for me to speak particularly of the interests and assumptions from which my own book derived.

The very term "nativism" has influenced profoundly our angle of vision in studying anti-foreign and anti-Catholic forces. The word is an "ism." It came into being in the middle of the nineteenth century to describe the principles advanced by a political party. Etymologically and historically, therefore, it refers to a set of attitudes, a state of mind. In contrast to words like assimilation, segregation, marginality, and the like, "nativism" does not direct attention primarily to an actual social process or condition. Those who study the phenomenon want to know why certain ideas emerge when and where they do, and how those ideas pass into action. Consequently, the histories of nativism have not tried, except incidentally, to clarify the structure of society. Instead, they trace an emotionally charged impulse.

While the word itself almost inevitably pulls our interest toward subjective attitudes, our contemporary culture has pushed us further in that direction. Since the 1930s the intellect and the conscience of America have been in revolt against what is called "prejudice," viz., the ill-treatment of ethnic and religious minorities. Now, prejudice is by definition subjective—a pre-judgment not grounded in factual experience. Nativism, of course, commonly qualifies as prejudice; and students regard it not only as a state of mind but as one which badly distorts the true nature of things. A good historian will certainly not consider nativism entirely as a set of prejudices; but since no one writes about it unless he shares the current revulsion against ethnic injustice, the subjective irrationality of nativism leaps to the historian's eye. He wants to know how we have mistaken one another and, perhaps too, he wishes to assure us that the mistakes were, indeed, mistakes in the sense that they arose from no compelling social need.

Along with the crusade against prejudice, another aspect of modern thought has affected the study of nativism. We live in an age that has an almost superstitious awe and distrust of ideologies. That is to say, we dread the power of ideas that are weapons in the hands of "hidden persuaders." Karl Mannheim, George Orwell, and others have taught us to see, behind the inhumanity of our day, the coercion of ideas which interpret life in terms functional to someone's bid for power. Disseminated by the agitator and the propagandist, ideologies distort reality, attack the foundations of belief, and threaten the independence and integrity of the human mind. Historians and social scientists alike have been fascinated by ideologies and have labored to expose their dynamics. There is a consequent tendency to fix upon ideology as the critical factor in many a social problem, in the perhaps tenuous hope that the problem will yield to a reasonable solution once the ideological magic is exorcised.

The relevant consideration here is that the concern over ideologies reflects, more systematically, the same assumption that underlies the concept of prejudice. Both owe a great deal to our distinctively modern emphasis on the irrational depths of human nature. The modern mind dwells on the unconscious savagery lurking in its own dark corners. At the springs of human action the irrationalist historian, novelist, or social psychologist is not likely to find realistic motives of solidarity or calculated self-interest; nor is he likely to find high ideals. Instead, he discovers a fog of myths, prejudices, stereotypes, and power-hungry ideologies. If he looks at the American past he may notice this miasma overhanging many scenes, but nowhere does he find it more densely exhibited than in nativism. Nativism displays all the terrors that beset his own sensibility. It is an ideology: a rigid system of ideas, manipulated by propagandists seeking power, irrationally blaming some external group for the major ills of society. It mobilizes prejudices, feeds on stereotypes, radiates hysteria, and provokes our outrage against ethnic injustice.

I have said enough, I hope, about the general frame of reference within which nativism is studied to indicate that interpretation of it almost inevitably stresses subjective, irrational motives. Whenever a contemporary point of view gives so much encouragement to a certain historical approach, should we not suspect that our angle of vision screens out a good deal? Specifically, should we not suspect that the nativist theme does little justice to the objective realities of ethnic relations? To answer this question concretely, let me turn to my own experience in studying the subject.

Nativism, I felt sure, would not submit to effective analysis unless it could be identified consistently as an idea. Its meaning must inhere in a set of beliefs protean enough to apply to a variety of adversaries yet definite enough to show the form and direction of its history. To unravel the strands of nativist ideology became, therefore, a central problem. I discovered that the main strands ran more or less independently of one another. There were, in fact, several nativisms, each of which fixed upon some internal alien influence as a gravely divisive threat to national unity. Generically, nativism was a defensive type of nationalism, but the defense varied as the nativist lashed out sometimes against a racial peril. Although on occasion nativists rallied against other kinds of disloyalty too, these persistent anxieties provided a framework for studying the nativistic mentality.

Notice what I was *not* doing by pursuing the subject in this way. I was not trying to explain the total complex of ethnic tensions in American society. I was not focusing upon the institutional rivalries of Protestant and Catholic or upon their religious beliefs. I was not dealing fundamentally with the living standards of Italian and Yankee or with the party affiliations of Irish and German. All these crowded the background, for all of them helped to shape the nativist temper. Yet such basic components of the American ethnic scene could not occupy the foreground of my picture without blurring the clarity and significance of nativism as an idea. The bad habit of labeling as nativist any kind of unfriendliness toward immigrants or Catholic values had to be resisted. If nativism is not a mere term of derogation, it can embrace only antagonisms that belong within the ideologies of a passionate national consciousness.

As I studied the main nativist traditions, I discovered that over a long span of time they had not changed conceptually as much as an historian of ideas might suppose. Except on the subject of race (and in related forms of anti-Semitism), the kind of accusations which nativists leveled against foreign elements remained relatively constant. Anti-radical and anti-Catholic complaints in the twentieth century sounded much like those bruited in the eighteenth. The big changes were not so much intellectual as emotional. The same idea might be mildly innocuous at one time and charged with potent feelings at another. For the history of nativism, therefore, emotional intensity provided the significant measurement of change. If nativism was an ideological disease, perhaps, one might best diagnose it by observing when the fever raged and when it slackened.

The outlines of an overall interpretation now became visible. During four scattered intervals in American history (only two of which I studied in detail) nativism erupted powerfully enough to have an immediate impact on national development. In the late 1790's it produced the notorious Alien Acts. In the 1850's it contributed to the breakup of the party system. In the decade from 1886 to 1896 it magnified a host of social problems associated with unrestricted immigration. And in the period of World War I nativism unleashed repressive orthodoxies on a grand scale. In each of these four periods the United States was undergoing a major national crisis. In the 1790's international conflict intensified the cleavage between political parties. Sectional cleavage came to a head in the 1850's, class cleavage in the 1890's. World War I confronted an unprepared nation with the shock of total war. In each of these crises, confidence in the homogeneity of American culture broke down. In desperate efforts to rebuild national unity men rallied against the symbols of foreignness that were appropriate to their predicament.

My appraisal was more complex than this sketchy outline suggests, of course. And I have no doubt that nativist ideas deserve still further study, particularly to elucidate their relation to our traditions of individualism and Puritanism. What bothers me most, however, is that the concept of nativism has proved serviceable only for understanding the extreme and fanatical manifestations of ethnic discord. It illuminates the frenzies of the mob, the nightmares of the propagandist, the repressive statute, and the moments of national frustration. Nativism owes its significance to this intensity of feeling: and historians, fascinated by the men of passion and the moods of alarm, have neglected the less spectacular but more steadily sustained contentions imbedded in the fabric of our social organization.

In order to have a short-hand designation for such underlying stresses, we may call them status rivalries. By this I mean all of the activities—political, religious, economic, and associational—through which men of different ethnic backgrounds have competed for prestige and for favorable positions in community life. Status rivalries have not arisen from irrational myths but rather from objective conditions; they have not usually reached the point of hatred and hysteria; they have not depended upon ideological expression; they have not risen and fallen in cyclical fashion. Instead, they are part of the slow processes of ethnic integration, and they have shaped profoundly the course of our social development.

For a generation historians and even most social scientists interested in the jostling of Protestant and Catholic, of Christian and Jew, of old and new Americans, have not wanted to understand these tensions as basic structural realities. To do so is to recognize that our divergent and unequal backgrounds are causes—not just results—of our difficulties. It is more comforting to think that everyone is pretty much alike and that our differences are foisted upon us by myths and stereotypes. Attributing ethnic cleavage to nativism or racism takes the curse off the fact of inequality.

By the same token, the nativist approach validates our sympathy with the out-group. Nativism is primarily a one-way street, along which the native American moves aggressively against the outsider. Thus, the history of nativism inevitably portrays minorities as victims rather than participants. It permits us to assume their relative innocence. We need not ask too closely why the Irish were the shock troops of the anti-Chinese movement in California, how the American Protective Association could attract a following among Negroes, or why the Scots in America brought so much wrath upon themselves during the Revolution.

At this point you may concede that many peripheral frictions do occur outside the orbit of nativism, but you may still insist that it explains the more persistent difficulties, such as those which Catholics and Jews have met. At times, of course, irrational myths have played the decisive part in these encounters, but not as commonly or exclusively as historians have suggested. The real issues of faith which set religious groups apart can not fairly be reduced to nativist terms. Moreover, struggles for status underlie much that we attribute too easily to irrational prejudice, and I suspect that the question of status has touched the daily life of most Americans more intimately than any ideological warfare.

Consider for a moment the situation of the Irish Catholic in the late nineteenth or early twentieth century. Did he suffer much from nativist visions of popish conspiracies? It seems unlikely. He worshipped freely and had no legal disabilities; the most extravagant propaganda against him circulated in completely Protestant rural areas remote from his own urban habitations. The great handicap he faced was his social and economic subordination to the older Americans, who treated him partly as a joke, partly as an underling, and partly as a ruffian. And when he compensated in politics for his inferiority in other spheres, all the forces of Yankee respectability mobilized in Republican ranks against him. In scores of communities throughout the North both political parties were essentially ethnic coalitions. Even the American Protective Association was, perhaps, chiefly effective as an instrument for ousting the Irish from the municipal jobs which they held to the disadvantage of their ethnic rivals. In the western cities where the APA's greatest strength lay, Yankees, Scandinavians, and British used it to get control of school boards, police forces, and fire departments. . . .

How swiftly a group advances after its arrival affects very strongly the reception it meets. American's have expected immigrants to move toward cultural homogeneity but not to crowd the social ladder in doing so. When a new group, relatively depressed at the outset, pushes upward rapidly in the status system, conflict almost surely ensues. This happened in the late nineteenth century in the cases of the Irish and the Jews. Both came up against cruel social discriminations designed to retard the large proportion of each group who were getting ahead quickly.

Contrarily, a group that stayed put might escape opprobrium, once the older Americans had become accustomed to its presence, even if it retained a good deal of its cultural distinctiveness. The Germans, who did not bear the stigma attached to the more rapidly Americanized Irish, are a case in point. Although measuring relative rates of social mobility is obviously difficult, the census of 1890 offers an illuminating comparison between the Irish and the Germans. By comparing, for each nationality, the proportion of the first generation in various occupations with the proportion of the second generation in the same occupations, it becomes evident that the Irish were climbing the social ladder rapidly while the Germans were remaining relatively static, the sons being more content to occupy the stations of their fathers. The proportion of Irish in professional occupations almost doubled between the first and the second generation; the proportion of Germans did not change. The Irish entered other white collar jobs and fled from common labor at twice the rate of the Germans. Here is an important reason why the ambitious Irish provoked a resistance which the more phlegmatic Germans did not face.

To explain such differentials between ethnic groups, historians must not shrink, finally, from studying their respective national or social characters. Surely the boisterous, free-and-easy manners of the Irish, the humble patience of the Chinese, and many other ethnic inclinations we have not yet learned properly to define have shaped the relations between our various peoples. Instead of washing all of the specific color out of our ethnic fabric in our fear of propagating stereotypes, let us look for the realities behind them.

What I miss, in the most general way, is any serious effort to study historically the structure of American society—to work out, in other words, the inter-relations between classes and ethnic groups, taking account of regional and local differences. This task transcends the dimensions of nativism. It transcends a preoccupation with conflict and discord, and urges us to confront our involvements with one another in comparative terms. But as this is done, the history of nativism itself should fall into a truer perspective.

ARTHUR M. SCHLESINGER, JR.

The Age of Roosevelt
[1957-1960]

I. The Crisis of the Old Order,
1919-1933 [1957]
II. The Coming of the New Deal [1959]
III. The Politics of Upheaval [1960]

Histories of the New Deal started coming out in late 1933 but *the* history of the New Deal for most readers is Arthur M. Schlesinger Jr.'s multivolume effort which began to appear in 1957 and is still in progress. No other treatment of the Roosevelt era exerted a comparable influence upon the minds of scholars, students, and the reading public. Those who knew Schlesinger's earlier work were not surprised at the sharp impact of *The Age of Roosevelt*. The Harvard historian had proven himself a master of literary craftsmanship, dramatic narrative, and clarity of exposition in his first book (a Pulitzer Prize winner), *The Age of Jackson* (1945). The Roosevelt volumes displayed these same qualities to a high degree, demonstrating again that Schlesinger had few peers not only in brilliant, readable, and lucid style but in sustained drama, personal characterization, and analytical power. The books also possessed a passionate but intelligently controlled commitment to the rightness of Franklin Roosevelt's cause and the essential success of his historic mission —giving them not only an aesthetic but a moral and political impact.

Schlesinger's literary talents were so prodigious, his books so frequent, and his scholarship so subordinated to communication (at least in the physical appearance of the books) that some historians expressed suspicions about the depth of his research in primary materials. Others pointed out that his skill with personalities, especially his absorption with the personality of Roosevelt, had led him into "too great a concession to biography" (Allan Nevins' words), and a resultant neglect of impersonal social forces. Others noted and criticized what they saw as an insufficient attention to Congress and to state and local politics.

Arthur M. Schlesinger, Jr., *The Age of Roosevelt:* Vol. I, *The Crisis of the Old Order: 1919–1933* (Boston, Houghton Mifflin, 1957); Vol. II, *The Coming of The New Deal* (Boston, Houghton Mifflin, 1959); Vol. III, The Politics of Upheaval (Boston, Houghton Mifflin, 1960), Paper: Houghton Mifflin, 3 vols.

These methodological and conceptual criticisms were often just, for Schlesinger had made certain sacrifices to achieve the dramatic appeal of *The Age of Roosevelt*. But the most important criticisms are substantive, touching his most influential interpretive positions: his treatment of the "two New Deals," his argument for Roosevelt's pragmatism, and the broad verdict that emerged very early in the series and which has not been altered, i.e., that Roosevelt's presidency was, minor exceptions aside and notwithstanding, an epochal success.

Contemporaries discerned a shift within the New Deal, in about 1935, from one reasonably coherent reform philosophy to another—from the first to the second New Deal. Basil Rauch in 1944 described the shift clearly and in some detail, noting that not only did programs change, and the presidential rhetoric, but one set of personnel gave way to another of quite different reform views. Schlesinger's third volume (*The Politics of Upheaval,* 1960) offered an important modification of the long-accepted Rauch interpretation, and quickened scholarly interest in the question of the guiding philosophy within the New Deal. Since 1960 several historians have looked again at the first and second New Deal "shifts," and with impressive agreement. They think the whole thing exaggerated. I am inclined at this time to agree that there was more confusion than consistency in Roosevelt's five years of concentration upon domestic problems. The early New Deal never came very close to national economic planning, except perhaps in Rexford Tugwell's mind, and never had the radical potential Schlesinger reconstructed from the memoirs of the liberals. And at the same time that the early New Deal was not planning very aggressively it was also framing reforms of the exchanges and banks, activities quite out of harmony with the New Nationalism philosophy supposedly dominant among the first group of advisors. The shift of 1935 did occur, but the antitrust, New Freedom cast of the 1935–1938 period was muffled by irresolution, a continuation of planning in agriculture, oil, and coal, and occasional hints from the White House that maybe the National Recovery Administration approach to the entire industrial economy ought to be revived. Schlesinger has a keen ear for

political tone and the guiding ideas of articulate people, and
detected an important difference in the two halves of the New
Deal. But the hard legislative facts of the 1930s give minimal
support to those like Schlesinger and Rauch who sense such
clarities, and what we know of the mind of Franklin Roosevelt suggests that he, like the legislative record, was innocent
of much theoretical consistency.

The discussion, though it may have about it an air of
pedantry, is highly illuminating. Schlesinger, favorable to the
president and much interested in intellectuals and ideals, finds
(and elegantly recreates) a reasonably coherent pattern in
the affairs of the American state during the hectic depression
days. Later historians, more neutral about Roosevelt and
more inclined to work with legislative history, bureaucratic
policies, and the field effects of New Deal efforts, find more
confusion and overlap. Each of the traditional period divisions in twentieth-century history—1916–1919, 1929—has
recently started to blur, and the differences between political
rivals such as Theodore Roosevelt and Wilson, Franklin
Roosevelt and Hoover, or even La Follette and Debs are
being minimized. The same process is at work on the only
clear division ever discerned in the New Deal. American
history from the 1960s does not seem devoid of sharply
different alternatives, but the liberal record has certainly
been squeezed into a more narrow, and presumably less
exciting, range.

Another distinctive feature of Schlesinger's *Age of
Roosevelt* is his characterization of the president. Roosevelt
was one of the most elusive political personalities in the
American past, but Schlesinger has created and sustained
throughout these volumes a vivid, subtle, penetrating portrait.
With acknowledgment of the warts, it is a warmly admiring
portrait—not the first of this sort, but for several reasons
the most brilliant. In a political leader what is wanted is the
right combination of enlightened ideals and tactical flexibility.
Too much of the former leads to a dangerous and self-
defeating moralism; a disproportion of the latter becomes
expediency. In Schlesinger's view Franklin Roosevelt possessed the proper balance, and this enabled him not only to
hold and manipulate power but to direct power toward enduring ends. Some ideology or other gripped most minds in

the 1930s, and to Schlesinger this threatening characteristic of the period makes Roosevelt's mental flexibility and willingness to experiment the most providential gift he brought to his office. Hoover was a man of conviction, but his convictions included a body of conventional economic wisdom which, since it was wrong, rendered government impotent in the face of depression. Roosevelt experimented, and his experiments brought not only relief but a renewed confidence in basic American political and economic institutions. Roosevelt's flexibility—which Schlesinger often called pragmatism —had led contemporary critics and political opponents to find him nothing but an opportunist, but Schlesinger argued strongly in his most recent volume (*The Politics of Upheaval,* pp. 651–57) that "at bottom he had a guiding vision with substantive content of its own." Thus he saw Roosevelt as a pragmatist, but a pragmatist with a rudder—a deep and steady "philosophy of compassion." As long as there are arguments about Franklin D. Roosevelt they will eventually center on this question, and Schlesinger's interpretation has provoked a notable body of comment.

The historian who basically approved of Roosevelt's leadership quite naturally approved of the New Deal. Many Americans, most of them Republicans, did not agree in the 1930s and do not like Schlesinger's volumes today. But virtually all the published criticism by historians and other intellectuals came from Schlesinger's left.[1] These critics push

[1] The literature is reviewed in Frank Freidel, *The New Deal in Historical Perspective* (Washington, D.C., Service Center for Teachers of History, 1965, rev.). Everyone acknowledges William E. Leuchtenburg's *Franklin D. Roosevelt and the New Deal, 1932–1940* (New York, Harper & Row, 1963) as the best one-volume study, and Leuchtenburg is somewhat to the Left of Schlesinger. Jerold Auerbach reviews some of the newer Left-radical treatments of the New Deal in "New Deal, Old Deal, or Raw Deal: Some Thoughts on New Left Historiography," *Journal of Southern History,* 35 (February 1960), 18–30. Two of the best such "revisionist" studies are Paul Conkin, *The New Deal* (New York, T. Y. Crowell, 1967) and Barton J. Bernstein, "The New Deal," in Bernstein (ed.), *Towards a New Past* (New York, Pantheon, 1968). One of the very few carefully researched historical accounts from a Republican point of view (the word "conservative" is often used, but seems to me inappropriate) is Edgar Eugene Robinson's *The Roosevelt Leadership: 1933–1945* (Philadelphia, Lippincott, 1955).

forward a number of arguments with considerable authority: the New Deal never brought full economic recovery, and it left many reforms unattempted and most of the others half-done. Schlesinger must have known this (no one ever questioned either his intelligence or his diligence), yet he nonetheless wrote approvingly of the New Deal. Some critics have argued that he simply mistook a few token welfare measures for a lot of social change, chiefly because his liberal heart overruled his historian's head. In the minds of these critics, welfare legislation and efforts to redistribute wealth were so overshadowed by the gains made by the business classes that Schlesinger has been dismissed as a man who, because of his pro-Roosevelt sympathies, had not identified the real authors and beneficiaries of the New Deal. Leading capitalists, among them Baruch, Swope, Harriman, Gianini, and Kennedy, approved of the New Deal and used it to advance their own interests. Schlesinger ignored such men, or minimized them; for him, the National Association of Manufacturers was "the business community." His critics have not yet massed the evidence to prove conclusively that he misunderstood businessmen in the 1930s, but they point to devastating forays by Barton J. Bernstein in his essay in *Towards a New Past,* and especially to Ellis Hawley, *The New Deal and the Problem of Monopoly* (1966).

Undoubtedly Schlesinger misrepresented the role of business interests in the New Deal. But neither this error—and we are not yet sure how great it was—nor his tendency to overrate the social effects of New Deal reforms make Schlesinger's interpretation untenable. As I see it, he is arguing that what was accomplished was in a broad sense all that could have been accomplished under the circumstances. He might be wrong on the role of businessmen, and wrong on the extent of New Deal reforms, and still be right that what was accomplished was praiseworthy. This fundamental question involves not matters of "fact" but of apparent historical alternatives facing the administration at literally hundreds of points. Perhaps the New Dealers were lucky to get anything at all. But we recognize here a scholarly extension of a debate which boiled around the president every day from the early spring of 1933 to the very end, a debate which has proven very difficult to conclude.

Volume I: The Crisis of the Old Order, 1919-1933 [1957]

CRITICAL COMMENTARIES

ALLAN NEVINS
[*1957*]

Mr. Schlesinger has written a book with every ingredient for a success with both scholars and the general public. Its well-annotated pages comprehend passages of absorbing narrative interest, graphic portraits, and an informed analysis of the surface movements that made up the American reaction in 1921–1929, and the slow-growing revolt that suddenly gained irresistible force in the crisis of 1930–1933. His book has an organization which marvelously succeeds in covering a broad

From *The New Leader,* 40 (May 13, 1957), 13–14. Reprinted by permission from *The New Leader.* Copyright © The American Labor Conference on International Affairs, Inc.

Allan Nevins, who taught for many years at Columbia University before his association with the Henry Huntington Library, San Marino, California, died in March, 1971. Although Nevins' chief interest was the Civil War period, he has written on a wide range of subjects, including the New Deal, and was one of the leading biographers in the country.

canvas while at the same time spotlighting many episodes with vivid, concrete detail. It gives evidence of gargantuan reading in the news, literature and polemics of the time, of wide delving in manuscripts and of conversations with many surviving actors on the scene.

Altogether, at first reading it is an irresistible book. On a second reading, it gives rise to some doubts and questionings; and although its enduring value is doubtless great, it may be that by 1960, when students have gone over it with a microscope and scalpel, it will look less satisfactory than now. Meanwhile, its merits and shortcomings may be given a preliminary assay.

It is a story of men, ideas and events, with the interplay among them presented in a kaleidoscopic succession of incidents, speeches and scenes. It opens with the twilight of Versailles, young men like Bullitt, Berle, Keynes and Herter in despair, Hoover and Smuts walking the Paris streets in deep distress; it closes with the tramp, bugles and bank proclamations of Inauguration Day in 1933. Mr. Schlesinger has a gift for making the sardonic epigram, the political anecdote, the picturesque tableau seem significant without artificial footlights. It is remarkable how deftly and entertainingly they follow each other.

Within the limits he has set himself, Mr. Schlesinger also deals fairly well with the ideas of his period. The main limitations (there are others) are that his study is purely cis-Atlantic and begins sharply around 1918, with a curt backward glance at Herbert Croly and Veblen. It is on the whole the best study yet made of middle-layer thinking about the archaism of progressive notions, the need for a radical new order, and the role to be given Government planning— thinking, that is, midway between journalism and fundamental probings. It takes some men and books too seriously. That Dewey, Croly, Simon Patten, Beard and Veblen were true thinkers is clear. W. T. Foster and Waddill Catchings at least gave a stimulus to thought, though the result might be only the line that FDR scrawled in their *Road to Plenty:* "Too good to be true. You can't get something for nothing." Donald Richberg's novels, however, Rex Tugwell's crude early divagations, and like flotsam seem less useful. Their value is, perhaps, that they give a comprehensive picture.

Yet, on a second reading of this captivating book we close it with some doubts. They do not concern its expertness, vitality or informative value, which are beyond question. Nor need we worry much about objectivity. Various critics have pointed out that, despite its air of scrupulous impartiality in places—the many generous references to Hoover, the balanced treatment of Al Smith—it is a highly partisan book. Canvassing an immense mass of evidence, Mr. Schlesinger has picked out incidents and quotations that buttress a predetermined pattern, passing over equally cogent bits that would weaken his thesis. For example, everybody, in the murk, confusions, despairs and hopes of 1930–1933, said some foolish and some wise things. Mr. Schlesinger shakes his sieve, and somehow practically all the foolish remarks come out under old-order Republican names, all the shrewd remarks under new-order Democratic attributions. But this is as pardonable as Macaulay's Whiggism.

The fundamental objection is that the book, so good on men, ideas and events, is not good at all on forces and, indeed, neglects forces almost entirely. Under the ships, the captains, the crews heaved a sea into which Mr. Schlesinger drops no plumb-line.

The serious student of the Great Reaction, the Crisis, and the incipient years of the Great Depression runs at once into some basic questions. What were the reasons for the moral, economic and political relapse after Wilson? To what extent did governmental inertia and reaction find a compensation in the constructive business and institutional achievements of the decade? (For, as Hoover has insisted, some large economic and cultural advances *were* made.) What was the central nature of the crisis that overtook the American economy in 1930–1933—financial, industrial or commercial? What in this period was the relation between world finance and American finance, the European economy and the American economy, and how much of the final malady began abroad as an inevitable after-shock of the Great War? If we look abroad, out of what economic and ideological developments sprang the workable ideas that Maynard Keynes gave the New Deal, so much more important in the long run than the unworkable ideas that Richberg and Tugwell gave it?

These are questions that cannot be answered without a searching inquiry into economic and social forces; and Mr. Schlesinger proposes no answers, for he does not even begin to inquire into these forces. Revolution is a word that comes readily to the pens of the writers he quotes. But revolutions occur in the foundations and not on the surface—otherwise they are not truly revolutions. This book is more brilliant in some ways that Hippolyte Taine's work on the old order in France; it at least has more journalistic brilliance. The Rooseveltian revolution may yet seem, in the long run, nearly as important for stable America as the Revolution of Mirabeau and Robespierre was for unstable France. But anyone who lays Schlesinger and Taine side by side will see that Taine is preoccupied with forces, and those of a fundamental nature are searchingly analyzed, while Schlesinger deals rather with the collisions and explosions produced by forces.

Primarily a history, this volume, the first of a series, makes too great a concession to biography. It includes a biographical interruption in the historical narrative, the long section entitled "The Happy Warrior," which gives an account of Roosevelt's birth, education, early political career, work as Assistant Secretary of the Navy, and Governorship. It is well done and highly interesting, but offers few essential additions to what Mr. Schlesinger's Harvard colleague, Frank Freidel, has so well told us in his multi-volumed biography now well under way. We could well exchange these 70 pages, or most of them, for equal space given to an analysis of the forces of the time.

Such an analysis would have had an additional value in that it would have done something to correct the partisan quality of Mr. Schlesinger's volume. We lack, for example, a really thorough study of the immense difficulties, the fearfully complex problems faced by Mr. Hoover; and, equally, a thorough analysis of the arms he took up against his sea of troubles. Fumbling, inept, tardy, unimaginative as he was, the unhappy Chief Executive did do much. We would welcome a fuller, fairer effort to resolve the problem stated by William Allen White: whether he was the last of the old or the first of the new Presidents. Even the [Reconstruction Finance Corporation] gets a brief narrative rather than a searching analysis. The fact is that peoples, governments, rulers were in the grip of forces which few then could clearly see, much less understand, and whose blind, gigantic and often pitiless operation would now better repay scrutiny than the details of the Chicago convention.

But let us be grateful to Mr. Schlesinger for a distinguished book, which all literate folk can read with pleasure, and all intelligent citizens with profit. It introduces a series of volumes from which we shall expect much.

THOMAS LE DUC
[*1957*]

This book need not long detain the scholar. Announced as the first of four volumes on the age of Franklin D. Roosevelt, it offers little that is new either in information or insight. Except for trivial gleanings from Hyde Park, there is nothing in the volume not already known to the historian. It is incredible that in this generation a professional scholar should try to write a history of the fifteen years after Versailles without using either the government records in the National Archives or the manuscript collections in the Library of Congress.

The content of the book belies the title. If by "the old order" the author means the structure and relationships of the American economy and public policy, it is clear that he has given us only the sketchiest account. Possibly analysis of the records would have made more persuasive his thesis that the Federal government betrayed the plain people not only by positive discrimination but also by refusing to assume the social functions realized in the New Deal. We are badly in need of a knowledgeable and sophisticated study of the Republican era. Mr. Schlesinger seems to promise such a work, but he gives us instead a tedious essay designed to rehabilitate Franklin D. Roosevelt as a kind of mystical leader, "armored in some inner faith," from whom "an impulse of courage now flowed out to the nation."

The technique of restoring luster to the repute of FDR embraces, however, is something more than this resort to the ineffable. One method is to deprecate either the intelligence or the morals of nearly every other public figure—Democratic and Republican. In condemning such a large fraternity of popular political leaders, Mr. Schlesinger leads one to wonder just how far he trusts the democratic

From *Journal of Southern History,* 23 (August 1957), 405–06. Copyright 1957 by the Southern Historical Association. Reprinted by permission of the Managing Editor.

Thomas LeDuc teaches history at Oberlin College.

process. Employed also in the book is the device of focusing attention on isolated episodes like the Bonus March or the Gastonia troubles. One finds here a richness of dramatic incident that places the book less in the category of scholarship than of morality play.

The book is so passionate in tone and so meager in new research that it need not be dignified by an extensive review. *The Crisis of the Old Order* will inevitably be viewed as evidence on the state of American historical writing. The lay audience will doubtless greet this book from the hand of a Harvard professor as a fair sample of academic scholarship. And young practitioners of the craft may well wonder if the way to glory is by skillful objurgation rather than by laborious, objective, investigation.

FRANK S. MEYER
[1957]

As far as the United States is concerned, "the revolution of our time" will have to be adjudged to a very large degree in terms of the meaning of the role of Franklin Delano Roosevelt. This is not because he was an ideologue in the sense that Lenin or Sun Yat-sen or Mussolini was. The pragmatic cast of American thought has long been such that it was not to be expected that the American protagonist of fundamental political and social change would be the prophet of a rigid system of ideas.

But, though not in this sense an ideologue, Roosevelt, in a typically experimental and pragmatic way, paralleled the ideologues who elsewhere led the revolt against the freedom of the individual in the name of "security," "society," the State. It was he who made the decisive breach in the American constitutional structure and the free

From *National Review*, (March 16, 1957), 263–64. Reprinted by permission of the *National Review*, 150 East 35th Street, New York, New York 10016.

Frank S. Meyer is a writer and member of the editorial board of *The National Review*.

American economic system. It was he who established the foundations of that statism which has continued to grow so mightily under
both political parties to this day. True, in previous years, under
Theodore Roosevelt and Woodrow Wilson, important preliminary
steps in this direction had been taken; but it is with the administra-
tions of Franklin Roosevelt that the transformation occurs.

Yet, despite the unquestionable primacy of FDR in the liberal
revolution, there has been no book from the liberal ranks that seriously assesses him and consolidates the man, the myth, and the age, in
the way that the theoreticians of the Establishment might seem to
owe him. A great mass of Rooseveltiana has been published, ranging
from the trivialities of Elliott Roosevelt and Frances Perkins to the
detailed biography of Frank Freidel; but no one has fixed the historical image, no one has presented him on the level of political principle.

For years it has been rumored that Arthur Schlesinger, Jr. was
working on a *magnum opus* that would do just this. At last the first
volume of his projected four-volume *Age of Roosevelt* has appeared
(*The Crisis of the Old Order, 1919–1933*). Having looked forward
for these same years to the opportunity of coming to grips with a
serious proponent of the Roosevelt revolution, I opened the book
with high hopes of battle. All the advance publicity had borne out
the rumors: Adlai Stevenson praised its "insight"; Frank Freidel compared it to Churchill; August Heckscher considered it "history as
only the greatest historians have written it." But when I began to read
the book, disappointment set in—not disappointment in that I dis-
agreed with Mr. Schlesinger's thesis. That I expected. But disappointment with the quality of his thought, with the vulgarity of his conceptual apparatus, with the slickness of his presentation.

Certainly the ideology is there, but it is not honestly and intellectually offered. It is projected by stereotyped portrait and amusing
anecdote and sentimental evocation. The message is powerful enough,
but it is powerful at the level of the sophisticated advertisement writer.
The very title carries it. "The old order" is, of course, a literal translation of *"l'ancien régime,"* with overtones of Marie Antoinette, bab-
bling "Let 'em eat cake," and the Bourbons, ruling with callous
indifference over starving multitudes.

Coolidge and Hoover, although they are granted a few human
characteristics, emerge, together with the bankers and businessmen of
the twenties, as the blind and bumbling architects of disaster, figures
introduced into the action but to enhance the glory of the shining hero
waiting in the wings. It is the devil theory of Charley Michelson's

campaign (which did so much to discredit Hoover and elect Roosevelt) raised to a more genteel level and decked out in the pretentious garments of History.

The structure of the volume is itself designed to present this simple contest. The first two-thirds are devoted to an impressionistic story of the twenties—all tinselled prosperity, intellectual and spiritual disillusionment and, at the end, muttering rebellion. It comes to its culmination in a purple passage describing the Democratic National Convention of 1932 and the nomination of Franklin Roosevelt.

And here the second theme begins, developed in the last third of the book—the life of Franklin Roosevelt from his birth to Inauguration Day, 1933. The lights change, the tone is reversed. Everything is portentous of hope—from the gay Russian sleigh in which "James and Sallie Roosevelt . . . skim along the frosty white roads" a few days before the happy event of January 30, 1882, until March 4, 1933, when, on the last page of the book, the hero moves towards his apotheosis:

> Many had deserted freedom, many more had lost their nerve. But Roosevelt, armored in some inner faith, remained calm and inscrutable . . . grim but unafraid. Deep within, he seemed to know . . . that catastrophe could provide the indispensable setting for democratic experiment and for presidential leadership. . . . The only thing Americans had to fear was fear itself. And so he serenely awaited the morrow. The event was in the hand of God.

The book leaves one with what Hollywood likes to call "an unforgettable message"—etched in corn. Still, with all the apparatus of close-ups and fade-outs, the blarney about "patrician" social responsibility, the "intimate pictures" and the hero-worshipper's loving lingering on detail, the lineaments of the real Roosevelt are discernible enough: a person of charm, of great influence over men, revealing himself fully to no one, intent always upon power and its achievement, unmeasured in his ambition. He was no firm ideologist, it is true; but one thing he understood as far back as his days in the Albany Legislature, and earlier, was that the road to power in the twentieth century lay in the statist and socialist direction.

This, at least, Mr. Schlesinger makes clear and in this he glories. There is a sense in which he has, after all, written the kind of ideological tract adequate to his purposes. It may be that the very style in which it is written, the very refusal to state openly his premises and argue for them is a tribute to his hero, the tribute of imitation. For

Roosevelt, who led this country far along the road to socialism, never himself publicly stated his premises nor argued for them. As he said to Tugwell about government "planning" in 1932: "That kind of thing would have to grow rather than be campaigned for."

In a very real sense, FDR never campaigned openly for what he fundamentally wanted. It simply "grew." That is, he put it over. His public efforts in campaign after campaign were based, not upon an open struggle for his goals, but upon a Machiavellian calculus directed towards the achievement of power.

Volume II:
The Coming of the New Deal
[1959]

CRITICAL COMMENTARIES

ROBERT E. BURKE
[1965]

With this volume Professor Schlesinger gets to the heart of the subject matter of his important and long-awaited magnum opus. He is
here concerned chiefly with the domestic aspects of the New Deal in
1933 and 1934. Although he does deal fully and convincingly with
the London Economic Conference (incidentally passing on a superb
Cordell Hull anecdote), he has reserved the foreign affairs of the
period for a subsequent volume. The result is a first-rate piece of historical writing, centering upon the President but skillfully developing
the major themes topically. . . .

The last four chapters are in a section called "Evolution of the
Presidency." In them Schlesinger passes his judgment upon Roosevelt,

From *Journal of American History,* 65 (October 1965), 148–50. Reprinted
by permission of the Organization of American Historians.

Robert E. Burke teaches history at the University of Washington.

both as President and as human being. FDR emerges as a traditional-ist who conceived of his program as a return to first principles of conduct. His deviousness and inconsistency, two of the major prob-lems facing the sympathetic historian, Schlesinger sees as tactical flexibility. The result is a picture that is fresh and exciting, the product of an author who has had experience with practical politicians and knows that politics is indeed the art of the possible. There is here none of the lament of the doctrinaire liberal intellectual, still remorse-ful because FDR failed to nationalize the banks, or of the die-hard conservative, whose image of the New Deal is that of a conspiracy of crackpot professors and grafting politicians.

If Schlesinger's sympathies are clearly with his hero through-out, in this volume he seems less partisan than in the introductory one. He affords little aid and comfort to the anti-New Dealers, but he does permit them to state their cases. He cannot resist quoting the pronouncements of doom uttered at the time by conservatives, and he cannot always escape from the present ("the president of the Stu-dent Association at Commonwealth in the spring of 1935 was an Arkansas youth named Orval E. Faubus"). But he seems willing to go where the evidence leads, as in his surprisingly friendly conclusion about Jesse Jones. The text is studded with superb analytical descrip-tions of people. . . .

The book is based upon truly exhaustive research—printed sources (including a full study of the contemporary periodical press), the manuscript collections at Hyde Park and the National Archives, the oral history materials at Columbia, his own interviews, and corre-spondence with survivors. . . .

Schlesinger has given us by far the best book yet produced on the first phases of the New Deal. Much still remains to be done—Congress deserves a fuller treatment (although the author justly ob-serves that it was anything but the rubber stamp of hallowed tradi-tion), the field of state politics of the era remains mostly unworked, intellectual currents of the period need careful examination, and the social history of the times remains to be written. But the main story of FDR and his efforts to restore the national economy and morale is here developed brilliantly. The result is a major work of recent history.

CARL N. DEGLER
[1959]

Judging from Arthur Schlesinger's *The Coming of the New Deal,* an historian who undertakes to write the history of a period as productive of commentary and analysis and as rich in documentary materials as the 1930s performs his task under a handicap. So much has been said already that little new can be added. This is true, it would seem, even of interpretations. Mr. Schlesinger has not found it necessary to foresake the traditional view that there were in fact two New Deals—a first one concerned largely with recovery and a second centered on reform—for this is apparently the interpretive framework of his larger study, "The Age of Roosevelt," of which this volume is the second. (Actually, there is a good deal of evidence, as Mr. Schlesinger tells the story, to show that this widely accepted division is more neat than accurate, though he does not so interpret it.)

But if there are no new significant facts or interpretations of the New Deal in these pages, there is excellent synthesis of the mountain of sources for the period. The structure of the book is carefully conceived. The evolution of New Deal policies is treated under broad headings, like agriculture, relief, money, and labor, from inception in March 1933 to that time in early 1935 when policy was firmly established. The book gains much from its well-wrought structure, for information gained in the opening chapters plays in again and again as the scope of the book broadens. That the book becomes increasingly compelling as one reads through it bears testimony to its excellence as narrative history.

Although in the first three chapters too close attention is sometimes paid to who-said-what-to-whom and whose-knife-was-going-into-whose-back, with the chapter on the growing labor unrest the nation as a whole comes in for attention. Similarly, in the chapter on

From *The Yale Review,* 48 (Spring 1959), 445–47. Reprinted by permission of *The Yale Review;* copyright Yale University Press.
Carl Degler teaches history at Stanford University.

the mounting opposition to FDR and the New Deal, one gets a sense of the times outside Washington and the title "The Age of Roosevelt" becomes appropriate. But all through this volume, the central concern is the Roosevelt administration, not the country.

It is in the last chapter, "The Evolution of the Presidency," that Schlesinger is at his best. His portrait of the President as leader and person is perhaps the most perceptive to be found anywhere. Persuasively he argues for an FDR who never revealed himself fully to any man. "At work or at play, the defenses remained intact," Mr. Schlesinger writes. Wisely he recognizes that not all of FDR's traits fit into neat patterns; for example, the meticulousness of stamp collecting is hard "to reconcile . . . with the disorderly, generous and flexible Roosevelt."

If there are understanding, perception, and verve in Mr. Schlesinger's presentation of Franklin Roosevelt, there is less critical evaluation of the New Deal than one has a right to expect at this distance. And it is the philosophical vantage point from which Mr. Schlesinger surveys the Age of Roosevelt that gives rise to the book's only serious weakness. His favoritism toward the New Deal, it should be said, is never as extreme as the anti-New Deal bias which marred Edgar Robinson's *The Roosevelt Leadership*. Nevertheless, a tone of warm sympathy, not detachment, pervades *The Coming of the New Deal*. As defenses of New Deal measures are piled upon one another, even a favorably disposed reader becomes uneasy. All save one of the principal New Deal actions are judged sound in retrospect. The exception is Social Security, but only in the manner of its financing. Mr. Schlesinger thinks the program should have been supported out of general taxation instead of by deductions from wages. (One unexpected fruit of Mr. Schlesinger's almost total defense of the New Deal is a spirited —and well supported—rehabilitation of the NRA, for many years the one sheep in the New Deal fold which both liberals and conservatives agreed was black.)

Hindsight is used to evaluate New Deal actions, but not always. For example, Mr. Schlesinger glosses over the pillorying of financiers and bankers at the hands of Congressional committees on the grounds that times had changed, though in our own day we have been painfully aware that two can play at that game. No comment is made on FDR's ignoring the Congressional revelation that Secretary of the Treasury Woodin and Norman Davis accepted favors from J. P. Morgan, though again contemporary analogies suggest themselves immediately. Today's continuing problem of an agricultural surplus seems to arouse no doubt in Mr. Schlesinger's mind of the soundness of AAA's [Agricultural Adjustment Administration] solution to agricultural distress in 1933. Instead, he seeks to exonerate the AAA of the charge of wantonly killing little pigs.

One of Mr. Schlesinger's contributions is to press once again the point that the New Deal was the work of many men and ideas and not just FDR or even the administration. Yet Roosevelt's apparent failure to measure up to the standard of a thorough-going New Dealer is sometimes underplayed. Only the careful reader, for instance, will learn that FDR opposed Federal Deposit Insurance almost to the last or that he was so slow in speaking out in favor of the Wagner Labor Bill that it was already through the Senate and in the House before the President was heard from.

But one no sooner mentions the uncritical viewpoint from which this book is written than one suspects that it is somehow irrelevant. *The Coming of the New Deal* was obviously planned not as a definitive history of an era but as an evocation of the spirit of the New Dealers and the administration which was dominated by Franklin Roosevelt. As such it is eminently successful. All the stirring events, the inevitable mistakes, the varieties of personality, the insistent problems of the early years of the first administration are here; so is the intellectual vacuity of the political opposition which, mercifully, the author does not comment upon, but lets speak for itself. Indeed, few historians of our day can excell Mr. Schlesinger in penetrating to the core of a personality; his sketches of the prominent New Dealers, which are scattered through the book, are as penetrating as they are brilliant. Moreover, the fun, the heady atmosphere close to power, the almost incredible dedication of some, the plain hard work which went into the making of the New Deal are also here as they were at the time.

REXFORD G. TUGWELL
[*1959*]

For those who read the first of Professor Schlesinger's "Age of Roosevelt" volumes—*The Crisis of the Old Order*—the manner of presentation in this second one—*The Coming of the New Deal*—will have no surprises. It tells its story in the same lucid language, it has the same orientation, and it seems to be powered by the same energy. It covers roughly Roosevelt's first two years in the White House; and this would seem to indicate that some half-dozen volumes may still be in prospect. It promises to be a remarkable addition to historical literature.

Aside from the literary talent shown throughout, so pleasurable to the reader, there is a special reason to value the Schlesinger books. The author is far from detached, is indeed obviously partisan to the progressive-liberal school of politics and statesmanship; and this involves him in feelings toward Roosevelt which are intense. For Roosevelt was the supreme practitioner of leadership in this genre. He showed how to translate theory into practice, at least on occasion, and so furnished the bridge intellectuals usually lack between their conceptions and the legislative-executive complex. To see long-advocated policies embodied in presidential speeches, in messages to the Congress, and finally in approved measures, was something the progressives of the twenties had hardly hoped ever to see; their exile had become so accustomed as to seem permanent.

Arthur Schlesinger was old enough to feel this sense of despair, but not old enough to participate in the sudden release of pent-up

From *The Virginia Quarterly Review,* 35 (Spring 1959), 342–48. Copyright *The Virginia Quarterly Review,* The University of Virginia.

Rexford G. Tugwell was one of Roosevelt's Brain Trust, an Assistant Secretary of Agriculture, and head of the Resettlement Administration. He has written extensively on Roosevelt and the New Deal, winning the Bancroft Prize with his *The Brains Trust* (New York, Viking, 1968) in 1968. He is associated with the Center for the Study of Democratic Institutions, Montecito, California.

policies into the public domain. He had no part in the New Deal. His book is a kind of vicarious participation, as his earlier one was a brilliant exposition of the ordeal of inaction when the old order was crumbling under the pressures of change and as its politicians were fumbling with irrelevant remedies for that society's ills. He was born in 1917 and this made him a young student while the country was suffering the preliminaries to the New Deal. He graduated from Harvard in 1938, just at the mid-point of the second Roosevelt term. There had been the tremendous victory of 1936, when he would have been a sophomore, the Supreme Court battle would have happened when he was a junior, and the gradual reorientation toward world problems would have been taking place when he was a senior. The impact of this student experience is evident everywhere. He was not in it, as his likeminded elders (by a few years) were; but he was of it —very much so. And he has been of it ever since.

His public service began in the Office of War Information and was continued in the Office of Strategic Services; so he did serve under Roosevelt, even if only in a minor way and only late in his administration. For the man who should have fallen heir to the Roosevelt tradition, and who would have been capable of fulfilling the expectations of the Schlesingers of the new generation, he offered a different kind of service. He was a hard and able worker in both the Stevenson campaigns. And he has never lost an opportunity to speak up for the attitude toward public affairs he represents. As I write this note about him, there lies on my table an issue of the New Republic in which he protests bitterly the policies being followed by the politicians of the Democratic party. They are in process, he says, of ridding the party of its intellectuals, and he cites in proof the selection of mediocrities as candidates in New York, Pennsylvania, and elsewhere. He ends his article with a characteristically explosive sentence: "A party which seeks to qualify itself for responsibility in an age of national and international crisis is not well advised to begin to do so by blowing out its own brains."

This same ability to focus a fierce light on current events makes the Schlesinger histories easy to read, or perhaps I should say, hard not to read, because he has one of the largest audiences of any living historian. . . .

The Hundred Days with which this volume opens is an extraordinarily difficult period to deal with in retrospect. There were so many, and such conflicting, forces converging so suddenly on Washington that sorting out the results and the events leading to the results is a task requiring much patience and understanding as well as orthodox historical carefulness. Much of what went on is very poorly documented. The busy New Dealers made very sketchy notes, when they made any at all, and the oral exchanges are quite lost except for the notoriously inaccurate recollections of later years. And the principal figure in the events—Roosevelt himself—kept no record of his multifarious conversations with those about him. There are the documents; but documents have depths behind them of discussion, argument, hostilities, alliances, pressures, trades—and even political blackmail—that have to be inferred if they are to be noticed at all. Something can be done still for this period by interviewing. And the Columbia oral history project will be a continuing source of interpretation. But all that can be done by a historian would not really tell much about the New Deal as it went on without the kind of detective sensitivity that Schlesinger shows.

It is not too much to say that he has entered into the personalities of the principal figures with a psychologist's deftness. But especially he has studied Roosevelt with a kind of anxious detachment as though he had the task of finding out enough about him so that another of the same sort could be discovered. It was an Age of Roosevelt and the next great one will be that of some one else. That some one else ought to understand himself and his responsibilities better for having read this history. . . .

It is this ability to convey the excitement, the confusion, the inspiring challenges of the New Deal that is to me the great attraction of the Schlesinger history. Back of it there is an immense industry, for the paper work has had to be gone through carefully, and there are mountains of documents. Not only that, it has had to be assessed in the light of the varied and conflicting accounts left by participants. If, as one of those participants, I can agree that a fair job has been done, as well as a wonderfully illuminating one, it shows how faithfully the understanding has been worked out. Perhaps this was mostly because Schlesinger has a genuinely exact conception of the presidency which so many others have seemed to lack. As to that, his conclusion is that

. . . one doubts whether the presidency can ever be effectively bureaucratized. Its essence is an independence, initiative, and creativity which requires and relies on its own lines of communication to the world outside. Vigorous government under the American system would seem almost impossible without something like the Rooseveltian sleight-of-hand at the center.

At any rate, that is the kind of president Roosevelt was. And whether it is true that it must always be done as he did it, it seems to me that it could have been done in no other way in his circumstances and in his time.

Volume III: The Politics of Upheaval
[1960]

CRITICAL COMMENTARY

DAVID A. SHANNON

[1960]

Schlesinger's research is wide, especially for a general book like this, which could be expanded into a shelf of volumes. The writing is first-rate. Schlesinger writes narrative history as well as any American historian of this century. He has a sense of drama, wit, and a sharp eye for irony. He relieves reader weariness—after all, it is a huge book—with apt quotations and revealing anecdotes. In a sketch of a few sentences, full of well-turned phrases, he gives the reader what is necessary to know of his characters' personalities. Sample: "The last of the prewar muckrakers, [Upton] Sinclair somehow kept a gentle but durable innocence while all around him—Steffens to his left, Mark Sullivan and Hearst to his right—capitulated to images of power and success. His books were brisk and sentimental, saturated with fact and suffused with moral indignation."

Not many historians of this generation write successfully for a wide nonprofessional audience. It is fortunate that one who does

From *The Progressive*, 24 (November 1960), 44–45. Reprinted by permission of the author and *The Progressive Magazine*.

chooses to write about Roosevelt and the Great Depression, for there seems to be after fifteen years almost as much popular misinformation and misconception about FDR as there is about Lincoln after almost a century. Just as the popular view of Lincoln as The Great Emancipator vastly oversimplifies and distorts reality without being absolutely wrong, so does the popular view of Roosevelt as The Great Liberal.

Americans of all shades of political opinion need to be reminded that Roosevelt "avoided ideological commitment . . . even avoided intellectual clarity," that even at the height of his most liberal period he maintained friendly relationships with Democratic city bosses of the most squalid sort and party conservatives such as Bernard Baruch and Jesse Jones, that in December 1934 even Morgenthau's tax plan was too radical for FDR's taste, that he never threw his support behind an anti-lynching bill, and that he hoped his "oratorical extremism would nullify the effect of . . . legislative and administrative moderation" and thereby give "new heart to his friends" while "diminish-[ing] the grievances of his enemies." People also need to be reminded that Alfred M. Landon was not by any means a nasal, naive Neanderthal. Governor Landon, incidentally, allowed Schlesinger access to his papers and consented to be interviewed, and the Landon that emerges from these pages is a somewhat more sophisticated and liberal person than was generally thought in 1936.

As excellent a book as this is—the best of the three volumes, in my opinion, because the subject-matter better fits the author's conceptions and interests—I must enter a few dissents. Schlesinger's decision to consider the legislative history of the Wagner Act in the previous volume blurs one important difference between the first and second New Deals and, because Roosevelt resisted Wagner's bill until he saw it would pass anyway, the author tends to give the White House too much credit for the record of the 74th Congress.

When one considers the background of the Wagner Act, one wonders about the validity of the assertions about the unreliability of the Senate progressives. Perhaps the Senate progressives were inadequate, perhaps Roosevelt was right in thinking that he could get more by working with Southern conservatives than with Northern and Western progressive prima donnas, but quoting statements by Harold Ickes and Rex Tugwell about the progressives' unreliability, rather than documenting the charge by close description of their actions, is not persuasive. The treatment of the Roosevelt coalition in 1936, which makes valid points not made before, would have been strengthened by more consideration of the American Labor Party of New

York than the almost passing references made. Indeed, more attention to state and local politics throughout the volume would have enriched the story.

Nevertheless, *The Politics of Upheaval* is impressive. It deserves the wide audience it will get, and the audience will be politically wiser and better informed for having read it.

Volumes I, II, and III

CRITICAL COMMENTARIES

JACOB COHEN

Schlesinger and the New Deal
[1961]

It would be hard not to admire the daring with which Schlesinger has imagined his task and the industry with which he is achieving it. In three volumes, *The Crisis of the Old Order: 1919–1933* (1957), *The Coming of the New Deal* (1959) and *The Politics of Upheaval* (1960) he has barely brought his story to the end of Roosevelt's first administration. He has not yet adumbrated the problems of foreign policy and the war is still to come. Since Schlesinger is presently making and taking notes for the Age of Kennedy, the job may never be completed.

A lucid but also a rather fussy writer, Schlesinger takes great pains to evoke the atmosphere of the moment. Many of his descriptions are enormously effective. What historian, or novelist, has cap-

From *Dissent,* 8 (Autumn 1961), 461–72. Reprinted by permission of the author and *Dissent.*

Jacob Cohen is Lecturer, Department of American Civilization, Brandeis University.

tured the depression so vividly, or, for example, retold the events
surrounding the court decisions of 1935 so dramatically? There is sus-
pense and drama and irony in his pages. Yet there is something
ceremonious and mechanical about all this mood music. Twelve or thir-
teen hundred pages into these volumes and we begin to predict when
Schlesinger is going to trot out his prose. (One begins to wish the sun
shone happily and hopefully throughout the first inaugural.) Schlesinger is fussy about his characters too. Each of them is meticulously
portrayed and provided with a pocket biography as he enters on stage.
Some came off beautifully; Harold Ickes, Huey Long, Father Coughlin,
Henry Morgenthau, and, over and again, Roosevelt. But, in addition
we are inundated with so much anatomical description, thirty-second
psychology, irrelevant and irreverent anecdote about so many New
Deal personages that soon we forget who it was that had the paunchy
face, who the shifty eyes and who wasn't paranoic.

Amidst this sound and fury Schlesinger fits a biography of
Roosevelt, and a superb one. We have detailed descriptions of the
principal New Deal legislation, analyses of social movements, weighty
discussions of economic policy, chatty reviews of congressional and
party politics, and brisk summaries of the books, ideas, and and
ideologies which were politically visible during these years. He offers
judgments on almost all the critical problems raised by his materials
and for the most part they are balanced and charitable.

And there is a unifying vision which gathers in the disarray in
these books. It is the unity imparted by Schlesinger's vision of the
vital center: Schlesinger has prescribed that the intellectual think
through broad social and political problems from the perspective of
working politics. In *The Age of Roosevelt* he has taken his own
advice.

Perhaps I can illustrate the point and draw out some of its implications. Schlesinger has punctuated his narrative with countless
prophecies of doom thundered against the New Deal during these
years. From the right we hear braintrusters accused of conspiring a
revolution in which Roosevelt, the Kerensky of America, would be
replaced by some appropriate Lenin. From the left we hear Roosevelt
accused of conspiring to bring Fascism to our shores. We are shown
farmers pouring milk on dusty roads, veterans beginning to march, a
nation singing hymns with Coughlin and Long, and we are informed
that many were of the opinion that revolution was rife. (William
Allen White, Raymond Swing, Sinclair Lewis, remember, all insisted
that Fascism could happen here.) Quotation is piled on quotation,

prophecies of doom from every quarter, contradictory, often absurd, invariably wrong. Schlesinger's purpose is, I suppose, to build a mood. But his method and his organizing vision conspire against him. Every prophecy, indeed nearly every criticism, is confronted through quotation. Hardly distinguishing between what is serious and what is not, Schlesinger enters into none of these prophecies and answers them feebly or not at all. Was Fascism a possibility, or socialism? Was a revolution in the farm belt possible? The questions are barely asked. Socialism, Fascism, revolution become as momentous as any other field report passing across a busy chief executive's desk. Schlesinger filters the political life out of his materials, and deprives historical moments of their reality.

This homogenization operates throughout the book. Philosophy, which must be excruciatingly honest to its own assumptions and is not itself when separated from those assumptions, is cut to the proportions of a political program. Social movements are weighed on the scales of political pressure, even suffering becomes a lobbyist among lobbyists. I say this with some care to the seriousness of what I am charging. I am aware of the many pages on which Schlesinger has recorded suffering vividly in these volumes. He has told us many times over that Roosevelt felt this suffering and acted upon his feelings. But I have not sensed in my journey with Schlesinger through the New Deal that he has made the suffering of the depression part of himself or indeed reexperienced anything but a narrow strand of the political sensibility of these years. Schlesinger lacks what for me is Niebuhr's surpassing quality, the quality of moral empathy, the ability to enter into the moral compulsions which raise men, all men, to action. A vital center without moral dimension (which may mean without transcendent dimension) presents as distorted a point of vantage upon history as the most doctrinaire ideology. . . .

The great task of pragmatism has been to apply the experimental method to man and society. The most important question we can ask of any pragmatist is, "What is the basic unity of society upon which you intend to experiment?" For John Dewey, the preeminent pragmatist of our day, the answer to this question (at least during most of his career) was "society itself." This effort to treat society-as-a-whole as the fundamental unit of experimentation is part of a development in American thought running through the work of Bellamy, Croly, Beard, Veblen, Mead, to Dewey himself. (For William James, the first great pragmatist, individual man was the unit of experimentation and therefore he developed no real social theory.)

For the latter pragmatists no social experiment which did not deal systematically and consistently with society itself was truly scientific. For this reason Dewey denied that the New Deal was pragmatic. "Experimental method," he wrote in 1935, "is not just messing around nor doing a little of this and a little of that in the hope that things will improve. Just as in the physical sciences, it implies a coherent body of ideas, a theory that gives direction to effort."

Consider now Schlesinger's use of the term pragmatism:

Faith in experiment implied a belief in a middle way. The pragmatic approach rejected equally those who would make no change at all in the social order and those who demanded total change. It sought increased government management of the economy but stopped short of government planning of all economic decisions.

As with nearly every political term, Schlesinger defines pragmatism by posing it *against* doctrinaire ideology. Pragmatism is both more and less than ideology: more successful because its methods are geared for success, less ambitious because it has learned how stubbornly history resists totalistic solutions. It is the method of the vital center and signals the end of ideology.

There are two reasons why I would insist that neither the New Deal nor vital center liberalism earns the name pragmatic. First, it is clear that neither of them are truly experimental in temper. There is no evidence in the *Age of Roosevelt* that the New Deal ever conducted a social experiment even approximating an experimental model, nor does Schlesinger in *The Vital Center* devise any potential experiments for our approval. Experimentation is impossible from the vital center. It has no over-all sense of the society upon which it is experimenting, and, more important, its implicit view of history conveys the suggestion that history is likely to resist experimentation. History from the perspective of the vital center is not only complex; it is also incongruous, a buzzing confusion of conflicting interests, the scene of diffused, interacting and overlapping sources of authority, full of contradictory ideas and ironic gaps. "Control" is the word we usually associate with the experimental method, and the history which Schlesinger perceives would hardly stand still long enough to permit any control. Improvisation is not pragmatism.

The second reason I would deny the New Deal the name pragmatic is that it lacked the set of unchallenged moral assumptions which are necessary to make pragmatism work. To conduct an experiment intelligently we must know beforehand what will constitute a successful experiment. To experiment intelligently on man we must be morally, I would almost say, ideologically secure, for what but a clear social ethic can distinguish a success from a failure with man? Schlesinger, who usually knows what to say, makes the point this way:

Without some critical vision, pragmatism could be a meaningless technique; the flight from ideology a form of laziness, the middle way an empty conception.

Well spoken. And since the point is now his we may properly ask Schlesinger what "critical vision" of the New Deal animated its pragmatism. More often than not an eclectic hodge-podge, a humanitarian "sense," an "instinct for the future." Devising one which satisfies a humanitarian sense or an instinct for the future is impossible. Schlesinger was wrong to begin with when he posited an antimony between pragmatism and ideology. One might better argue that pragmatism is impossible without ideology. What else is this "critical vision" of which Schlesinger speaks if not ideology of some sort? The question is not whether we have an ideology but whether that ideology is explicit. The danger of Schlesinger's doctrinaire opposition to ideology is that it will dull the moral and critical faculty itself and make pragmatism indeed a form of laziness, an empty conception. . . .

Like the serious Southerners who cried havoc (also Communist) at the inroads which abstract equality would make upon Southern life, so too were there industrialists and bankers who hollered Communist about the inroads the New Deal was about to make upon our sacred institutions. Schlesinger has conveyed the density of life in America well enough to reveal how ludicrous, how hypocritical, the cries and threats of the business community were. Yet is is clear from his account that the violence of their reaction to developments in the New Deal helped block avenues of reform and moved the vital center somewhat further to the right. I am convinced that if the New Deal had been more realistic it would have seen through the opposition, [it could have] calmly and persistently . . . [seen] . . . how inordinate were their fears, and [it] could have safely moved further along the road to reform than it did. Historical realism is quite properly a prelude and reminder to ideology, but it cannot be a substitute for it. I am unhappy that a liberal of Schlesinger's importance can spend three columns depicting a pageant of reform without ever asking the profoundly historical question of whether more could have been done. This uncritical acquiescence to what he selectively defines as historical reality not only makes for an inadequate *Age of Roosevelt,* it also indicates the perils residing in vital center liberalism. . . .

America had more to fear than fear itself: it had an economic system addicted to cycles of boom and bust to fear; it had a world movement of totalitarianism to fear; it had the complications which attend mass society to fear and it had much that could be stated explicitly to accomplish as well. It is the Rooseveltian political flair which always seems to attract Schlesinger's admiration and which he renders most heartily. He records too the rhetoric, the vague goals, the intuitions of the man, though not with the same fidelity. But democratic society must be run by more than a kind of political existentialist and must scrutinize itself in more intelligible terms than Schlesinger provides. What could have Roosevelt accomplished which he didn't? This is the question we should ask. To what further use could he have put the dextrous powers of his office? An answer to these questions which has no sense of the style of the man is empty of life (and Schlesinger has infused his portrait with much that is of life), an answer to this question which has no element of systematic criticism, no explicit sense of what is possible and what is desirable, no thoroughgoing commitment to the notion that history not only is but that it can be improved, is empty of meaning.

I do not accuse Roosevelt of fatalism, I accuse Schlesinger of it. We have not said enough when we have established convincingly that a chief executive has the leeway to influence the course of history. If we are to be free ourselves we must ask whether he influenced events in the direction they ought to have and could have gone. I find in Schlesinger's treatment of Roosevelt a reflection of his treatment of the entire New Deal. Here is the same mood of acquiescence, the same liberal yes-saying, the same know-nothingism in the name of good history. And all of them examples of some of the perils which reside in the vital center.

OTIS L. GRAHAM, JR.

Historians and the
New Deals: 1944–1960
[*1963*]

That Franklin D. Roosevelt's New Deal would eventually be seen as two separate and, in many ways, contradictory movements was not apparent to harried Americans in the Thirties. Conservatives were too busy damning the entire experiment as subversive and dangerous, while liberals were too busy drawing up legislation and finding money and office space to support their unlimited projects, to take thought as to the internal logic of the dynamic "New Deal." It was not until the middle Forties that an American historian, standing back a brief distance from events, was able to discern in the six-year period a division—both theoretical and actual—into two parts. The useful distinction between first and second New Deals was made in 1944 by Basil Rauch, and has served to orient scholars and commentators in the years of assessment that followed.

Rauch described the first New Deal—built largely in the so-called Hundred Days, and having as its heart NRA [National Recovery Administration] and AAA [Agricultural Adjustment Administration]—as a conservative, cautious beginning, aimed at recovery, and proceeding through an understanding with the business community. The second New Deal, according to Rauch, began late in 1934 as Roosevelt drifted toward a political alliance with progressives. It produced a burst of legislation in the spring and summer of 1935, and again in 1938. This second period was marked by a "leftward" shift, and was preoccupied, now that recovery was assured, with reform.

Rauch's book, although based of necessity upon limited sources

From *The Social Studies,* 54 (April 1963), 133–40. Reprinted by permission of McKinley Publishing Co. (Footnotes have been deleted.)

Otis L. Graham, Jr. teaches history at the University of California, Santa Barbara.

and perspective, established initial, plausible, and therefore durable categories. No scholar came forward to dispute or dispense with the notion of two New Deals, and Rauch's characterization of the periods was not fundamentally altered by subsequent writers. Only recently, building upon a slender but stubborn body of dissent from men who had been close to Roosevelt, has an historian challenged the Rauch analysis and description. Arthur M. Schlesinger, Jr., in the third volume of his *Age of Roosevelt* series published in 1960, altered the earlier idea of the intellectual underpinnings and long-range intent of the two New Deals. The novelty of Schlesinger's new interpretation was noted briefly by Frank Freidel in an essay summarizing New Deal historiography in 1961, and by Schlesinger himself. It deserved, whatever its persuasiveness, wider notice. The traditional conception could not be reconciled with Schlesinger's view, and it was apparent that not only the two New Deals, but the recent American reform tradition indirectly, had come under a searching re-evaluation. I shall attempt a brief survey of the growth and development of these divergent views concerning the New Deals, with a side glance at the recent shift of historical perspective which has made a reinterpretation of the New Deals seem necessary.

It was Rauch's contention that both the legislative record of the period 1933–1939, and the loose congeries of presidential advisors responsible for the philosophy and functioning of the New Deal, underwent a marked change in mid-stream. In the beginning, unhampered by organized opposition and determined to act, Roosevelt and his associates put together a body of legislation at first startling in its novelty, mass, and free use of Federal power. The National Recovery Administration and the first Agricultural Adjustment Administration were the heart of this phase, which despite its novel features constituted a generally conservative effort to forge co-operation between government and business in the interests of recovery. The President was apparently satisfied with the work of 1933, but attacks from the Right and a disturbing growth of strength on the Long/Coughlin Left were eventually to force Roosevelt into a new path of political action. "A fundamental change in the political philosophy and policies of the Roosevelt administration did occur during 1934," Rauch states, and "its importance justifies the designation first and second New Deals." As the second phase began, an emboldened Roosevelt glued together a new coalition including Labor and small farmers, and surrounded himself with new political advisors. He then proceeded to enact a program more liberal and daring, less responsive to the needs of business, than before. This second New Deal took its personnel and tone from the progressive movement, submerged but not extinguished by the Twenties, and whereas the aim of the first New Deal had been recovery, the aim of the second was reform.

Rauch did not argue that the shift was absolute or sudden, and stipulated that in two areas the New Deals were the same—in foreign policy, and in the "extension of government regulation of the kind first imposed on railroads by the Interstate Commerce Act of 1887." But "in agricultural, industrial, labor, tariff, money, and unemployment relief legislation the policies of the first New Deal were fundamentally altered and in some sense reversed to create the second."

The reconstruction of events, as Rauch presented it, was clear and winning. Roosevelt, under pressure from Right and Left in late 1934, veered leftward to enter a second New Deal, flying henceforth the battered but proud banner of the progressives. If "liberal" may be taken to mean favorable to labor, Rauch went on, and if "conservative" means favorable to business, "in this broad sense the first New Deal was conservative and the second New Deal liberal." The Rauchian designations, conservative to liberal, recovery to reform, stuck fast, and the unmanageable six year period was reduced to order—an order which seemed to do little violence to the facts, and to illuminate the sharp twistings and turnings of the hectic era. . . .

Not until the third volume of his *The Age of Roosevelt* did Arthur Schlesinger, Jr., consider the shift from first to second New Deals. *The Politics of Upheaval* (1960) argued that the novelty of the first had been greatly underestimated because of its tone of solicitude for business interests. At the same time, the anti-business animus of the second appeared to establish its right to radical title. Yet the second New Deal, Schlesinger pointed out, for all its radical language, aimed lower than the first. The Banking Bill of 1935, the "Soak-The-Rich" Tax, the Holding Company Bill, these were still interventionism, but with a difference. In place of telling businessmen what *to* do, the second New Deal told them what *not* to do. Schlesinger identified the shift by more than the passing of the NRA attempt at planning. He made much of the changing of the guard among advisors—Tugwell, Moley, Berle, Hugh Johnson being traded in for Corcoran, Cohen, Eccles, and in the background, Brandeis. Added to the decline of NRA, came the increasing domination of AAA by the more prosperous farmers, the shift in TVA from regional planning into a "corporation for the production of power and fertilizer," the defeat of the attempt to make RFC "an instrument of governmental capital allocation," and the decision to put unemployment compensation on a Federal-State rather than a national program basis. What was involved, then, was a retreat from a fledgling collectivism, an attempt (however weak) at planning. For Schlesinger, the second New Deal represented the two steps slipped backward after the timid step foreward. Whatever Brandeis' devotion to reform, he "was speaking for an America that was dead. His words were morally bracing but socially futile." Attempting to skirt the pit that had entrapped earlier historians, Schlesinger said of the second New Deal: "The basic conservatism of its economics was disguised by the aggressive radicalism of its politics."

Certain qualifications went along with this re-interpretation. While Schlesinger cited the concurring opinions of Charles Beard and Hugh Johnson, who at the time of the change had both branded the second New Deal a backward step (a "throw-back, Johnson snapped), he re-printed in the "Notes" to Chapter XXI a letter of demurrer from Leon Keyserling. Further, Schlesinger, admitted that not all of the second New Deal was tired doctrine; the Brandeisians made common cause—however reluctantly—with the Keynesians or "Spenders," and deficit spending of the sort resorted to in 1938 represented something new on the American scene. The Harvard historian noted, as well, that the degree of unanimity within the first New Deal was generally exaggerated. Still, on balance, his judgment was decisive; there had been an important shift in 1935, a change of tack that left behind one body of theories inherited from the reform tradition, and replaced it with another. The change was not a salutory one. "In the end, the basic change in 1935 was in atmosphere—a certain lowering of ideals, waning of hopes, narrowing of possibilities, a sense that things were, not opening out, but closing in." The second New Deal, "ostensibly more radical but essentially more conservative," reflecting an upturn in the economy and a loss of boldness born of emergency, was a return to the safe and the traditional.

Thus the sixteen years since the appearance of Rauch's pioneering study had seen the parallel, but uneven, growth of two views of the New Deals. The question of the nature of both phases of Rooseveltian reform broadens out to include the problem of what is truly progressive in American progressivism.

PAUL CONKIN

The New Deal
[1967]

Reprinted below is a brief section from Paul Conkin's book The New
Deal, *in which he discusses Schlesinger's use of the word "prag-
matism" in describing the New Deal, and a short discussion of* The
Age of Roosevelt *drawn from Conkin's bibliographical essay.*

Roosevelt's beliefs, though broad and unexamined, were never
equivocal. In fact, few men have exhibited as complete a continuity
of belief as Roosevelt. Not only did he refuse to accept new systems
of belief, but he rarely understood them fully. When he applauded
Christians and Democrats, he assumed everyone, at his best, was included. He sincerely commended both Jefferson and Jesus, without
trying to understand the complexity of either man. Atheism was beyond his ken. New political ideologies surely reflected evil instead
of possible alternatives. His opponents were either won over by persuasion or dismissed as traitors. He simply never had the type of
intellectual discrimination to understand fundamental but subtle philosophical differences. But his beliefs, so ill-defined, so lacking in structure, were generously assumed to include almost anyone. He never
concerned himself with nuances, with careful definitions. But he was
not so generous at the level of power. Here he could be as ruthless
and as intolerant as the occasion demanded, since he always too easily
felt that he worked in behalf of the vast majority of righteous people.

Above all, Roosevelt was not a pragmatist. In Arthur M. Schlesinger's *Age of Roosevelt,* Vols. I, II and III (New York, 1957–1960),
and in a less insistent way in almost every book about Roosevelt, he
has been referred to as a pragmatist, but never with a very precise or

From *The New Deal* (New York, Thomas Y. Crowell, 1967), 11–13, 110–
11. Reprinted by permission of the author. Copyright © 1967 by Thomas Y.
Crowell Company, Inc.
Paul Conkin teaches history at the University of Wisconsin.

philosophically correct use of the word. If the term "pragmatism" has any specific meaning, it is as a very loose label for a major philosophical movement, which originated in the moral and esthetic thought of Puritanism and Transcendentalism and in the epistemological innovations of Charles S. Pierce, which acquired a psychology and other suggestive, if confused, ideas from William James, and which climaxed in the neo-Hegelian system of John Dewey. For pragmatists, the method of inquiry, although developed in a very complex and technical fashion, was only a prelude to intense moral, religious, and, most important, esthetic concerns and, beyond these, a distinctive and very pious stance toward Being or Nature. Thus defined, pragmatism represented the most comprehensive, and possibly the most difficult, of modern philosophical movements. In his traditional attitudes and beliefs, his lack of philosophical concern, his generalized but simplistic religion, his lack of esthetic sensitivity, Roosevelt was the very antithesis of pragmatic.

Because of its vast scope, pragmatism incorporated some beliefs that almost everyone shared (including Roosevelt), but these took on quite a definite and subtle meaning in the context of the whole philosophic outlook, and all rooted in a distinctive metaphysical position called radical empiricism. There is nothing to indicate that Roosevelt ever studied pragmatism or even came close to understanding it. Few people have, and nothing in his intellectual makeup invited such a strenuous effort. Even the idea of experimentation, as articulated by Dewey and implied in modern science, does not relate to Roosevelt's haphazard, theoretically attenuated programs. His rejection of formal and theoretical ideas was close to the anti-intellectualism and common sense of most active men but bore no relationship to the technical interplay of reason and experience in the pragmatic conception of inquiry. In fact, Roosevelt was most unpragmatic in not appreciating the vital instrumental role of formal thought. Only if pragmatism becomes a poor synonym for practicality (a term ambiguous enough for anyone) can Roosevelt, by some miracle of historical inexactitude, become a pragmatist. Even his acclaimed willingness to learn by experience (not distinctive to pragmatism by any means) has been overemphasized. In very few cases did he ever repudiate any of his past choices or frankly admit the failure of one of his policies. This is not to deny the large number of pragmatists or near pragmatists who were in the New Deal and who helped shape the policies of some agencies. But, as a whole, they envisioned much more sweeping reforms than Roosevelt ever desired or supported. John Dewey, the grand old man of the movement, was always a persistent and penetrating critic of the New Deal. . . .

In both scope and literary appeal, the major study of the New Deal is now underway by Arthur M. Schlesinger, Jr. His three completed volumes of the *Age of Roosevelt*—I. *The Crisis of the Old Order;* II. *The Coming of the New Deal;* III. *The Politics of Upheaval* (New York, 1957–1960)—exploit almost all the dramatic possibilities of the New Deal. Frankly and deliberately partisan, Schlesinger nevertheless accepts a scholarly discipline and incorporates abundant and valuable factual detail, much nowhere else available. His forte is brilliant characterization, heightened by a moralistic tendency to fit his sharp vignettes into alternative galleries of heroes and rogues. Throughout he uses a common-sense, simplistic, interpretative scheme which apotheosizes Roosevelt's type of nontheoretic expedient leadership. Schlesinger incorrectly identifies this distaste for disciplined intelligence and formal thought with experimentalism and pragmatism.

HERBERT FEIS

~~~~~~

The Road
to Pearl Harbor
[1950]

PAUL SCHROEDER

~~~~~~

The Axis Alliance
and Japanese-American
Relations, 1941
[1958]

FOLLOWING AMERICAN INVOLVEMENT in each of the World
Wars there has emerged a group of historians who argued,
usually with some bitterness, that American participation
was tragically unnecessary and unwise. This revisionism has
been attributed to a number of factors: it is a part of the inevitable public reaction against the war once it is seen that
the promises held out to those who fight, promises of eternal
peace and security following victory, were greatly inflated;
it is a part of the isolationist counterattack against entering
the war at all, and it comes after the war only because books
take a while to produce; or it is a reflection of a return to
sanity among intellectuals who regretted having set aside
their usual pacifism and skepticism to support just this one
final war and who do penance by writing lucid accounts, in
retrospect, of how foolish the whole thing was. Revisionists
have not set a high standard of cool, detached, "scholarly"
prose. They are usually either highly excited or downright
furious (no wonder, given their assumptions; a number of
fine young men died for nothing, as they see it, and to their
credit they find it difficult to remain calm), and some cannot
resist a concept of unusual explanatory power—treason.

Although the revisionist school after World War I produced a body of writing not only of considerable size but in
a number of cases of impressive quality, most historians
with an interest in these subjects tend to regard revisionism
with some disdain. In the revisionist ranks one finds a high
proportion of isolationists, moralists, idealists, and quasi-
pacifists, and while these are attitudes easily tolerated or
even admired in the ministry, they are not highly regarded
among modern diplomatic historians. The style of these
scholars since 1945 has been pragmatic, realistic, tough; they
understand the need for military readiness, for an active, re-

Herbert Feis, *The Road to Pearl Harbor: The Coming of War
Between the United States and Japan* (Princeton, Princeton Uni-
versity Press, 1950. Paper: Atheneum). Paul W. Schroeder, *The
Axis Alliance and Japanese-American Relations, 1941* (Ithaca,
Cornell University Press, 1958).

sourceful foreign policy, for shouldering our responsibilities around the world. They can understand the wistful touch of isolationism in World War I revisionists, and occasionally read those books, although they are not persuaded by the arguments against Wilson's decision to intervene. But the revisionist position in World War II seems inexcusable to the average historian of the postwar period. How many times must history demonstrate the fact of America's world involvement before reasonably intelligent men will face reality?

Thus the revisionists who wrote after World War II have had nothing like the influence of those who criticized Wilsonian policy in the 1920s and 1930s. Their major work is probably not known to most readers: Charles Beard's *President Roosevelt and the Coming of War, 1941*, Charles C. Tansill's *The Back Door to War*, some of the essays in that wide-ranging book edited by Harry Elmer Barnes, *Perpetual War for Perpetual Peace*.[1] The failure of this body of work to convince most intelligent readers (and scholars have probably been even more critical than the reading public) has not, of course, been simply a matter of their accusatory tone, the partiality some of them have shown for the conspiracy theory of Pearl Harbor, or the fact that their sentiments about war and international activism were markedly more negative than those of most people in the postwar years. The principal reason was—and, is—that revisionist criticism of Roosevelt's diplomacy was simply not as strong a case as Walter Millis, Tansill, Barnes, Borchard and Lage, and others had been able to marshall against Wilson in books they published in the 1920s and 1930s. There are many points that could be made here, but the chief difference is of course that a much stronger case can be made that the vital interests of the United States were menaced in 1939–1941 than can be made for 1914–1917. It has seemed to virtually everyone that the best and truest histories were those written by Langer and Gleason, Donald Drummond, Basil Rauch, Herbert Feis, and Robert Divine [2]—books which, while varying

[1] Beard (New Haven, Yale University Press, 1948); Tansill (Chicago, Henry Regnery, 1952); Barnes (Caldwell, Idaho, Claxton Press, 1953).
[2] William L. Langer and S. Everett Gleason, *The Challenge to Isolation, 1937–1940* (New York, Harper, 1952), and *The Un-*

in detail, see Roosevelt's willingness to arm, support Britain, and run the risks of war against the Fascist dictatorships as the only wise and possible course of action.

The best of these studies for the Pacific area is Herbert Feis' much-respected and even much-read book, *The Road to Pearl Harbor*. Feis' account, based on extensive research in both Japanese and American archives and private manuscript collections, offers that solid procession of relevant detail which scholars always hope for, but manages also to sustain a high sense of tension and drama, and to project a very appealing dual sympathy. A few critics complained that Feis paid insufficient attention to the social forces behind foreign policy—economic, political, and psychological pressures in Japanese society, American economic interests in Asia, public opinion in both countries, the structure of party politics—and pointed out that only a "diplomatic" historian, preoccupied as he is with cables, State Department papers, military reports and other "official" paper, would have commenced a study of Japanese–American relations in the year 1937. In this way they were undoubtedly on firm ground, but much the same criticism could unfortunately be said for most diplomatic history. Feis, former State Department official and the author of ten fine books in the field of American foreign relations, was credited with having written what must long be regarded as the standard account of Japanese–American relations in the period just prior to the outbreak of war—an account which was superior in both technique and judgment.

Yet if Feis had in the end written a book which placed the blame for war at the door of (a few of) the Japanese,

---

declared War, 1940–1941 (New York, Harper, 1953); Donald Drummond, *The Passing of American Neutrality, 1937–1941* (Ann Arbor, University of Michigan Press, 1955); Basil Rauch, *Roosevelt from Munich to Pearl Harbor* (New York, Creative Age Press, 1950). This book, written to counter Beard, is probably the most favorable treatment the Roosevelt policies will ever get. Herbert Feis, *The Road to Pearl Harbor;* and Robert Divine, *The Reluctant Belligerent* (New York, John Wiley, 1965). Probably the best article offering this general view is Dexter Perkins, "Was Roosevelt Wrong?", *Virginia Quarterly Review,* 30 (Summer 1954), 355–72.

there was evidence along the way which might have led him to a different interpretation. Beard, Barnes, and the revisionists found Roosevelt and Hull devious, mendacious, and bent upon war (in FDR's case) at least partially for political reasons. Feis did not agree, but he did find American policy, at crucial points, unusually uncompromising. He did not make much of this; others, on an island near China, were more unreasonable. Yet some historians, not "hard" revisionists, have argued for a viewpoint which is nonetheless quite critical of American policy. Ambassador Joseph Grew gave this view its first and classic expression when he argued, in diplomatic cables and years later in his autobiography, that war could have been avoided if the President and Hull had not insisted on immediate Japanese withdrawal from China.[3] A number of historians have agreed with Grew, but none put the argument so impressively as did Paul Schroeder in his *The Axis Alliance and Japanese–American Relations, 1941.*[4]

Schroeder's book is titled as a study of the Japanese–German Pact of September, 1940, but its argument that the pact was by the summer of 1941 no longer a barrier to Japanese–American understanding served only as a step to his larger thesis. The Roosevelt administration, he argued, knew by June, 1941, that it was within reach of an agreement with Japan to nullify the Axis Alliance and abandon the drive southward toward the Dutch East Indies, in return for certain economic guarantees and diplomatic assurances. But Washington decided to insist also upon an immediate Japanese withdrawal from China, and held rigidly to this position through the Fall, declining Prince Konoye's offer of

[3] Joseph Grew, *Turbulent Era,* ed. Walter Johnson (Boston, Houghton Mifflin, 2 vols., 1952). The review of Feis by Richard Van Alstyne, below, perceives Feis' ambivalence about Hull.

[4] Others pointing out the rigidity of American policy were Francis C. Jones, *Japan's New Order in East Asia: Its Rise and Fall* (Toronto, Oxford University Press, 1954), and Akira Iriye, "Japanese Imperialism and Aggression: Reconsiderations," *Journal of Asian Studies,* 23 (November 1963), 103–15. Iriye's article is a valuable review of recent Japanese scholarship. In his *Journey to the 'Missouri'* (New Haven, Yale University Press, 1950), Toshikazu Kase, a Japanese moderate, provides support for Grew's speculations about the potential strength of moderate elements.

talks with the President on Guam, until the Japanese decided in December to choose war over humiliation. Schroeder, as he made explicit, was making basically the same indictment which Ambassador Grew had offered in his postwar writing, a realist critique of American diplomacy in the Pacific. The crucial issues between Japan and the United States were resolvable that summer, he felt, and war came primarily because Roosevelt and Hull (with the strong support of many others in the inner circle of advisors, such as Secretary of War Stimson and Secretary of the Treasury Morgenthau) took an unbending position on China, where American vital interests were not at stake but Japanese interests were deeply engaged. This was done not because Roosevelt and Hull were eager for war, but because they, and the country behind them, were inclined toward a moralistic diplomacy. America's imperialistic past was totally forgotten, Japan's imperialistic future totally condemned. Schroeder thus underlined that the war was fought over China, a perspective which in itself strongly sustains the suspicion that someone was not thinking very clearly. As did Grew, Schroeder assumed that more time —which we could easily have obtained—could have allowed both sides to observe the drift of the European conflict. If it went badly for Germany, the Japanese would have confirmed their retreat on the Axis Alliance and the southward drive, and ultimately abandoned their determination to "win" in China. If not, the United States had bought time to rearm.

Schroeder's book did not offer an entirely new view, but it was the best presentation of the view of the soft revisionists, critical of American policy yet free of suggestions that the administration desired war with Japan. The points of contrast between the Schroeder (Grew, Jones, et al.) interpretation and that offered by Feis (Langer and Gleason, Drummond, Rauch, et al.) may not be readily apparent to the nonspecialist, since historians almost never directly confront prior arguments in any controlled way. But in these two books—and in these two general schools—one is offered two descriptions of American policy, one emphasizing its defensiveness and reasonableness, the other its (typically American) inability to distinguish between areas of vital interests and areas where it could not and should not hope to exercise a predominant influence; and two descriptions of the

Japanese ruling classes, one emphasizing the potential strength of moderate elements, the other reluctantly convinced that by 1940–1941 one dealt with men who understood only force. We can agree, of course, that both sides miscalculated, and—although neither of these authors stresses the point— that there was precious little energy deployed in the last few months on either side toward finding that compromise which we can now theoretically construct, and that there was a great deal of fatalism and moral weariness on both sides which inclined statesmen to let these incredibly thorny issues slide into the hands of the generals and admirals. The larger questions are still unanswerable. Were there the political raw materials within Japan which a differently shaped and timed American policy might have nursed into a government willing and able to liquidate the Chinese venture short of victory, and shrink Japanese ambitions until they became acceptable to the older imperial powers? Did power realities in the United States—Congressional and public opinion, military and economic pressures—allow Franklin Roosevelt enough discretion, both in the direction of a credible firmness or a timely concession to power realities, so that he might pursue that wiser, flexible diplomacy which both Feis and Schroeder, each in different ways, would have wished? Neither man, nor indeed any other writer, has yet produced sufficient information of the sort we need to answer these questions and begin to narrow this debate toward the possibility of a broad agreement.

HERBERT FEIS
The Road to Pearl Harbor
[1950]

CRITICAL COMMENTARIES

EDWIN O. REISCHAUER

[1951]

Herbert Feis has done a remarkably clear and complete job of mapping for us every twist and turn of "the road to Pearl Harbor." The decade since this road was traveled has laid bare most of its secrets. Mr. Feis had access to the State Department archives, the Stimson, Morgenthau, and Grew diaries, and selections from the Roosevelt papers, and had the opportunity to talk at length with many of the Americans involved in the negotiations which preceded the outbreak of war with Japan. On the Japanese side he had the records of the International Military Tribunal at Tokyo, the records of the similar

From *American Historical Review,* 56, 3 (April 1951), 617–18. Reprinted by permission of the American Historical Association.

Edwin O. Reischauer, former U.S. Ambassador to Japan (1961–1966), is a professor of history and international relations at Harvard University.

230

tribunal at Nuremberg, and the very revealing Kido and Saionji–Harada diaries, as well as other documents and studies. In time new materials may come to light, but there is little probability that they will alter the story appreciably.

Mr. Feis starts his recitation in 1937, but he makes it particularly full after April, 1940. He presents as complete and detailed an account of diplomatic maneuverings of the next twenty months as most students of history will wish to read, giving a full and well-documented account of what was said and done and, whenever possible, what the principle actors recorded as their actual thoughts. No one will feel that Mr. Feis has slighted his subject. The only objection can be to the dreary repetition of the same thoughts and same speeches by a limited *dramatis personae*. All that is left in question are the exact motives of some of the actors in their minor decisions, but never in the major stands they took, and the fascinating but fruitless question of what would have happened if something different had been done at each stage. But such problems will still remain no matter how many scholars may study this same subject in the future.

Mr. Feis rarely injects himself into the book, preferring to leave the reader to his own decisions. His occasional judgments, however, appear to be both stimulating and sound. He thinks that in 1937 the Western Powers had their last good chance to stop Japan short of a major war, but that this chance was lost when "the only concurrent action taken was to do nothing." [p. 9] The later efforts to stop Japan he feels were doomed to failure. He sides with Hull against Morgenthau in feeling that the stronger action advocated by the latter in 1940 would have "caused Japan to move farther and faster." [p. 107] And, while admitting that Hull's arguments were "dull and inflexible," he believes that Grew and Dooman were too sanguine in their hopes that something would come of the Konoye–Roosevelt meeting proposed in the summer and early autumn of 1941. [p. 274]

Mr. Feis stays very close to the diplomatic road he has chosen to map. He describes each recurring rut in the conversations—each repetition of American principles and of the mystically phrased ambitions of the Japanese leaders. But he pays little attention to the lay of the land which determined each major turn in the road as it led closer and closer to the chasm of war. We learn how crucial oil was—how its denial to Japan was the one sure weapon the Western Powers had against Japan and how this denial forced Japan into the final decision for war. But we do not learn why or how the Japanese came to be embarked on their dangerous course of conquest. We hear of the deep divisions within the Japanese government but nothing of the forces which produced these divisions. Even the dynamics of American politics, with its crosscurrents of isolationism and interventionism, needs explanation. One cannot read Mr. Feis's book without being impressed with the futility of the whole weary course of the diplomatic negotiations. Ambassadors, foreign ministers, prime ministers, and President alike appear to be mere puppets, waving their hands and speaking their pieces with vigor, but carried along by forces over which they have no control. Mr. Feis has told us with ample detail and scrupulous accuracy what happened in the field of diplomacy, but he has not really attempted to explain why it happened. That has been his self-imposed limitation, but within it he has written a book which should remain for some time the standard account of the diplomatic relations leading up to the war with Japan.

M. MATSUO
[1951]

Dr. Feis's scholarly, yet eminently readable, study of the situation presented by the deterioration in relations between the governments of the United States and Japan in the years before the attack on Pearl Harbor is an important contribution to the history of that critical period. His account of the actions of key personages and of the interplay of domestic and international political factors is of absorbing interest. Even readers who gave close attention to those developments as they occurred are likely to encounter many unsuspected and revealing facets in this book—a significant indication of how foreign policy is formulated and executed without effective reference to the broad mass of the people concerned.

From *Pacific Affairs,* 24 (September 1951), 320–21. Reprinted by permission of *Pacific Affairs.*
    M. Matsuo is the National Secretary of the Japan Institute of Pacific Relations, Tokyo.

Dr. Feis's account of United States policy, which he has based on numerous official documents, memoirs, interviews, and personal experience in the Department of State during the period in question, appears sound on the whole, although the reviewer is not in a position to evaluate all of the material cited. One wonders, however, whether in appraising the determinants of the foreign policy of a democratic country like the United States, it might not have been helpful to give more detailed consideration to such factors as public opinion and Congressional attitudes, passive though their roles seem to have been.

In dealing with the formulation and execution of Japanese policy relating to the diplomatic negotiations with the United States, Dr. Feis employs a similar method, basing his interpretation on official documents, depositions of Japanese defendants and witnesses before the International Military Tribunal for the Far East, the private diaries of Marquis Kido and Baron Harada, and Prince Konoye's private papers. In considering Japan, however, this method is less effective because, although in the oligarchy that existed before the surrender the opinions and actions of those in power were far more decisive determinants of national policy than would have been possible in a democratic country, their attitudes and behavior cannot be properly understood unless these are considered in the context of prevailing political and social conditions. It would have been extremely helpful, therefore, particularly to readers unfamiliar with the state of affairs in prewar Japan, if Dr. Feis had afforded even a very brief explanation of the background against which the Japanese statesmen and militarists had to formulate national policy. Alternatively, he might have referred such readers to other books that do so.

In general, the account of events is documented less satisfactorily on the Japanese side than on the American. While not wishing to belittle the importance of the materials already referred to, on which Dr. Feis chiefly relies, the reviewer believes that recourse to other sources in addition would have been useful in accounting for various aspects of Japan's prewar course of action. Thus, although in comparison to their Western counterparts, Japanese political and military leaders are for the most part inferior memoirists, yet such prominent prewar leaders as Issei Ugaki, Seihin Ikeda, Reijiro Wakatsuki, Hachiro Arita, Kichisaburo Nomura and Saburo Kurusu —to mention only a few—have already published their memoirs. Parenthetically, it may be noted that many other persons of former prominence in national affairs are still living and may possibly be inclined in future to express their thoughts more freely than they have hitherto done, thus clarifying certain phases of prewar Japanese–American relations. Certainly, much ground remains to be explored, at least on the Japanese side. It may be some years before a reasonably full, critical study is made; the project is one in which collaboration between Western and Japanese scholars might prove fruitful.

Aside from this general impression, Japanese readers will notice the misspelling of the names of certain well-known individuals and organizations, such as Nagai (Miziko) for Nagai (Matsuzo) [p. 29], Shumpeitai for Shimpeitai [p. 78], Hocho for Hochi [p. 119], Wikawa for Ikawa [p. 175], and General Hoshino for a noted civilian bureaucrat, Naoki Hoshino. [p. 291]

In summary, then, Dr. Feis has made a useful addition to public knowledge of an important phase of international relations before the last war. He has, indeed, done more than this: his book has vital contemporary significance because it presents a thoughtful, solidly-documented account of a "failure of diplomacy"—not a failure of the diplomacy of any particular country, but the failure of diplomacy as a means of peaceful regulation of international relations. The book contains much food for thought at a time when, ten years after the attack on Pearl Harbor, the world is once again confronted with the threat of a general war and is still dependent on international procedures that were not conspicuously effective a decade ago.

RICHARD W. VAN ALSTYNE
[*1951*]

Mr. Feis's work differs considerably from its predecessors in that it is an analysis of both Japanese and American policies between the years 1937 and 1941. Through sources not hitherto available, he is able to hold up to the reader a double mirror in which the problems

From *Far Eastern Quarterly*, 11 (November 1951), 107–09. Reprinted by permission of *Far Eastern Quarterly*.

Richard Van Alstyne teaches history and international relations at the University of the Pacific.

and issues as viewed first in Tokyo and then in Washington may be studied. Differences of opinion and conflicts over policies that took place within the governments of both countries are given close attention, and decisions taken in Tokyo are made to synchronize with measures decided upon in Washington. Because of this breadth and thoroughness of treatment, Mr. Feis's book will undoubtedly be without a peer for some time to come.

The point of departure is the Brussels Conference, "a funeral rather than a birth." Meanwhile a secret agreement attached to the Anti-Comintern Pact between Japan and Germany in the preceding year provided for cooperation against Russia. Within the American government the demand for strong measures against Japan, especially for an embargo on oil, came chiefly from the Treasury Department under Morgenthau, who formulated a plan for collaboration with Britain as early as July 1940, while Hull was absent at Havana. A draft of an executive order drawn up by Morgenthau in the following December and providing for the freezing of funds was so worded that, if signed by the President, "Morgenthau would become the works, Hull the front" of American foreign policy. Of the Japanese–German alliance of the preceding September, Hull took the view that it meant that Japan would soon strike southward against Indo-China; but, supported by Welles and Maxwell Hamilton against Hornbeck and Norman Davis, the secretary insisted on caution. One immediate effect of the Tripartite Pact, however, was the opening in November 1940 of staff talks with the British regarding strategic cooperation between the two powers in the Far East. Germany in the meantime tried her hand at mediating between Chiang Kai-shek and the Japanese; but the Chinese united with the British, Australians and Dutch in urging Washington to join with them in economic action against Japan. Ambassador Nomura's mission to Washington during the ensuing year is given full attention, and the reader is left with the impression that Nomura had some influence in delaying the American decision, reached by July 23 after long hesitation and internal division of opinion, to freeze Japanese funds. Whether the freezing order of July 26 meant a complete embargo remained even then in doubt until the committee set up to administer the order decided the matter *de facto* by refusing to issue licenses. This committee, made up of three lawyers from the State, Treasury and Justice Departments, appears in the last analysis to have decided the matter, not merely for the United States but for the Dutch and British as well.

Meanwhile opinion inside the government at Tokyo remained

tortured on the dilemma of how to use the Tripartite Pact and the Non-Aggression Pact with Soviet Russia. Prince Konoye urged repudiation of the Pact and an agreement with the United States on the basis of Japan's having a free hand in China and Indo-China in exchange for a pledge of neutrality in Europe. Tojo, however, insisted that Germany would win and Japan would then get her chance to gain all she wanted, including the Russian maritime provinces. The decision to invade southern Indo-China was made on July 2 on the assumption that Germany would win over both Britain and Russia before the winter. The United States, it was hoped, would not retaliate; but to meet eventualities the Japanese army and navy at once began preparations for war, including practice for the Pearl Harbor attack.

The freezing order of July 26 caused Prince Konoye, with the support of the Navy, to seek a personal meeting with Roosevelt. Ambassador Grew was a strong advocate of such a meeting, but his recommendations on this as well as on other matters carried little weight in Washington. Hull, "the man of rigid doctrine," persuaded Roosevelt against the meeting. If a compromise was to be reached, it had to be done before the end of November: Japan's rivals in the southwest Pacific were growing steadily stronger, the economic plight of Japan was getting stringent, and the best months for Japanese landing operations in the south were October and November. The alternatives which the desperate Japanese faced by November were either a foreign war or a civil war.

A number of criticisms of Mr. Feis's book seem justified. In the reviewer's judgment, he struggled for but fell somewhat short of the viewpoint of the long perspective. American diplomacy, we are led to believe, was at fault because of its rigidity. There is implied criticism of the prosiness of Hull's successive notes to Tokyo, repeating abstract principles "like a litany to the very hour of war." And Japan in 1941 could not execute a simple withdrawal from China, as Hull thought she should, without the direst consequences internal and external. After building up evidence to justify these conclusions, the author suddenly reverses himself and pronounces a sweeping *ad hoc* opinion against Japan for not capitulating to the Hull demands of November 26. To the Japanese mind, he says, compliance "amounted to national suicide." Yet Feis, suddenly turned moralist, declares [p. 327] that this "was not a valid attitude. The idea that compliance with the American terms would have meant 'extinction' for Japan, or so deeply hurt it that it could not guard its just interests, is an absurdity. . . . Its independence was not in peril. . . ." What is this but a precipitate re-treat to "the litany" of Hull? Nor does Feis seem disposed to question the wisdom of the American support of the Chinese National Government, much less to look critically at the propaganda activities of Chiang Kai-shek and his advocates in the United States. The American romance with Chiang, it would seem, deserves a chapter in a book on the coming of the war.

The Kurusu mission is not treated objectively. Here the author has accepted all of Hull's prejudices. Kurusu went to Washington to get a *modus vivendi,* one part of which was to the effect that Japan would at once withdraw from southern Indo-China. As an excuse for rejecting the proposition out of hand, Hull said that the truce would still leave Japan a member of the Axis pact. "To this," declares Feis [p. 310], "Kurusu had no answer." To this reviewer, a draft letter handed by Kurusu to the secretary on November 21 (*Foreign Relations: Japan, 1931–1941,* II, 756–57) reads very much like a repudiation of that pact. Nor is Hull's singular conduct during the next five days given much of an airing: the preparation of a note offering Japan a *modus vivendi* calculated to stave off hostilities for at least three months; the preparation of a ten-point note intended to be delivered simultaneously with the *modus vivendi* proposal; the submission of the Japanese proposal and of the proposed American *modus vivendi* to the British, Australian, Dutch and Chinese envoys, but the failure to show them a copy of the ten-point note; the frantic appeals of Chiang, who conceived he was about to be deserted, and the decision of Hull to give up the idea of a *modus vivendi.* Hull's delivery to the Japanese envoys of the ten-point note, coupled with a gruff rejection of a plea from Kurusu for a *modus vivendi,* closed all doors to compromise. Yet Roosevelt's last minute appeal of December 6 to the Emperor was in effect a return to the *modus vivendi.*

The book has serious faults of diction. Grammatical slips are not uncommon. The author has an irritating fondness for treating dependent clauses as whole sentences, and occasionally he resorts to slang. His figures of speech are sometimes brilliant, but their frequency leaves the reader with the feelings of their being forced. The work is a tool book primarily, if not exclusively, for the use of scholars, yet Feis gives the impression of making gestures in the direction of readers of *Time* magazine. One can ascertain the sources from the footnotes, but a bibliography would help.

JOHN E. WILTZ

From Isolation to War, 1931–1941
[1968]

The historian Herbert Feis has viewed the Brussels conference as a modern tragedy: "The last good chance to work out a stable settlement between China and Japan was lost in 1937." Still, it is hard to see what the conferees might have done. Isolationism and military weakness precluded coercive action by the United States. That left one option: a negotiated settlement legitimizing Japan's position in Manchuria, North China, and Shanghai. Given the temper of Americans—strong sympathy for China, hostility toward Japan—it would seem that the United States could not have acquiesced in such an arrangement. And without American concurrence any agreement would have been meaningless. Ambassador Grew probably made the best appraisal of the conference when he wrote in his diary . . . that the meeting never should have convened. It had been evident from the start that delegates "could never in the world agree to take *effective* measures" and would only encourage Japanese militarists by exhibiting the "lack of unity and impotence of the Powers." Grew then asked: "Why can't statesmen think things through?" . . .

If Japanese moves in Southeast Asia had touched off the crisis in Japanese–American relations in 1941, it was clear by autumn 1941 that China was a main obstacle to settlement in the Far East. Paul W. Schroeder (*The Axis Alliance and Japanese–American Relations*) believes this was unfortunate and unnecessary. He writes that down to July 1941 the United States had "sought to attain two limited objectives in the Far East, those of splitting the Axis and of stopping Japan's advance southward." Both objectives, Schroeder thinks, were

From *From Isolation to War: 1931–1941* (New York, Thomas Y. Crowell, 1968), 64, 122–23. Reprinted by permission of the author. Copyright © 1968 by Thomas Y. Crowell Company, Inc.

John E. Wiltz teaches history at Indiana University.

within reach. Then, "on the verge of a major diplomatic victory, the United States abandoned her original goals and concentrated on a third, the liberation of China." According to Schroeder, "this last aim was not in accord with American strategic interests" and "was completely incapable of being achieved by peaceful means."

One may make several observations about Schroeder's argument. First, Japanese leaders never intimated that they might consider a settlement without reference to China. Proposals emanating from the Foreign Office consistently listed resolution of the "China incident" as a condition of any agreement with the United States, and when the special envoy to Washington, Saburo Kurusu, proposed a truce in November 1941 that would have left the China question in abeyance he received a sharp rebuke from Tokyo. Also, American leaders were less committed to the idea of liberating China than Schroeder suggests. Kurusu's overtures sparked interest in Washington and late in November 1941 Secretary Hull drafted a proposal for a *modus vivendi* similar to that outlined by the Japanese envoy. "Magic" having reported the Tokyo's government's rebuke to Kurusu, Hull concluded that such a proposal had no chance, and in face of rumors that he and Roosevelt were considering a "sellout" of China dropped the idea. . . .

JOHN T. FARRELL
[1952]

Mr. Feis is an obviously friendly witness when it becomes a question of interpreting American policy in the Far East before Pearl Harbor. His work will not meet with approval on the part of those who have been the severe critics of the late President Roosevelt or his advisers; nevertheless, these critics may conceivably be put upon their mettle to produce a work as temperate, judicious, and well docu-

From *The Catholic Historical Review,* 37 (January 1952), 477–79. Reprinted with permission from The Catholic University of America Press.

John T. Farrell is professor of history at the Catholic University, Washington, D.C.

mented as this book. Perhaps, an offer to try could open to others what was made available to this former official of the Department of State, and the argument might then develop on a much higher level than heretofore. What makes the present work attractive is that it does raise the dispute over diplomacy from the level of insinuations about personal motives, and the author is quite willing to consider the possibility of error in the American position. Indeed, if the order of time were reversed, if the history could have been written as we have it here before the consequences, Mr. Feis' book could have served as an argument for peaceful adjustment and the avoidance of war in the Pacific area.

A point of departure for such an argument would be the implied evidence of Japan's marked though not complete independence of Axis ties in the period between the German invasion of Russia (June 22, 1941) and the fall of the Prince Konoye cabinet (October 16). It is hard to resist the impression, even if Mr. Feis is successful in doing so, that all of the Japanese leaders, including Tojo, were convinced that a retreat was in order, and that they might even have modified their position on the China Incident, if only we had not (and this was Ambassador Grew's reasoning) lacked insight, suppleness, and maybe even the desire to reach an accord. We were already pinching the empire's arteries of trade severely, and as the author paraphrases Grew's opinion: "Wise American statesmanship, thus, would have bartered adjustment for adjustment, agreeing to relax on economic restraints little by little as Japan, little by little, went our way. Instead [the statesmanship] was dull and inflexible." Mr. Feis admits [p. 275] that these words constitute a reasonable position, but to them he opposes the statement that such measures would not have been adequate in order to impose upon Japan "the terms for which we had stood since 1931." Half a loaf taken might have avoided a two-ocean war; and what happened to the whole loaf at Yalta, where the integrity of China was bargained away for Russian promises, was a bitter, if unnecessary, consequence which may indicate that the officials concerned thought very little of the 1931 terms as such. Besides, what one has heard frequently since that time is that diplomacy must be tried even if there is no assurance of success. The unhappy climax to the Konoye attempts to reach an agreement was the refusal on the part of Roosevelt, in August, to meet the Japanese prime minister for a personal interview.

Another point, not so much stressed by Mr. Feis, but always there for the reader to discern, is the pressure which was exerted on

Secretary of State Hull by the other cabinet members, Stimson, Morgenthau, and Ickes, and these were backed up by Stanley K. Hornbeck who was the Department of State adviser on political relations, to the end that every proposal made by the Japanese was construed in the most pessimistic way, and every suggestion of bargaining was condemned beforehand as appeasement. Such were the attitudes taken in the department, at the very beginning of the long Hull-Nomura conversations, toward the original subject matter supplied by the private intermediaries, Bishop James E. Walsh, Superior General of the Catholic Foreign Mission Society at Maryknoll, and Father James M. Drought of the same society, these two having gained access to the administration through Postmaster-General Frank C. Walker. It would be a mild judgment upon our former Secretary of State to say that he seems to have been as helpless as was Prince Konoye in dealing with more belligerent colleagues. But Hull was more adept at clinging to office.

This is an extremely worthwhile addition to our diplomatic history. Other scholars will now wish to follow Mr. Feis, to go through, as he did, the originals, not just the published fragments, of the Stimson and Morgenthau diaries, the Department of State records, to have unlimited access to the Roosevelt Papers, and to consider these along with the Japanese materials which were made of record by the International Military Tribunal for the Far East. They will be indebted to Mr. Feis for his broad survey based upon all of these significant materials.

PAUL SCHROEDER
The Axis Alliance and
Japanese-American Relations, 1941
[1958]

CRITICAL COMMENTARIES

DAVID LINDSEY
[1959]

Winner of the American Historical Association's Beveridge Award for 1956, Paul Schroeder's volume is a welcome and valuable addition to the growing shelf of works dealing with the origins of World War II. Traversing much of the ground already covered by Langer and Gleason, Feis, Rauch, Beard, and others, this study subjects the available evidence to a searchingly penetrating analysis. Japanese–American relations for the crucial twelve months preceding Pearl Harbor are probed with meticulous care and refreshing candor.

From *World Affairs Quarterly,* 30 (July 1959), 191–92. Reprinted by permission of *World Affairs Quarterly.*
David Lindsey teaches history at California State College, Los Angeles.

Although the title suggests that Japan's adherence to the Axis Alliance forms the work's chief focus, the volume covers a broader range. Scrutinizing Japanese–American relations in 1941, the author demonstrates convincingly that the Axis Pact, so far as it concerned Japan and the United States, was largely a dead letter by the summer of 1941 and played virtually no part in determining the course of Japanese negotiations with the United States.

Rejecting the "back-door-to-war" thesis as well as the view that war was America's only effective response to Japan's aggressive policy in the Far East, Schroeder offers a third view. In a cogent, tightly reasoned argument he contends that more astute and flexible American negotiation in the summer and fall of 1941 not only could have averted war with Japan but would have developed a *modus vivendi,* satisfying American concern for checking Japan's southward advance in east Asia and holding in abeyance for later settlement the time and conditions for Japanese withdrawal in China. Such an accommodation reflects not entirely *ex post facto* wishful thinking on the part of the author. That Japan was willing to disregard her Axis Alliance, pull back from Indo-China, and disengage her bogged-down forces in China in return for lifting of American economic pressure seems amply supported by the evidence, especially Ambassador Grew's extensive testimony. The chief stumbling block to settlement proved to be the stubborn intransigence of the American State Department officers (backed, to be sure, by American public opinion) who rebuffed Japanese overtures with unyielding insistence upon supposed moral principles and outworn shibboleths regarding China. Having by mid-1941 successfully checked Japan's southward advance by economic embargo and asset-freezing pressure, Secretary Hull regrettably began making even tougher demands on Japan in the fall. This hardening American attitude and "new offensive policy" killed chances of an accommodation, which Japan appeared willing to make as late as November 6, 1941, and "made the crucial difference between peace and war."

The author does not suggest appeasement of Japan as proper American policy but maintains that a more realistic appraisal of American interests and capabilities in the Far East should have led to a more effective American policy. He has examined the primary sources perceptively and offers a strongly convincing case supporting his position, which the historian and general reader will do well to ponder thoughtfully.

FOREST C. POGUE
[*1958*]

Two themes of revisionism are developed in this valuable study of Japanese–American relations during the year before Pearl Harbor. One consists of an effective demonstration that fear of Japanese aid to Germany had little influence on the United States Far Eastern policy in the late summer and fall of 1941. The other is a vigorous argument that the United States, in demanding too much of Japan in this period, lost the chance to win its essential requirements in the Far East and succeeded only "in making inevitable an unnecessary and unavoidable war."

The first is thoroughly documented as the author points to basic differences in Japanese and German interests—aside from a mutual desire to share the spoils of the British, French, and Dutch empires —which made the alliance largely ineffective from the beginning. He holds that American leaders had ceased to worry about it to any extent by the late summer of 1941.

In the secondary theme, which threatens to overshadow the one described in the title, the author sharply criticizes Secretary Hull's inflexible policy for the application of moral principles to the China question. But for the Secretary's unrealistic demands for Japanese retreat from China, Mr. Schroeder believes, the United States could have won its pre-July desires for a halt to Japanese expansion southward and a split in the Axis. This would have gained time for a long-range solution of the China problem.

Despite his strictures on American policy, the author denies membership in the Beard-Morgenstern-Tansill-Theobald back-door-to-war school of revisionism. He concludes that "Roosevelt's fault, if any, was not that of deliberately provoking the Japanese to attack, but

From *Mississippi Valley Review,* 45 (December 1958), 524–25. Reprinted by permission of the Organization of American Historians.

Forest Pogue, biographer of George Marshall, is Director of the George C. Marshall Library, Lexington, Virginia.

of allowing Hull and others to talk him out of impulses and ideas which, had he pursued them, might have avoided the conflict." Mr. Schroeder notes that while he feels that American policy from the end of July to December, 1941, was a grave mistake, it "should not be necessary to add that this does not make it treason."

Despite his recognition "of Japan's chronic ambivalence in foreign policy and the deep rift between the Court party and the Army in her internal political structure," the author is excessively sanguine about the Japanese government's desire or ability to come to terms which would stick. As a result, he is unduly severe on Mr. Hull for the failure of negotiations. The plain fact is that Prime Minister Konoye and, later, Foreign Minister Togo were never able to negotiate with a free hand. From the summer of 1941, the moderates worked against time limits set by the Japanese army leaders who agreed to negotiations with the greatest reluctance and continued military preparations which were known to the United States through the breaking of the Japanese code. Foreign Minister Togo has aptly said that he was handed a time bomb when he took office in mid-October. His chances of staying in power, like those of Konoye before him, depended on persuading the Americans to offer terms acceptable to the army. They were always in the position of saying to the United States, "please speak softly or our demented brothers will allow the bomb they have lighted to explode." In the light of ten years of Japanese army aggression in Manchuria and China, of a military extremist policy of assassination or threat of murder of Japanese leaders who worked for peace, and of the continuing preparations for war, it was a little hard for Mr. Hull and his advisers to set great store by the promises, however sincere, of the moderate leaders of Japan.

JOHANNA M. MENZEL
[*1959*]

This is a valuable new contribution to the Pearl Harbor controversy. The author of this prize-winning study (recipient of the Beveridge Award of the American Historical Association) approaches that controversy from a fresh vantage point by analyzing the role of the Tripartite Pact in American– and German–Japanese relations and its significance for American public opinion. . . .

The analysis is lucid, yet on some major points the thesis fails to satisfy. The author exaggerates Washington's worries over the possibility of a two-front war brought on by Japanese adherence to the pact. In May 1941, the state department learned that the Japanese cabinet was divided in its interpretation of the pact, particularly Article III, and, as evidence of this accumulated in June and July, there was less and less reason to assume that Japan would make a German–American incident in the Atlantic the cause for entry into the war. Of the two sides of the apparent paradox [p. 46], "If the Axis Alliance was America's biggest worry, it was also the most expendable part of Japan's policy," the second in fact largely cancelled out the first. If America increased its aid to Great Britain but cautiously between April and July 1941, it did so not because of American fears of anything the Axis alliance might impel Japan to do. On the contrary, so far as Japan was concerned, Washington feared most what Nippon might do in southeast Asia for reasons of its own, with the resulting deterioration of the strategic position of Britain, Holland, and China. But Schroeder also argues that the conclusion of the pact "contributed more than anything else to the deterioration of Japanese– American relations during this critical year of 1940." [p. 19] While this is probably true for the response of the American public, the

From *Journal of Modern History,* 31 (December 1959), 390–91. Reprinted by permission of the University of Chicago Press. © 1959 by the University of Chicago.

Johanna Menzel, now Johanna Menzel Meskill, teaches at Lehman College in New York City.

pattern of American governmental response during 1940, particularly the timing of the embargoes on aviation gasoline and different grades of scrap, shows no relation to the Axis alliance. Washington reacted much more sharply to Japanese moves threatening southeast Asia than to Japan's entanglement with the Axis.

The second part of the analysis, which deals with the role of the Tripartite Pact in Axis diplomacy, appears to be substantially correct. But it hardly goes beyond the story told by F. C. Jones in *Japan's New Order in East Asia,* still the most thoroughly researched published account to date.

In his concluding chapters, Schroeder returns to the broader aspects of the Pearl Harbor controversy, especially the wisdom of America's "hard" policy vis-à-vis Japan after July 1941. Here he agrees basically with Ambassador Grew; he argues skillfully and temperately and carefully weighs the major objections which have been advanced against the Grew thesis. There is no need or space to enter here into the merits of this position, except to say that whatever its magnitude and precise nature, the change in Japanese–American relations after July 1941 had very little to do with the Axis alliance issue, and very much with questions of time, a slowly shifting balance of military forces, and the substantive issue of the future organization of Asia which had been at the heart of Japanese–American disagreements for years.

GEORGE F. KENNAN

~~~~~~

American Diplomacy, 1900-1950 [1951]

F SOME SORT OF CEREMONY had been planned in the year 1950 to commemorate and reflect upon a half century of American foreign relations, it would have been a dismal affair. In fifty years the United States had fought two world wars at tremendous cost for dubious gains, and seen her happy isolation reduced until she was forced to accept a permanent state of near war with the Soviet bloc. Her "victory" over the Axis powers had evaporated in the five years after 1945, to be replaced by a military, economic, and psychological crisis which was if anything greater than the threat posed by militant Fascism. The Truman government had attempted to devise policies appropriate to the new situation, but against modest successes in Greece and in Western Europe there were the failures to prevent Soviet domination of Eastern and Central Europe, the unresolved crisis over Berlin, the shocking "loss" of China to a hostile ideology. In June 1950, communist forces from North Korea attacked southward against the America-supported government of South Korea, apparently sensing the sizeable internal and external difficulties in which the United States was caught. Republican Senator Joseph McCarthy began to batter the government with charges of internal subversion and virtual treason in the spring of 1950.

Against this background George Frost Kennan, 46, a career diplomat with twenty-five years experience in the Foreign Service, former (and first) head of the Policy Planning Staff of the State Department, and principal influence behind the Marshall Plan, left government service. America's overseas problems, Kennan admitted, were not entirely due to her own mistakes, but his resignation reflected his discouragement that his efforts on the Policy Planning Staff had produced so little real change in American foreign policy.

George F. Kennan, *American Diplomacy, 1900–1950* (Chicago, University of Chicago Press, 1951. Paper: New American Library).

"Never before," he wrote in August 1950, "had there been such utter confusion in the public mind with respect to U.S. foreign policy. . . . Only the diplomatic historian . . . will be able to unravel this incredible tangle and to reveal the true aspect of the various factors and issues involved . . . No one in my position can contribute very much more . . . unless he first turns historian, earns public confidence and respect through the study of an earlier day, and then gradually carries the public up to a clear and comprehensive view of the occurrences of these recent years." [1] He therefore accepted a position at The Institute for Advanced Study, Princeton, New Jersey, from which he has produced a number of impressive and influential pieces of history and historical reflection, among them *American Diplomacy, 1900–1950.*

The book, a brooding, melancholy search for the errors which had brought America into the mortal hazards of midcentury, became, despite its brevity, a major contribution to the "realist" critique of American diplomacy. Others had preceded him, and many more would follow,[2] but the realist argument, in my view, has not received another statement at once so compact and so powerful. Kennan concentrated in four areas—American policy in 1898–1899, the development of the Open Door policy, the decision to intervene in 1917,

[1] George F. Kennan *Memoirs: 1925–1950* (Boston, Little, Brown, 1967), 500. Kennan officially was on leave from the State Department in 1950. In 1952 he was appointed Ambassador to the Soviet Union, and returned briefly to government service. He retired finally in July 1953.

[2] The "realist school" is a phrase used to group a number of scholars whose views of American foreign policy have a philosophic identity. The boundaries of the school, and its internal variations, challenge the descriptive powers of the most talented observer, but there is little controversy over the leading figures and books: the columnist Walter Lippmann [see, for example, *The Cold War* (New York, Harper, 1947)]; the political scientist Hans J. Morgenthau [see, for example, *The Defense of the National Interest* (New York, Alfred A. Knopf, 1951)]; Senator J. William Fulbright [see, for example, *The Arrogance of Power* (New York, Random House, 1966)]; and the historian Norman A. Graebner [see, for example, *Cold War Diplomacy: 1945–1960* (Princeton, N.J., Van Nostrand, 1962)].

and the handling of relations with Japan and Germany leading up to the attack on Pearl Harbor. In each case Kennan found errors of the same general type: a preoccupation with what he called "the legalistic-moralistic" issues rather than the realities of power; American self-righteousness, untempered by the suspicion that the aspirations of other nations might be either legitimate, or, at worst, not properly the subjects of theological or moral examination; an oscillation between ignorant isolation and excited crusades to reform the world when a sensible course would have been an informed, steady, but carefully limited involvement in world affairs. These errors he invariably traced not to individual policy-makers, but to the American character and to American public opinion.[3]

Some have thought that realists like Kennan and Morgenthau, because they talk of power impulses, have some penchant for militaristic solutions to external problems. Kennan's book holds a surprise for those with such suspicions. This realist (it is true also of Lippmann, Morgenthau, and the others) identifies the idealist as the man most susceptible to the bugle of total war. Kennan continually urges that the level of excitement be lowered, that wars be undertaken with greater skepticism and greater infrequency, and that military power be regarded as a means to equilibrium, not to victory. Critical of America for an isolationist unwillingness to employ her influence to support order in a world clearly interdependent, Kennan nonetheless wound up advocating less

[3] The book also contains the "Mr. X" article, published in *Foreign Affairs* in July 1947, under the title "The Sources of Soviet Conduct." The article expressed views which Kennan pressed upon Secretary of State George C. Marshall and President Truman, views which most observers assumed to be the underpinning of the containment policy which the U.S. was to follow for many years (it is not clear what has happened to it). Kennan was later to express regret that the article did not make it entirely clear that he saw the Soviet threat as political rather than military, that he did not think the Soviets intended to invade anyone after 1945, and that he had hoped for a containment which was selective rather than global, political rather than military, and a prelude to an early diplomatic settlement of the grievances of 1945–1957 instead of a semipermanent state of armed seige. Kennan's reflections on the misuse of his analysis of Soviet intentions appears in his *Memoirs: 1925–1950,* and should not be missed.

force, less intervention, and a greater receptivity to international change than the nation had employed in 1898, 1917, even 1941. As a realist, he seemed to expect the employment of force in international life; but his advice to his own country, an advanced and even "satisfied" power, was almost invariably that she should learn to accept alterations in the international map as one of the morally neutral facts of life rather than as an affront to some moral order whose lone champion was the United States of America.

Critics of the realists have wondered, among other things, if they themselves understand the hard facts of life in the twentieth century. The realists urge that nations employ force with a degree of restraint and an absence of popular excitement which were barely possible in the age of Louis XIV, and virtually impossible in a century in which all wars involve ideological passions and threaten the existence of entire populations. They point out that the realists, after an effective criticism of those who allow moralism to intrude into the shaping of foreign policy, are unreasonably vague in describing that national interest which is the center of their own diplomatic concern. Legalistic positions are easy to ridicule, but the line between where the realist will fight and where he will negotiate and compromise remains obscure. Others take scholars like Kennan upon another flank, arguing that they overestimate the acknowledged American penchant for abstraction and moralism in the shaping of American foreign policy, and underestimate the expansive thrust of economic interests.[4]

Although these and other reservations will occur to the reader of Kennan's book, a generation of readers, both professional and nonprofessional, have gradually swung to the realists' view. American foreign relations does seem in retro-

---

[4] The essay by Lloyd Gardner, somewhat abbreviated below, ought to be read in full in Barton J. Bernstein (ed.), *Towards a New Past* (New York, Pantheon, 1968). The parental work of this sort, excluding the turn-of-the-century writing of John A. Hobson, is William Appleman Williams' *The Tragedy of American Diplomacy* (Cleveland, World, 1959). Notice that Kennan sees American businessmen as unanimous for peace in 1898 [p. 16], a judgment which seemed quite sound until the publication of Walter LaFeber's *The New Empire: An Interpretation of American Expansion, 1860–1898* (Ithaca, Cornell University Press, 1963).

spect unduly burdened by self-righteous, moralistic modes of thought rather than the cool, ideologically neutral, slightly cynical thought of the professional diplomat whose memory is good on geographical details and poor on moral principles. There is no uniform agreement as to the sources of the distinctive American foreign policy, but the "legalistic-moralistic strain" has been powerfully at work in the minds of American newspaper editors and clergymen, Senators and journalists, presidents like Wilson and both Roosevelts, secretaries of state like Dulles, Hull, and even Stimson. The unfortunate effects of this turn of mind and temperament are not hard to list.

The persuasiveness of the realist critique of this tradition, combined with Kennan's incomparable style and the philosophic richness and confident range of his argument, would have been enough to earn *American Diplomacy* a continuing popularity, but the book's appeal has been further enhanced by developments in American foreign relations since it was published. American policy under Eisenhower, Kennedy, and Johnson took on a scope and aggressiveness (some called it "shouldering our responsibilities") which made it seem that the realists had indeed seen deeply into the soul of American diplomacy, and that their critique was more accurate with every passing year. This seemed especially true of the Vietnamese adventure, a crusade which any rational diplomat would have liquidated long ago if it had not been for some blurry but incredibly powerful notions about "international obligations," "the free world," and so on. Of all the witnesses who testified in opposition to American involvement in Vietnam, none spoke with such authority as Kennan, who had been struggling against inflamed rhetoric and a substitution of military for economic and political containment since the end of World War II.

Roger Hilsman, in his *To Move a Nation*,[5] tells of a sign which was displayed in the State Department briefing room during the Cuban Missile Crisis: "In a nuclear age, nations must make war as porcupines make love—carefully." In such an age, full of the combustible materials of nationalism and ideology, it is not hard to understand another reason for the deep appeal of Kennan's realism. It makes equilib-

[5] (New York, Dell Publishing Co., 1968).

rium and stability its ends, distrusts all abstractions, expects and seeks no total victories, discourages indignation and enthusiasm, exalts steadiness, patience, and expertise. This is conservatism at its best, with its deep aversion to conflict. In an excitable, deadly time, we can hardly get enough of it. The problem with realism, at least as Kennan embodies it, arises from the limitations of all conservatism. Its critical vision is clear; it deflates, it reminds men about to go on bloody crusades how little may be accomplished, how little they know. Its forte is restraint. But it can seldom tell us what we ought to do, if anything. Twice in the course of his argument in *American Diplomacy,* in a reference to Weimar Germany and another to Japan in the 1920s, Kennan suggests that American security rested ultimately upon the progress of liberal, social-democratic reform movements. Much could have been done by American policy to encourage such movements, but Kennan, because he is a conservative, is not at home in discussions of social reform, and does not develop the point. Toward the end of the "Mr. X" article Kennan spoke of what America might do, after containment, to promote moderate tendencies within the Soviet Union. Compared to the analysis of Soviet society which preceded it, the discussion is perfunctory. The United States must solve its own internal problems, he wrote, and live up to its best traditions. Kennan knew that the U.S. must accomplish more than the maintenance of economic prosperity. He knew, or seemed to know, that for America to be secure in the world she must be more than just armed, resilient, alert, firm. It was not enough that she repel; she must also attract. But he was a conservative, merely an expert in foreign affairs. He hinted at, but could not expound in anything like adequate detail, the necessity for a progressive domestic life inside the United States, based on a social vision which included not just economic growth and formal political liberties, but also the progressive realization of the most vital of our traditional ideals—human equality. This dimension of American foreign policy, requiring both idealism and social conflict, the realists have left to others.

CRITICAL COMMENTARIES

ARTHUR M. SCHLESINGER, JR.
[1951]

Until rather recently, foreign policy has been on the periphery of our national attention. For the main part of the nineteenth century, Americans devoted themselves to political consolidation and economic development within the nation. The very success in building up national power had the ironic effect of thrusting the United States into the very center of the world equilibrium of power; but the crushing international responsibilities descended on a people intellectually and morally ill-prepared to receive them. Only in the past decade, indeed, has the magnitude of these responsibilities begun to be adequately recognized.

The essential problem is that foreign policy demands to be thought about in its own way and according to its own principles. The issues of international relations are not to be solved by simply applying principles already developed in domestic politics or in jurisprudence or in personal ethics (or, even, despite certain columnists, in the playing of chess or of poker). Like any serious art, foreign policy is a craft for professionals. Though we had a professional tradition in the early days of the republic, when our very security depended on our external relations, this vanished in the course of the nineteenth century. It is only in the past generation that this tradition has begun to revive.

From *Partisan Review,* 18, 6 (November–December 1951), 706–11. Reprinted by permission of the author. © 1951 by *Partisan Review.*

Arthur M. Schlesinger, Jr., author of studies of Andrew Jackson, Franklin D. Roosevelt, and John F. Kennedy, among other books, is Albert Schweitzer Professor of Humanities of the City University of New York.

George Kennan's *American Diplomacy, 1900–1950* is a professional's meditations upon the half-century of awakening. Kennan, of course, is a foreign service officer of unusual literacy and thoughtfulness. Years of writing dispatches to the Department in Washington usually have a benumbing effect on the literary style of our diplomats, and often in the long run, on their intellectual habits as well. Kennan has amazingly escaped from the inhibitions of professionalism. His attack on problems is fresh, direct and penetrating; his style is graceful, subtle and sometimes moving. Above all, he approaches the past with a firm and developed philosophy of diplomacy.

The first essay (most of the book consists of lectures delivered . . . at the University of Chicago) deals with the Spanish-American War; the second, with the Open Door policy. Both illustrate for Mr. Kennan the combination of fecklessness, happenstance and confusion which attended America's stumbling entry into the great world. People occasionally had flashes as to what it was all about—Theodore Roosevelt, in certain moods, Admiral Mahan, Lewis Einstein—but in general, the key problems of foreign policy were misunderstood and ignored.

The besetting sin, in Mr. Kennan's judgment, was the legalistic-moralistic approach to international problems—the effort to define international relations in terms of abstract and formal principles of behavior, accompanied by the belief that the promulgation of these principles was a contribution to world order. This habit of mind drew on both the juridical proclivities of the lawyers who dominated our government and on the sentimental idealism of all upright Americans confronting a wicked world; in Cordell Hull, Mr. Kennan might have added (but diplomatically did not), the two motives came to classical union. Their dominance prevented Americans from thinking systematically and professionally about the concrete realities of power.

To the American mind, Mr. Kennan writes, it is implausible that people should have aspirations more important than the preservation of international peace; but this, alas, is not true; the world is far more dark, willful and turbulent than we imagine. We cannot assume that nations, like people, are moral beings (it is an insecure enough assumption about people). Thus, the only safe basis for foreign policy is national interest; "our own national interest is all that we are really capable of knowing and understanding." International stability comes from the accommodation of competing national interests at the "point of maximum equilibrium." What we call peace is therefore a dynamic and unstable equilibrium, threatened alike by internal change and by external rearrangement. When the equilibrium is shattered, the forces released are fanatical in their intensity and incalculable in their consequences. The problem of statecraft is to avert the extremities of force by reconciling the paradox of balance and change.

National interest, in Mr. Kennan's thinking, is simply what is good for the nation; and he readily recognizes that this is a conception which different people will charge with different implications. His own concern in this book is clearly more to make the case against legalism and moralism than to make the case for any particular version of the national interest. But he does emphasize the indispensable point that force cannot be treated as a concept outside of the given framework of purpose and method; it must be included within the philosophy of national interest. "If this were better understood, there could be neither the sweeping moral rejection of international violence which bedevils so many Americans in times of peace nor the helpless abandonment to its compulsions and its inner momentum which characterizes so many of us in times of war." And he emphasizes too that the conception of the national interest cannot be imposed upon a country; it grows out of the country; it is the outward expression of the spirit and purpose of national life. The attempt to separate foreign and domestic policy is artificial and mischievous.

If you say that mistakes of the past were unavoidable because of our domestic predilections and habits of thought, you are saying that what stopped us from being more effective than we were was democracy, as practiced in this country. . . . A nation which excuses its own failures by the sacred untouchableness of its own habits can excuse itself into complete disaster.

In discussing democracy, Mr. Kennan cannot avoid a certain skepticism and even pessimism of tone. It is this perhaps which leads him eventually to seek refuge in the hope that the nation may yet be saved in foreign policy by learning to respect a professional elite of trained diplomats.

Beyond this, he looks for American security to be preserved by preventing any single power from dominating the Eurasian land mass; which means, he argues, that we have a special stake in the prosperity and independence of "the peripheral powers of Europe and Asia." This would presumably commit us to Britain and Japan as the keystones of our policy; and it is somewhat in these terms, though not very explicitly, that Mr. Kennan conducts his critique of U.S. foreign policy since 1914. If the worst danger was to shatter the world equilibrium and the next worst was to forsake the peripheral powers, then clearly we should have sought a negotiated peace in the First World War, intervening only if necessary to avert the destruction of Britain; we should have revived Germany more quickly after the war, thereby repairing the gap in the international fabric; we should never have fooled around with a Chinese solution in our Far Eastern policy, which could only have meant the abandonment of the periphery in order to enthrone chaos; and, if we had backed Germany and Japan under moderate leadership, we might have forestalled the devotees of the Thousand Year Reich and the Greater East Asia Co-Prosperity Sphere.

No one would be quicker than Mr. Kennan to admit the speculative character of his observations. One may well wonder, for example, whether the preservation of Imperial Germany or the support of Imperial Japan against China might not have whetted more appetites than it satisfied; or why the balance of power requires that we must always back the island power against the mainland, especially when the island is the seat of aggression. Badly stated, indeed, Mr. Kennan's whole thesis may seem only a more urbane version of the *Realpolitik* to which innocents tend to turn when the facts of international life suddenly burst upon them.

But what differentiates the Kennan approach from that of, for example, the followers of Professor Hans J. Morgenthau is that he takes the revelations of international amorality in his stride; more than that, he comprehends them in his understanding of the tragedy of history. Mr. Kennan, in other words, is deeply moral, rather than moralistic, like Judge Hull, or immoral, like the boys who have just discovered that politics involve power. He does not think that international questions can be solved by the enunciation of ethical generalities; nor does he think they can be solved by a cynical division of the spoils. The fact that international relations are amoral does not mean to him that moral factors play no part; nor does it absolve the individual from moral responsibility. This, indeed, is in his view the tragedy of history: man cannot escape decision, but the complexity of events diffuses the burden of guilt, and, beyond this, so much is inherently insoluble.

In order to fill out the book, the publishers have added Mr. Kennan's two notable *Foreign Affairs* essays on the Soviet Union. They show admirably the realism, the equability and the compassion with which he approaches the problems of current policy. . . .

The bitter experience of the past generation will be entirely wasted if Americans do not accept Kennan's . . . basic point—that the only solid foundation of national action is national interest. But they must understand, as Kennan does, that this point is the beginning, and not the end, of wisdom. They must accept it within the framework of a larger acceptance of the complexity, indeterminacy, insolubility, and above all, deep sadness of history. Only such an acceptance can prevent a sense of national interest from turning into a conviction of national infallibility.

HANS J. MORGENTHAU
[1957]

This constructive critique of the last half-century of American foreign policy is written by a man who has had wide experience in important diplomatic posts in Central Europe and the Soviet Union; who, during a number of crucial years, held key positions in the State Department as head of its Policy Planning Board and as its counselor; and who through his endowments of mind and heart stands head and shoulders above the common run of diplomats (if I remember correctly, it was Dean Acheson who called Kennan "the most intelligent man in America"). As was to be expected, such a book by such a man sheds light upon the foreign policy of the United States.

American Diplomacy consists of two parts: the lectures which Kennan delivered . . . at the University of Chicago, and two articles, one of them the famous "Mr. X" article of 1947, reprinted from *Foreign Affairs*. The difference between these sections of the book is striking. The first betrays in form and content its origin as a series of lectures. Although it appears on its face to be an exercise in the

From *The New Republic,* 125 (October 27, 1957), 17–19. Reprinted by permission of *The New Republic;* © 1957, Harrison-Blaine of New Jersey, Inc.

Hans J. Morgenthau, a leading scholar in the field of American foreign relations, teaches at the University of Chicago.

diplomatic history of the last half-century, it is neither historical narrative nor systematic comment, but rather a series of brilliant and profound aphorisms on the nature of foreign policy in general and of American foreign policy in particular, grouped around the major international problems that have confronted the United States in the last fifty years. The two articles which form the second part are closely reasoned, subtle arguments, presented in a highly polished prose and concerned with understanding the Soviet Union and the requirements for a successful American foreign policy in regard to it. Moreover, behind these differences in presentation and approach lies a difference in concept and philosophy which makes it at times difficult to believe that the two sections were written by the same man.

In his lectures, Kennan finds that the theories and assumptions which American statesmen have brought to bear upon American foreign policy since the Spanish—American War are faulty. It is to a defective philosophy of foreign policy, rather than to the weaknesses and errors of individual statesmen, that he traces the deficiencies of United States diplomacy. He summarizes that erroneous philosophy as "the legalistic-moralistic approach to international problems.". . .

Kennan traces the effects which this philosophy of foreign affairs has had on our policies before, during, and after the war with Spain, on our policies with regard to the Far East, and on the ways we dealt with the problems which arose from the two world wars. Under the influence of this philosophy, we fought wars which we did not need to fight, such as the war against Spain. We acquired territories which we did not need to acquire, such as the Philippines. We embraced certain principles, such as the Open Door in China, which in their vagueness were incapable of providing guidance for our foreign policy and had no recognizable connection with our national interest. We sometimes did the right things for the wrong reasons, such as our intervention in World War I and our support of Great Britain in World War II before Pearl Harbor. Habitually we told other nations how they ought to behave in terms of international law and morality without considering either the interests of the nations involved or the power necessary to make those legal and moral principles prevail.

These faulty tendencies in American foreign policy are powerfully supported by the influence of what Kennan calls "short-term trends of public opinion" upon the decisions of the executive; ". . . In the short term our public opinion, or what passes for our public opinion in the thinking of official Washington, can be easily led astray into areas of emotionalism and subjectivity which make it a poor and inadequate guide for national action." The lectures illustrate with impressive examples the extent to which the most fallacious foreign policies of the United States have either been initiated upon the pressure of public opinion or have been supported by it.

This reviewer has nothing but admiration and approval for Kennan's critique of recent American foreign policy and for the corresponding plea for a foreign policy which receives its standards for evaluation and its guides for action from the national interest—both of the United States and of other nations—rather than from abstract legal or moral principles. But the test of statesmanship is in the application of theory to a concrete situation, and that is what the second part of this book provides. Kennan's theory of foreign policy is admirable; how is his foreign policy?

The first of the articles here reprinted presents the famous justification for the policy of containment, "designed to confront the Russians with unalterable counter-force at every point where they show signs of encroaching upon the interests of a peaceful and stable world." I must confess that I am more impressed by this presentation of the policy of containment now than when I first read it four years ago. There can be no doubt that the restoration of the balance of power in Europe and Asia through the development of counter-force is an indispensable prerequisite for a successful American policy toward the Soviet Union. The only question is how that counter-force is to be applied and in what terms it is to be conceived. On these points Kennan's presentation of the containment policy leaves itself open, at the very least, to misinterpretation.

The United States lacks the power to contain the Soviet Union "at every point" of its 20,000-mile perimeter. To try to do so would be to scatter the limited resources of the United States and invite the Soviet Union to press upon the weakest point with maximum strength. Since that is so, it is imperative for the United States to differentiate among those prospective points of hostile contact which, in view of American security, must be defended at all costs, those which may be defended in certain circumstances, and those which can hardly be defended at all. That is to say, the sweeping terms of the policy of containment must be qualified by those considerations of interest and power to which Kennan has called attention in the first part of his book.

Moreover, the policy of containment has been transformed in practical application into a kind of Maginot Line policy which, in the opinion of this reviewer, stems from a profound misunderstanding of the nature of American power and of the sources of its deterrent effect. The policy of containment has thus far been successful, even at those points of contact which lie completely defenseless at the borders of the Soviet Empire, not because of the power which the United States would have been able to bring to bear "at every point," but because the Russians could be certain that, in case of an attack upon the vital interests of the United States, the totality of American power would be used in defense and retaliation, not "at every point," but at those points which would vitally affect the interests and security of the USSR.

The other article reprinted in this book deals, under the heading of "America and the Russian Future," with the kind of Russia with which we could get along, and with the means of creating such a Russia. Much that is profound and wise is said in this article about the futility of direct intervention, especially through the instrumentality of war, about the narrow limitations of propaganda and about the importance of our own domestic policies. Yet, if one again applies Kennan's own standards of interest and power, it is impossible not to doubt the soundness, or at least the relevance, of his solution.

He thus summarizes his argument:

These, then, are the things for which an American well-wisher may hope from the Russia of the future: that she lift forever the Iron Curtain, that she recognize certain limitations to the internal authority of government, and that she abandon, as ruinous and unworthy, the ancient game of imperialist expansion and oppression. . . . If she is prepared to do these things, then Americans will not need to concern themselves more deeply with her nature and purposes; the basic demands of a more stable world order will then have been met. . . .

Are we to understand that once these things are done, the conflicts of interest and power which for the last two centuries have pitted Russia against her European and Asiatic neighbors will disappear, or at least cease to threaten the peace of the world? Does Kennan really mean to suggest that, with these things done, the traditional Russian interests in Manchuria, of which he has some very wise words to say on page 42, will either be as nothing or at least be no longer in conflict with the interests of China, Japan, and the United States? With these things done, will the "Polish Question" become a mere historical remembrance and cease to be, to quote Stalin, "a question . . . of life and death for the Soviet state," as it was for Russia of the Czars? And will the accomplishment of these things obviate the return to diplomacy, so emphatically proposed by Kennan in the lectures, with its bargaining and accommodation of conflicting interests? In a word, even if the Russian government were to meet the requirements stipulated in this article, would not the task of American foreign policy, though made easier in detail, remain precisely what it is today?

The contradiction between intellectual insight and the actual foreign policies pursued, which has vitiated much that is sound in conception in the foreign policies of the Truman administration, can well be explained by the domestic pressures which have traditionally played upon the conduct of American foreign policy and to which a weak administration is especially susceptible. The contradiction between the insights of Kennan's theory of foreign policy and the actual policies he advocates cannot be explained in such a fashion. Perhaps it is a testimony to the strength of those "pernicious abstractions" in American thinking on foreign policy which he so brilliantly exposes that even a man of Kennan's stature is not completely immune from them.

LLOYD C. GARDNER

American Foreign Policy 1900–1921:
A Second Look at the
Realist Critique of American Diplomacy
[1968]

For more than a decade, George F. Kennan's "realist" critique, *American Diplomacy, 1900–1950,* has dominated debate in American universities and elsewhere. Though these famous lectures were hardly

From *Towards a New Past,* edited by Barton J. Bernstein (New York, Pantheon, 1968), 202–226. Reprinted by permission of Pantheon Books, a solely responsible for the rise of this critique of American foreign policy to its present position, they have yet to be rivaled by any other writing on twentieth-century American foreign relations. The book is now in its twentieth printing.

Since many key points Kennan sought to establish in these lectures pertained to the earlier years (1900–1921); and since many of these contentions have served as foundation, not only for the author's discussion of later policy decisions, but for the realist school in general, it may be useful to review these events from a radical perspective with the hope that meaningful distinctions may emerge separating that view from other efforts to make sense out of the developments and personalities of these years. Hopefully, also, there will appear something of a general dialogue between what is really a conservative criticism of the American liberal "world view," and a radical explanation of the development of that outlook at the beginning of this century.

Kennan saw an overriding theme in the events leading up to John Hay's Open Door Notes on China in 1899 and 1900, in the rapid growth of the arbitration movement before the First World War, and in the aura cast by Woodrow Wilson's crusade to make the world safe for democracy. Reduced to its simplest expression, that theme was the American's "legalistic-moralistic approach to international problems." It ran "like a red skein through our foreign policy of the last fifty years."

Before testing specifics against this generalization, as he set it forth during the lectures, Kennan gave his audience an atmospheric description of the State Department at the turn of the century when it was "a quaint old place, with its law-office atmosphere, its cool dark

---

Division of Random House, Inc., and Chatto & Windus Ltd. Copyright © 1968 by Random House, Inc.

Lloyd Gardner recently published a study of the economic aspects of New Deal diplomacy which identified him with those who, like William Appleman Williams, understood American foreign policy as the product of economic forces indigenous to advanced capitalism. The realist position would naturally seem inadequate to a scholar with Gardner's sympathies, not only because it locates the dynamic in American policy as being a national mode of thought, but also because it demonstrates a conservative distrust for all idealisms, including those of the contemporary Left.

Lloyd Gardner teaches history at Rutgers University. The footnotes have been deleted from this portion of his essay, and students are urged to read this and all other abridged essays in this book in their entirety in the original source.

corridors, its swinging doors, its brass cuspidors, its black leather rocking chairs, and the grandfather's clock in the Secretary of State's office."

After that marvelous word picture of an institution at the end of an "innocent" era, one expects an amiable, if slightly condescending, discussion of the origins of the Open Door policy. We are not disappointed. Kennan assures his audience that John Hay's Far Eastern policy "was not an American policy but one long established in British relations with China." A strong Anglophile, the Secretary of State thought he was being "responsive to a request the British had made of us." Indeed, there was no evidence that . . . [Secretary Hay] understood fully its practical significance." The policy apparently was as innocent and parochial as the institution and its inhabitants. As for commercial motives, these took a very small place, sandwiched in between the really important matters. "The formula had a high-minded and idealistic ring; it would sound well at home; it was obviously in the interests of American trade; the British had been known to advocate it—still did, so far as he knew—and it was hard to see what harm could come from trying it on the other powers."

State Department officials from the time of the Open Door Notes to the Second World War were indeed constantly frustrated by the failure of the "Great China market." But the ongoing assumption behind the policy was that American Far Eastern trade, and our national interests in general, would be better served by equal access to all of China than by a preferred position in a sphere of influence. It was, in theory and in fact, the foreign policy of a confident industrial power. And as such it soon became the United States approach to its dealings with other areas of the world, particularly colonial and underdeveloped areas.

From this point of view, as another career Foreign Service officer, Stanley K. Hornbeck, wrote in 1918 (and in contrast to the emphasis in *American Diplomacy, 1900–1950*), the specific matter of how the actual notes came to be sent to the powers interested in China was of little significance, as the "Republican administration was enthusiastic over the possibilities of American commercial expansion in the Pacific." America had sent the notes instead of Great Britain because the world order was at a crucial transition point, but the "idea of defending China's integrity and of gradually securing wider opening of her doors to foreign trade on terms enjoyable mutually by all comers had long been cardinal features of the policies of both countries." And a number of recent monographs have drawn upon similar evidence to establish the strength and variety of domestic economic pressures behind the inauguration of a more forceful China policy. . . .

Turning from the China policy of the McKinley administration, Kennan explains the similar phenomena of the arbitration movement, the League of Nations, and finally the United Nations as resulting (on the American side) from an idealization of our own past political experience projected onto the world at large. His criticism of these efforts was directed at the unreal expectations stemming from such delusions in the first place, and at the American assumption that "the things for which other peoples in this world are apt to contend are for the most part neither creditable nor important and might justly be expected to take second place behind the desirability of an orderly world, untouched by international violence."

The American policy maker's attempt to impose an American-organized and American-led security system on the world at the end of the First World War was premature; but his world view had developed from a much keener insight into the nature of his society (and its needs) than would appear from the realist critique. We may criticize his naive moralism or idealism along with the realists, but a full account of the development of that outlook is a much more difficult problem. The rhetoric of all great nations and empire builders is, after all, usually sounded in moralistic themes. The American policy maker in the progressive era was confronted with a set of conditions at home and abroad, and a collection of traditions about himself and his role in the world. As world conditions changed, so did the formulas he used to match them to the new opportunities and challenges. World conditions changed very rapidly in these years; so rapidly, in fact, that his formulas were often outdated at once. Even so, these formulations need much more analysis than is presently available in the realist critique. . . .

The realist critique questioned certain manifestations of American foreign policy. Its contributions may be appreciated for what they are without admitting that its criticisms go to the center of the problem. On the other hand, one fears that this critique has been distorted too often in order to deny the relevance of all save the most "tough-minded" alternative in a given situation. Its major use seems to be to justify "elitism" as opposed to "popular" diplomacy. If it falls short as an explanation, it may well prove disastrous as a justification for basically unsound policies. And if Kennan set out to question America's extended commitments, his followers (as he now seems aware) have ironically increased those dubious undertakings in the name of realism. In the end, the realist critique leads one to believe that the rhetoric surrounding the foreign policy of a John Hay, or a Woodrow Wilson, was in fact the core substance of the policy: the radical perspective, on the other hand, sees the development of America's world view as a logical result of national expansion.